Battlegroun

GALLIPOLI
ANZAC – SARI BAIR

Battleground series:

Stamford Bridge & Hastings *by* Peter Marren
Wars of the Roses - **Wakefield / Towton** *by* Philip A. Haigh
Wars of the Roses - **Barnet** *by* David Clark
Wars of the Roses - **Tewkesbury** *by* Steven Goodchild
Wars of the Roses - **The Battles of St Albans** *by* Peter Burley, Michael Elliott & Harvey Wilson
English Civil War - **Naseby** *by* Martin Marix Evans, Peter Burton and Michael Westaway
English Civil War - **Marston Moor** *by* David Clark
War of the Spanish Succession - **Blenheim 1704** *by* James Falkner
War of the Spanish Succession - **Ramillies 1706** *by* James Falkner
Napoleonic - **Hougoumont** *by* Julian Paget and Derek Saunders
Napoleonic - **Waterloo** *by* Andrew Uffindell and Michael Corum
Zulu War - **Isandlwana** *by* Ian Knight and Ian Castle
Zulu War - **Rorkes Drift** *by* Ian Knight and Ian Castle
Boer War - **The Relief of Ladysmith** *by* Lewis Childs
Boer War - **The Siege of Ladysmith** *by* Lewis Childs
Boer War - **Kimberley** *by* Lewis Childs

Mons *by* Jack Horsfall and Nigel Cave
Néry *by* Patrick Tackle
Retreat of I Corps 1914 *by* Jerry Murland
Aisne 1914 *by* Jerry Murland
Aisne 1918 *by* David Blanchard
Le Cateau *by* Nigel Cave and Jack Shelden
Walking the Salient *by* Paul Reed
Ypres - **1914 Messines** *by* Nigel Cave and Jack Sheldon
Ypres - **1914 Menin Road** *by* Nigel Cave and Jack Sheldon
Ypres - **1914 Langemarck** *by* Jack Sheldon and Nigel Cave
Ypres - **Sanctuary Wood and Hooge** *by* Nigel Cave
Ypres - **Hill 60** *by* Nigel Cave
Ypres - **Messines Ridge** *by* Peter Oldham
Ypres - **Polygon Wood** *by* Nigel Cave
Ypres - **Passchendaele** *by* Nigel Cave
Ypres - **Airfields and Airmen** *by* Mike O'Connor
Ypres - **St Julien** *by* Graham Keech
Ypres - **Boesinghe** *by* Stephen McGreal
Walking the Somme *by* Paul Reed
Somme - **Gommecourt** *by* Nigel Cave
Somme - **Serre** *by* Jack Horsfall & Nigel Cave
Somme - **Beaumont Hamel** *by* Nigel Cave
Somme - **Thiepval** *by* Michael Stedman
Somme - **La Boisselle** *by* Michael Stedman
Somme - **Fricourt** *by* Michael Stedman
Somme - **Carnoy-Montauban** *by* Graham Maddocks
Somme - **Pozières** *by* Graham Keech
Somme - **Courcelette** *by* Paul Reed
Somme - **Boom Ravine** *by* Trevor Pidgeon
Somme - **Mametz Wood** *by* Michael Renshaw
Somme - **Delville Wood** *by* Nigel Cave
Somme - **Advance to Victory (North) 1918** *by* Michael Stedman
Somme - **Flers** *by* Trevor Pidgeon
Somme - **Bazentin Ridge** *by* Edward Hancock
Somme - **Combles** *by* Paul Reed
Somme - **Beaucourt** *by* Michael Renshaw
Somme - **Redan Ridge** *by* Michael Renshaw
Somme - **Hamel** *by* Peter Pedersen
Somme - **Villers-Bretonneux** *by* Peter Pedersen
Somme - **Airfields and Airmen** *by* Mike O'Connor
Airfields and Airmen of the Channel Coast *by* Mike O'Connor
In the Footsteps of the Red Baron *by* Mike O'Connor
Arras - **Airfields and Airmen** *by* Mike O'Connor
Arras - **The Battle for Vimy Ridge** *by* Jack Sheldon & Nigel Cave
Arras - **Vimy Ridge** *by* Nigel Cave
Arras - **Gavrelle** *by* Trevor Tasker and Kyle Tallett
Arras - **Oppy Wood** *by* David Bilton
Arras - **Bullecourt** *by* Graham Keech
Arras - **Monchy le Preux** *by* Colin Fox
Walking Arras *by* Paul Reed
Hindenburg Line *by* Peter Oldham
Hindenburg Line - **Epehy** *by* Bill Mitchinson
Hindenburg Line - **Riqueval** *by* Bill Mitchinson
Hindenburg Line - **Villers-Plouich** *by* Bill Mitchinson
Hindenburg Line - **Cambrai Right Hook** *by* Jack Horsfall & Nigel Cave
Hindenburg Line - **Cambrai Flesquières** *by* Jack Horsfall & Nigel Cave
Hindenburg Line - **Saint Quentin** *by* Helen McPhail and Philip Guest
Hindenburg Line - **Bourlon Wood** *by* Jack Horsfall & Nigel Cave

Cambrai - **Airfields and Airmen** *by* Mike O'Connor
Aubers Ridge *by* Edward Hancock
La Bassée - **Neuve Chapelle** *by* Geoffrey Bridger
Loos - **Hohenzollern Redoubt** *by* Andrew Rawson
Loos - **Hill 70** *by* Andrew Rawson
Fromelles *by* Peter Pedersen
The Battle of the Lys 1918 *by* Phil Tomaselli
Accrington Pals Trail *by* William Turner
Poets at War: Wilfred Owen *by* Helen McPhail and Philip Guest
Poets at War: Edmund Blunden *by* Helen McPhail and Philip Guest
Poets at War: Graves & Sassoon *by* Helen McPhail and Philip Guest
Gallipoli *by* Nigel Steel
Gallipoli - **Gully Ravine** *by* Stephen Chambers
Gallipoli - **Anzac Landing** *by* Stephen Chambers
Gallipoli - **Suvla August Offensive** *by* Stephen Chambers
Gallipoli - **Landings at Helles** *by* Huw & Jill Rodge
Walking the Gallipoli *by* Stephen Chambers
Walking the Italian Front *by* Francis Mackay
Italy - **Asiago** *by* Francis Mackay
Verdun: **Fort Douamont** *by* Christina Holstein
Verdun: **Fort Vaux** *by* Christina Holstein
Walking Verdun *by* Christina Holstein
Verdun: **The Left Bank** *by* Christina Holstein
Zeebrugge & Ostend Raids 1918 *by* Stephen McGreal

Germans at Beaumont Hamel *by* Jack Sheldon
Germans at Thiepval *by* Jack Sheldon

SECOND WORLD WAR

Dunkirk *by* Patrick Wilson
Calais *by* Jon Cooksey
Boulogne *by* Jon Cooksey
Saint-Nazaire *by* James Dorrian
Walking D-Day *by* Paul Reed
Atlantic Wall - **Pas de Calais** *by* Paul Williams
Atlantic Wall - **Normandy** *by* Paul Williams
Normandy - **Pegasus Bridge** *by* Carl Shilleto
Normandy - **Merville Battery** *by* Carl Shilleto
Normandy - **Utah Beach** *by* Carl Shilleto
Normandy - **Omaha Beach** *by* Tim Kilvert-Jones
Normandy - **Gold Beach** *by* Christopher Dunphie & Garry Johnson
Normandy - **Gold Beach Jig** *by* Tim Saunders
Normandy - **Juno Beach** *by* Tim Saunders
Normandy - **Sword Beach** *by* Tim Kilvert-Jones
Normandy - **Operation Bluecoat** *by* Ian Daglish
Normandy - **Operation Goodwood** *by* Ian Daglish
Normandy - **Epsom** *by* Tim Saunders
Normandy - **Hill 112** *by* Tim Saunders
Normandy - **Mont Pinçon** *by* Eric Hunt
Normandy - **Cherbourg** *by* Andrew Rawson
Normandy - **Commandos & Rangers on D-Day** *by* Tim Saunders
Das Reich – **Drive to Normandy** *by* Philip Vickers
Oradour *by* Philip Beck
Market Garden - **Nijmegen** *by* Tim Saunders
Market Garden - **Hell's Highway** *by* Tim Saunders
Market Garden - **Arnhem, Oosterbeek** *by* Frank Steer
Market Garden - **Arnhem, The Bridge** *by* Frank Steer
Market Garden - **The Island** *by* Tim Saunders
Rhine Crossing – **US 9th Army & 17th US Airborne** *by* Andrew Rawson
British Rhine Crossing – **Operation Varsity** *by* Tim Saunders
British Rhine Crossing – **Operation Plunder** *by* Tim Saunders
Battle of the Bulge – **St Vith** *by* Michael Tolhurst
Battle of the Bulge – **Bastogne** *by* Michael Tolhurst
Channel Islands *by* George Forty
Walcheren *by* Andrew Rawson
Remagen Bridge *by* Andrew Rawson
Cassino *by* Ian Blackwell
Anzio *by* Ian Blackwell
Dieppe *by* Tim Saunders
Fort Eben Emael *by* Tim Saunders
Crete – **The Airborne Invasion** *by* Tim Saunders
Malta *by* Paul Williams
Bruneval Raid *by* Paul Oldfield
Cockleshell Raid *by* Paul Oldfield

Battleground Europe

GALLIPOLI

ANZAC
SARI BAIR

Stephen Chambers

Series Editor
Nigel Cave

Pen & Sword
MILITARY

First published in Great Britain in 2014 by
Pen & Sword Military
An imprint of
Pen & Sword Books Ltd
47 Church Street
Barnsley
South Yorkshire
S70 2AS

Copyright © Stephen Chambers

ISBN 978 178159 190 1

The right of Stephen Chambers to be identified as Author
of this work has been asserted by him in accordance with the
Copyright, Designs and Patents Act 1988.

A CIP catalogue record for this book is
available from the British Library.

Typeset in Times New Roman by Chic Graphics

Printed and bound in England by
CPI Group (UK) Ltd., Croydon, CR0 4YY

Pen & Sword Books Ltd incorporates the imprints of
Pen & Sword Archaeology, Atlas, Aviation, Battleground, Discovery,
Family History, History, Maritime, Military, Naval, Politics,
Railways, Select, Social History, Transport, True Crime, and
Claymore Press, Frontline Books, Leo Cooper, Praetorian Press,
Remember When, Seaforth Publishing and Wharncliffe.

For a complete list of Pen & Sword titles please contact
PEN & SWORD BOOKS LIMITED
47 Church Street, Barnsley, South Yorkshire, S70 2AS, England
E-mail: enquiries@pen-and-sword.co.uk
Website: www.pen-and-sword.co.uk

CONTENTS

Acknowledgements

Without the help of many individuals and organisations this book would not have been possible. Special thanks are due, in no particular order, to Peter Hart, IWM Oral Historian, who has again been of tremendous help throughout the journey of this book. To the late Patrick Gariepy for providing so much help and information on the casualties mentioned here. The Gallipoli campaign can only truly be understood by treading the very ground that the men, from both sides of the trenches, had fought, bled and died; a huge thanks, therefore, goes to Guy Marner, who has accompanied me on battlefield trips to north Anzac. Peter Trounson and Simon Jervis have been kind in providing first hand veteran accounts and allowing me to use them for this book. Thanks must also go to Ian Gill for furthering the knowledge of the Australian Light Horse and Hill 60. In Turkey, thanks must go to the experts who live and breathe the Gallipoli campaign, or *Çanakkale Savaşı* as it is known. To Haluk Oral, who has helped me see Gallipoli through Turkish eyes and to both Şahin Aldoğan and Kenan Çelik, who have been studying the campaign and walking the ground far longer than most. Thanks also need to go to both Bill Sellars and Eric Goossens, who are not only excellent hosts but are also knowledgeable of the battlefield itself. And of course, by no means least, to Nigel Cave, Series Editor, whose guidance along the way has kept me on the straight and narrow as always.

From individuals to organisations, museums, libraries, websites and the like, the list of thanks is almost endless but to start, thanks need to go to the staff at the National Archives, the Imperial War Museum, the Australian War Memorial, The Alexander Turnbull Library and pals on both the Great War Forum and the Gallipoli Association Forum, growing hives of valuable information on the campaign. The indefatigable work of the Commonwealth War Graves Commission cannot go without mention for their caring for the British and Commonwealth war dead in Gallipoli and elsewhere around the world. The Gallipoli Association, which since 1969 has been helping keep the memory alive, is an association worth joining, which has a website worth visiting and a journal worth reading.

Sadly, the veterans have long since faded away, but they are not forgotten, their stories continue to be told and are used here to show the human aspect of war. Contemporary material in the form of war diaries, divisional, regimental and battalion histories have also been referenced. The published diary of Sir Ian Hamilton and also Cecil Aspinall-Oglander's Official History are both a 'must' read, although both stand in the shadow of the Australian official historian, Charles Bean, whose detailed account of Anzac is second to none. I have made full use, as appropriate, of many personal accounts in the form of letters and diaries as well as a large assortment of maps and photographs, many never having been published before. The originators of these must all be thanked, because without this material there would be no story to tell. With historical documents it is always difficult to trace all the copyright holders, so for any who have not been contacted, please accept my sincere apologies, and feel free to contact me if you feel it necessary. To all these people and any I have mistakenly forgotten to mention, please accept my sincere apologies and thanks.

Stephen Chambers
West Sussex and North Anzac, 2013

Ottoman Turkish recruitment poster.

Series Editor's Introduction

This latest book in Stephen Chambers' series on Gallipoli covers the last concerted offensive by the British, Anzac and Indian Army forces on the peninsula in that ill-fated campaign of 1915. Like so many others in the fighting, it is a tale of opportunities missed through a series of errors and omissions, some predictable, some a matter of both the fog and the fortunes of war. A significant factor in the failure was, of course, the truly heroic, fiercely aggressive defence of the Turkish defenders.

It makes tragic reading – not so much the failure of the offensive, for that happens frequently in warfare. At Gallipoli the failures have a peculiarly poignant narrative, which has captured popular imagination. Who cannot be moved by the fate of so many wounded who were incinerated by the fires that broke out in the scrubland – such a characteristic of the countryside there? The tales of heroism in impossible conditions, often undertaken with a very strong likelihood of death or maiming, are one of the notable features of the whole campaign; but here they are particularly plentiful.

This latest book enables those of us who come after to understand, as best we can, what went wrong and how it went wrong. To appreciate the issues facing both sides, it is even more than usually important to understand the ground in addition to all the other contributory factors – misdirected artillery, the late delivery of orders, failures in communications, the setting of impossible start times, the jumbling up of units in the confusion of battle or in moving through difficult, often unknown, country.

An understanding of the campaign, with all its twists and turns, of optimism dashed by outcome, is best made with a personal visit and to see for oneself: to appreciate the difficulties of moving through the country to start line positions; of maintaining control amongst the attacking (and then defending) units; to comprehend how hard it was for higher command to have an adequate appreciation of what precisely was happening at the front line; to see why there were such problems with supply and reinforcements; to view the difficulties faced by the artillery and the support shelling by the navy.

This volume guides the visitor to the key points in a series of, sometimes quite challenging, walks and tours; and provides a commentary that helps to make sense of it all. The heroism of individuals and units is, as usual, covered in the author's own effective style.

Lord Kitchener Says Enlist To-day.

The several volumes on Gallipoli that Steve has written over the last few years provide by far the most detailed series of tours available in print. Many visitors come to Gallipoli and take away a sense of the haunting beauty and tragedy that still pervades the peninsula; now they have the books to come away with a greater understanding of what took place a hundred years or so ago, to interpret what they see.

The outcome for the allies was, in the end, a noble failure; those who come on pilgrimage or on tour owe those who served and died here a conscious effort to see beyond tragedy and futility, to appreciate the what, the how and the why. These books go a long way to enable us to achieve those desirable objectives.

Nigel Cave

Introduction

The Allied strategic objective in the Gallipoli Campaign was, by capturing Constantinople (now Istanbul), to force German's ally Turkey and its Ottoman Empire out of the war. In addition, this would open a warm water sea supply route from the Aegean through the Dardanelles and into the Black Sea to Russia. It was also hoped that pressure on Turkey would influence the neutral states of Bulgaria, Romania and Greece to enter the war on the allied side, and in a combined effort to assist the Entente powers in removing the weaker allies of Germany; namely Turkey and Austria-Hungary. But the campaign would be a risk with a far from certain outcome. If successful it was hoped to shorten the war, but if it failed, the consequences were

General Sir Ian Hamilton.

beyond comprehension. Would the war be lengthened by not concentrating efforts on the Western Front against the main power, Germany? Would it weaken Britain's influence in the east, threatening the British Empire? Although a valid gamble, the campaigns poor planning and execution shattered any glimmer of hope in a catalogue of mismanaged sea and land battles that would finally end in January 1916.

After the failure of the naval actions, which culminated on 18 March 1915, when British and French battleships attempted to force a passage through the Dardanelles, a land campaign was planned. The purpose was to aid the Navy in passing through the Dardanelles by capturing the forts and neutralising the strait's minefields.

The amphibious landings on 25 April 1915 were the beginning of Sir Ian Hamilton's Mediterranean Expeditionary Forces' (MEF) invasion on the Gallipoli Peninsula. Ashore, but with many casualties and little more to show than a beachhead, the following months witnessed heavy fighting, but no breakthrough. In the north, the Australian and New Zealand Army Corps (ANZAC) were hemmed in and attempts at a breakout in May failed; equally, attempts by the Turks to force the Anzacs into the sea failed. Further south, at Helles, the British and

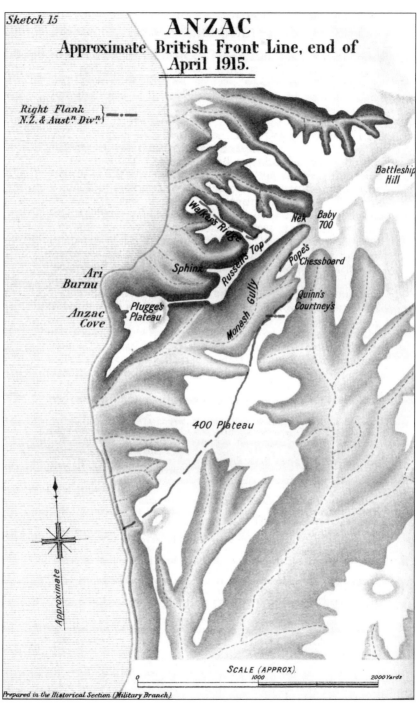

Sketch 15

ANZAC
Approximate British Front Line, end of April 1915.

Right Flank
N.Z. & Austn. Divn.

Battleship Hill

Walker's Ridge

Nek

Baby 700

Ari Burnu

Sphinx

Russell's Top

Pope's

Chessboard

Anzac Cove

Plugge's Plateau

Monash Gully

Quinn's

Courtneys

400 Plateau

Approximate

SCALE (APPROX).
0   1000   2000 Yards

Prepared in the Historical Section (Military Branch).

North Anzac (Official History).

French had repeatedly failed to capture the village of Krithia or the hill of Achi Baba, let alone threaten the Kilid Bahr Plateau, which was the real key to unlocking the Dardanelles. By June there was no doubt that Helles, the main offensive front, had reached a stalemate. Hamilton now looked for a strategic surprise elsewhere to break the deadlock.

The August offensive was born out of the earlier failures and is described in the following pages. It was critical that Hamilton made this a success in order to turn around his earlier misfortunes and place his troops in a position where they could finally capture the Peninsula, and thus command the Dardanelles. In a previous Battleground Europe book, *Suvla: August Offensive*, the story of the British IX Corps' landing at Suvla Bay was covered. This book is the story behind the adjoining events at Anzac, equally heartbreakingly tragic in failure, costly in casualties but daring in ingenuity. The Anzac objective was the high ground, the Sari Bair ridge that had been one of the very same goals for the attack on 25 April. Without controlling the heights, the allied forces would remain trapped. Many names associated with this offensive quickly became famous; Lone Pine, The Nek, Chunuk Bair, Hill 971, Hill 60. Unfortunately, although close to achieving its immediate objectives, the offensive hammered itself to a stalemate, which many believe was inevitable. Hamilton had played his last card and lost; the allied evacuation was foreseeable. This is the story of Gallipoli's last great battle; the forlorn hope to bring the campaign to a successful close.

In *Anzac: The Landing* we studied the Gaba Tepe landings and the fighting that followed in the attempt to capture the Sari Bair heights and the Third Ridge, the stepping stones across the Maidos plain to the Dardanelles. This over ambitious plan failed as the Turks quickly checked the Anzacs' advance. On 27 April the Turks tried a second counter attack with the aim of pushing the Anzacs back into the sea, but this in turn failed and a temporary respite in the fighting occurred.

On 28 April the Anzacs were reinforced by four battalions from the Royal Naval Division (RND). For three days and nights, the besieged Australians and New Zealanders had been fighting without a stop, so the bolstering by new men was a welcome relief. However, the Turks had also been reinforced and were planning another counter attack. On 1 May the attack came, hammering the Anzacs and the newly arrived RND, but the line held and once again the Turks were beaten back. During the recent fighting, a dangerous gap in the line near Monash Valley, at the top of the Anzac perimeter, had been identified, from where the Turks could enfilade the Anzac positions. Here, between the New Zealand positions on Russell's Top and the Australian positions holding the Second Ridge posts (Quinn's, Courtney's and Steele's), was

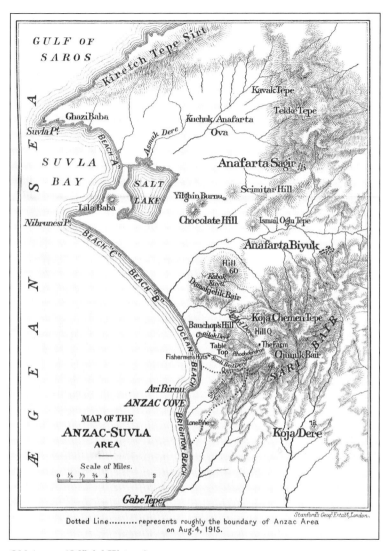

Old Anzac (Official History).

the Turkish held Chessboard and The Nek. Both of these positions gave the Turks a field of fire into the backs of the Australians holding positions along the Second Ridge. This gap needed plugging. At dusk, on 2 May, a joint New Zealand and Australian attack, with support from the RND, was launched to eradicate the Turks from these positions and to capture Baby 700. This hill was tactically very important. Briefly held during the first day of the landings, it needed recapturing in order to strengthen the Anzac position. During the attack some trenches were taken near the Chessboard, but elsewhere the rest of the attack failed, forcing a withdrawal back to the starting line. By 3 May it was apparent to both sides that there was stalemate at Anzac. The Turks had not given up, though, and 19 May witnessed the largest Turkish counter attack of the campaign so far. Result: another failure.

At Helles, the main Gallipoli front at this time, Hamilton planned a general attack to clear the beachhead finally and to capture the first day objectives of Krithia and Achi Baba. This half-hearted attempt, later known as the First Battle of Krithia, was fought on 28 April, but failed. The Turks then tried to throw the British and French back into the sea during 1-3 May, but ended in the same predicable results. Victory, for either side, was not going to be easy. Hamilton then renewed the offensive between 6-8 May; result was another disappointment, and he again repeated the old style attack on 4 June, with similar results, although British and French attempts to straighten the lines towards the end of June did meet with limited success. However, a similar bite and hold attack during the second week of July went to show that this type of small-scale attritional tactic would be slow and costly, and time and troops were at a premium. There was also a naive expectation that the Turks would offer little resistance and were, by July, low in morale. This was far from the truth and, although the Turks were on the defensive and had suffered devastating casualties, they were a long way from conceding. There would be no quick and easy win.

Chapter One
Planning and Preparation

So bold it might be successful

Lieutenant General Sir William Birdwood, commanding the ANZAC Corps, was one of those not content with the stalemate. He worked on a breakout plan with his Chief of Staff, Lieutenant Colonel Andrew Skeen. Raids to gain intelligence of the ground had been conducted into the immediate area; these occurred at Gaba Tepe to the south and Suvla to the north. What was presented to the Commander in Chief, General Sir Ian Hamilton, was not revolutionary in objective but was imaginative in the series of complex stages to reach that goal. This bold and daring plan was essentially a flanking manoeuver that consisted of a major night break out to the north of Anzac and a left hook sweeping move to capture the two highest peaks of the Sari Bair range, Chunuk Bair and Kocaçimentepe (Hill 971), by dawn. With the heights secured there would be a follow on advance to push the Turks off the Second Ridge and to capture Baby 700, Battleship Hill and 400 Plateau. With Anzac Ridge captured, an advance to capture the Third Ridge would follow, followed by Gaba Tepe and then Mal Tepe, the hill overlooking Maidos and the Dardanelles. Birdwood

Lieutenant General Sir William Birdwood, ANZAC Corps.

thought rather optimistically that a single division would be sufficient for this! Hamilton saw potential in this plan, but only if he had more men available. One division would not be enough.

In early June 1915, the political scene was changing back in London. The beginning of the shells scandal, amongst other problems, had toppled the Liberal government; although Asquith continued as Prime

Minister in a newly formed coalition government, Winston Churchill was forced to leave his position as First Lord of the Admiralty. The War Council, in charge of the strategic direction of the war, was reformed under Lord Kitchener, Secretary of State for War, and was meaningfully named the Dardanelles Committee. Hamilton had a request pending for three more divisions in total, in addition to the 52nd (Lowland) Division that Kitchener had already promised him. Initially he would have had to make do with this division, but then a change of tack fell in Hamilton's favour. Kitchener and the War Council's focus was Gallipoli and they needed an early conclusion to the campaign. For this Hamilton received his three additional divisions as well as the 52nd. The

Field-Marshal Horatio Herbert Kitchener, Secretary of State for War.

three New Army divisions consisted of the 10th (Irish), 11th (Northern) and 13th (Western) Divisions, who were volunteers who had answered Kitchener's 'Your Country Needs You' recruitment campaign of 1914. These were mainly civilians, but what they lacked in training and experience was made up for by enthusiasm and determination to get to the fighting before the war was over. Christmas 1914 had come and gone, but there was still talk that it would all be over soon. Hamilton did not have to think long about how the extra resources should be deployed, and agreed to General Birdwood's proposal.

On 11 June, barely a week after the failure of the Third Battle of Krithia, the optimistic Hamilton now looked at Anzac becoming the focus. Hamilton wrote in his diary:

Sailed over to Anzac with Braithwaite. Took Birdwood's views upon the outline of our plan for entering the New Army against the Turks. To do his share, durch und durch (God forgive me), he wants three new Brigades; with them he engages to go through from bottom to top of Sari Bair. Well, I will give him four, perhaps five! Our whole scheme hinges on these crests of Sari Bair which dominate Anzac and Maidos; the Dardanelles and the Aegean. The destroyers next took us to Cape Helles where I held a pow-wow at Army Headquarters, Generals Hunter-Weston and Gouraud being present as well as Birdwood and Braithwaite. Everyone keen and sanguine. Many minor suggestions; warm approval of the broad lines of the scheme. Afterwards I brought Birdie back to Anzac and then returned to Imbros. A good day's work. Half the battle to find that my Corps Commanders are so keen. They are all sworn to the closest secrecy; have been told that our lives depend upon their discretion.

General Esat Pasha, Turkish Northern Group Commander.

At about the same time in June, Turkish *Northern Group* Commander General Esat Pasha and divisional commander Colonel Mustafa Kemal were on Battleship Hill discussing risks from the north and south to the Anzac area. The groups Chief of Staff, Fahrettin, recounted the conversation between the two officers. Esat Pasha asked Mustafa Kemal, *Where will the enemy come from?* Kemal then made a sweeping hand gesture, from Ariburnu and up along the coastline to Suvla, and said, *From there!* Esat Pasha then said, *Let's assume that they do come from there! How will they be able to move?* Kemal used his hand to draw a semi-circle that began from Ariburnu and continued towards Chunuk Bair Kocaçimentepe: *Like that.* Esat Pasha reportedly began to laugh and patting Kemal on the shoulder, said, *Don't you worry, they will not do that.* Kemal replied, *God willing, sir, may it turn out the way you expect.*[1]

During late June, in Helles, the French had launched a successful attack at Kereves Dere and a week later the British at Gully Ravine. At Anzac it had been quiet since May, with the exception of small scale raids and minor tactical operations. This posed a question for Turkish commanders as to where the next attack, large or small, would be happening. The Turks knew that the Gallipoli campaign would continue, especially after Winston Churchill's speech on 5 June in Dundee when he stated, *Through the Narrows of the Dardanelles and across the ridges of the Gallipoli Peninsula lie some of the shortest paths to a triumphant peace.* The Kereves Dere and Gully Ravine successes did cause the Turks concern, but these were isolated bite and hold attacks, not an all-out offensive to end the campaign. It was now time for the Turkish command to work out the best way to counter the next offensive, but for that they needed to know where the next allied offensive was to fall.

Enver Pasha, the Turkish Minister for War and *de facto* Commander

17

in Chief, still believed that Bulair and Enez at the Gulf of Saros was the main threat, but General Otto Liman von Sanders, his German military adviser and commander of *Fifth Army*, largely disagreed, although he did keep troops in the area. Sanders wrote to Corps Headquarters, requesting their opinions on possible enemy offensive locations. Vehip Pasha, commander of the *Southern Group* at Helles, responded that he did not believe there would be another major attack there; one main reason was the area was surrounded on three sides by the sea, so any advance would have to be due north. The previous slaughter during the Krithia battles proved this was not a viable route, and the nature of the ground elsewhere on that coastline prohibited a new major landing. He thought that a breakout at Anzac was most likely, combined with a new landing either

General Otto Liman von Sanders.

north or south of that position. Esat Pasha, Vehip's brother, who commanded the *Northern Group* at Anzac, expected a southerly break out from Anzac towards Gaba Tepe, discounting a breakout to the north, towards Chunuk Bair and Hill 971. Colonel Mustafa Kemal, who was still a divisional commander at the time, had not ruled out north Anzac.

In the middle of July, Liman von Sanders reorganised the *Fifth Army* on Gallipoli. On the Asian side of the Dardanelles three divisions, supported by the Çanakkale Gendarme Battalion, were organised as the *Asian Army Group*. On the Peninsula itself, six divisions were positioned at Helles whilst four divisions were at Anzac. At Suvla there were only four battalions, two of infantry and two of gendarme. Much further north, *4 Cavalry Regiment* defended the Tayfur region whilst the *Saros Army Group* defended Bolayir, Enez and Kavak. The gendarmerie was organized by the French in the 1870s along the lines of their system, and served in rural areas where there were no police. Due to the shortage of soldiers in the war, they became part of the Ottoman Army.

By early July Birdwood had submitted the final plan, which he wanted to execute the same month to take advantage of the fine weather; however it had to be delayed until August due to delays in the extra troops arriving. The plan was less ambitious in objectives and concentrated on capturing Hill 971, whence he could capture the remainder of the Sari Bair ridge to the north; whilst to the south he would sieze Baby 700. Capturing the Third Ridge and advances to Maidos could wait. Five miles north of Anzac, the British IX Corps would land at Suvla Bay and, by securing the surrounding high ground, would make safe the area as a base to support the overall operation. In support of the main Anzac operation, Hamilton had planned several diversionary demonstrations. These consisted of a British naval squadron bombarding a cove named Sigacik Koyu, near Smyrna (Izmir), to a force of some 300 Greek soldiers who actually landed near Enez, on the Turkish coast. During the lead up to the offensive Hamilton did not try to hide the troop build-ups, and had spread them out over various Greek islands. These islands, full of spies and close to the Turkish coast, would add to the misinformation that the Turks were receiving. Added to this, maps of various parts of Turkey were printed, which it was hoped would keep the Turks guessing as to where the main offensive, or new landing, would take place. The week before the offensive von Sanders had sent up daily aerial reconnaissance flights over Anzac and Helles, but these all returned inconclusive results. A larger diversion would come at Helles, where the attack hoped to focus the Turkish forces' attention whilst the Anzacs attempted their breakout and the British IX Corps landed at Suvla. Locally at Anzac there would also be an assault to capture Lone Pine, details of which will be covered later.

Under the overall command of Major General Sir Alexander Godley, the main Anzac attacking force comprised of the New Zealand and Australian Division, the British 13th (Western) Division plus two attached infantry brigades. Godley was a professional soldier who had seen service in the British Army since 1885. In 1910 he was appointed Commandant of the New Zealand Military Forces, which he soon turned into an organised and professional force that became the New Zealand Expeditionary Force at the outbreak of the First World War. When the Anzac Corps was created under Birdwood, Godley was

Major General Alexander Godley, NZ&A Division and commander of the Sari Bair attack.

19

appointed commander of the New Zealand and Australian Division. Godley was considered by many a callous and somewhat snobbish general and, if he was not already unpopular with the troops before August, he most certainly was after the offensive. Entrusted with him was not only the largest but the most risky offensive that Gallipoli had so far seen since the landings themselves.

Godley approved the plan for two main assaulting columns to march out of Anzac on the night of 6 August. The Right Assaulting Column, comprising the New Zealand Infantry Brigade under Brigadier General Francis Johnston, would head for Chunuk Bair, whilst Major General Herbert Vaughan Cox's Left Assaulting Column, that comprised Brigadier General John Monash's 4 (Australian) Brigade and Cox's 29 (Indian) Brigade, would head for Hill 971 and Hill Q. Both objectives were expected to be captured by dawn. The right column that would head for Chunuk Bair would have a simpler navigation task, as their route was to some degree visible from the old Anzac perimeter. They would advance by way of Sazli Beit Dere and Chailak Dere onto the Rhododendron Spur and then to Chunuk Bair. The left column's task was more complicated, having a dual objective. After reaching the head of the Aghyl Dere where it forks, the column would split: one half would cross the Damakjelik Spur and ascend the Abdul Rahman Spur to capture Hill 971, whilst the other half would ascend the right side of Damakjelik Spur to capture Hill Q.

The weakness of the plan was the reliance of coordinated timings of both columns to take their objectives, so if one failed the other would also. The risk of this plan was it being over ambitious and very complex in nature. This, coupled with the poor health of most of the men, who were suffering from dysentery and general fatigue, meant that the cards were not stacked in Birdwood's favour. Take into account the men's condition and then look at the rugged and rocky cliffs and spurs that even lightly equipped fit men in daylight would struggle doing, let alone sick and tired men with full loads at night.

It was described as:

... mad country. Watercourses change direction, seemingly gentle slopes conceal a precipitous and treacherous surface under the scrub, there is no method in anything ... One ravine is very much like another, the levels are all wrong, and without a compass or the summits to guide one, it is surprisingly easy to scale a tortuous ravine only to find oneself farther away from the summit than one began.

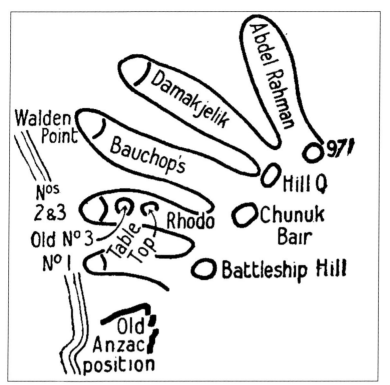

North Anzac.

Knowing the ground is important to understand the challenges that faced the men. To the west of the Sari Bair ridge was a labyrinth of spurs. The three major ones, from south to north, were Rhododendron Spur, Damakjelik Spur and Abdul Rahman Spur. Between them were five important ravines that run down from the heights, Sazli Beit Dere, Chailak Dere, Aghyl Dere, Kaiajik Dere and Asma Dere, all dry in summer. On each spur were several Turkish outposts, namely Old No.3 Post, Destroyer Hill, Table Top and Bauchop's Hill. Each was lightly entrenched, often consisting of shallow, disconnected trenches, which in some places had a thin belt of barbed wire, but on the whole the area behind this was undefended and unfortified. Within this whole area were only two Turkish battalions, the remaining elements of about 20,000 Turkish rifles from the Turkish *19th*, *5th* and *16th Divisions*, were clustered around Battleship Hill, Scrubby Knoll and Pine Ridge. Against this force, Birdwood had about 37,000 rifles available for the operation, 20,000 of which were under the command of Major General Godley, whose New Zealand and Australian Division were occupying the northern part of Anzac, and which were soon to be reinforced with several British New Army battalions.

In order to clear the path for the two assaulting columns, the foothills, which were lightly held by the Turks, were to be captured first. This included Turkish outposts on Destroyer Hill, Table Top, Old No.3 Outpost, Bauchop's Hill, Walden's Point and ultimately the task was to occupy the Damakjelik Spur. On the left flank the plan was to land British IX Corps during the night at Suvla, where it would help to protect the Anzac northern flank.

Moving soon after dark, it was hoped that both the covering forces would have captured their objectives by 10.30 pm. To coincide with this, the two assaulting columns would begin their assault at 10.45 pm and were calculated to reach the summits of Hill Q and Hill 971 about an hour before dawn. The left hand column would secure the flank and consolidate whilst the right hand column would capture Chunuk Bair and then send units to capture Battleship Hill and Baby 700.

From Russell's Top, in the old Anzac area, the Australian Light Horse would assist this advance by attacking The Nek and Baby 700 at dawn. The Nek, already a fortress where neither side had gained dominance, was recognized as a tough nut to crack; so, to attract attention away from here, there would be attacks from the garrisons holding Pope's Hill and Quinn's Post. These would be nothing more than subsidiary attacks, and again they would be launched against known strong defences on the Chessboard and the trenches opposite Quinn's Post, known as Turkish Quinn's. Neither of these attacks had much hope of success as both Australians and Turks had failed in similar assaults previously.

This was not the end of the plan. Once Battleship Hill was carried, the units would advance down the spur that led onto the Third Ridge (Gun Ridge) and occupy Scrubby Knoll, creating a new line of advance that would unlock the Old Anzac area. It was a tall order by any stretch of the imagination, but a coup if Birdwood could pull it off. To put this in context the objectives were no different than those set for the original Anzac landings in April.

To distract the Ottomans from the impending offensive, during the afternoon of 6 August, two diversionary attacks were to be made; at the Vineyard in the Helles sector, and at Lone Pine in Anzac. Both actions were designed to prevent the Turkish forces from sending reinforcements north to the Sari Bair range. During the night of 6 August the British IX Corps, under Lieutenant General Frederick Stopford, would land north of Anzac at Suvla Bay, and capture the surrounding hills in order to make the bay a safe harbour to support the overall operation.

It was expected, rather ambitiously, considering the condition of the

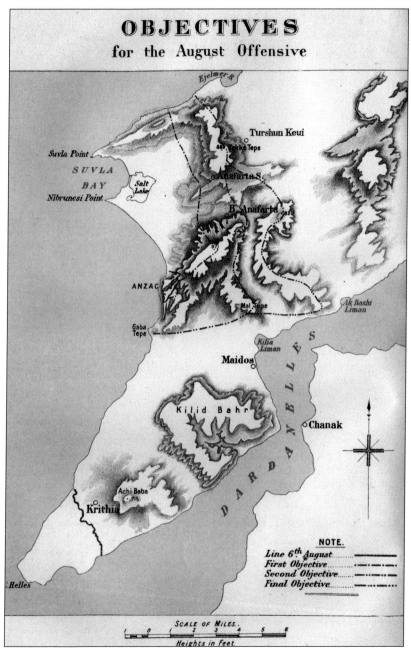

Objectives for August Offensive (Official History).

troops as well as the difficult country that needed navigating during the night, that the whole Sari Bair ridge from Kocaçimentepe (Hill 971) to Battleship Hill would be in Birdwood's hands by dawn on 7 August. This would make the Turkish positions untenable at Anzac, once again giving the upper hand to Sir Ian Hamilton. The key to success was speed and surprise; to maintain the advantage before the Turks could react, and thus avoid a long and costly battle that Hamilton could ill afford. Once the British had captured the high ground, it was widely thought that this would be the key to unlocking the Dardanelles. However, even though the views down to the Narrows would have been spectacular, the British possessed no artillery that was capable of accurately hitting these defences nearly fifteen kilometres away. A follow up advance would then be required to seize the Narrows, destroy the defensive guns, torpedo tubes and mine fields and at last allow the allied fleet through. None of this was planned for.

Many were deeply skeptical when they came to hear about the plan, especially in relation to both the complexity and the enormity of the task, as well as the nature of the ground where the operation was to be performed. On 2 August, Major Cecil Allanson, 6/Gurkhas, 29 (Indian) Brigade, wrote in his diary:

When the method of attack was disclosed to me confidentially that afternoon I gasped. It is to be remembered that Anzac is completely invested by the enemy; that no one has been able to reconnoitre the ground outside and that no one can absolutely guarantee the map. There are no villages and no inhabitants to help one, and the whole country seemed to be stiff with very sharp rocky cliffs, covered with thick scrub. I have a few ideas about night marches, their great difficulty and the need of careful reconnaissance, but when I was told that we were to break through the opposing outpost line at 10 pm on the 6th, march along the sea coast for three miles then turn at right angles and attempt to get under this big ridge about two miles inland, by dawn, and covered from the sea by innumerable small hills and nullahs, I felt what one would have done to a subaltern at a promotion examination who made any such proposition. The more the plan was detailed as the time got nearer, the less I liked it, especially as in my own regiment there were four officers out of seven who had never done a night march in their lives. The one hope was that the scheme was so bold it might be successful.

During the moonless nights of 3, 4 and 5 August, the Anzac piers and

Sari Bair showing the proposed direction of Godley's attack - Column ①, Australian and Indian assault on Hill 971 and Hill Q , Column ②.

jetties were busy bringing ashore men of the New Army, totalling 12,000 men, along with supporting artillery. Work continued until dawn, when all went quiet. There was then not a boat to be seen, and from the air the positions were camouflaged to hide the men ashore. The anticipation of a grand battle was growing. It was not just men brought ashore, but also their associated supplies. As sleepy as Anzac may have appeared during the hot sunlit days, the dark hours shrouded a scene of energy and resolve. As soon as the evening light had gone, a trail of heavily laden men and mules would take their huge loads nearer to the front. Growing piles of bully beef, biscuits, sealed petroleum tins of water, containing up to 80,000 gallons, and ammunition were hidden, ready to feed the impending storm. Field Ambulances repositioned themselves ready for the pending advance.

Hidden from the eyes of the Turks, large platforms were cut below the skyline of the hillsides to accommodate the troops, some capable of holding up to five hundred men. Existing communication trenches were widened, whilst new ones were dug silently during the night. Whilst all this was going on, life between the lines continued as normal, with sniping, bombing and shelling continuing like clockwork. To the Turks all appeared to be normal, although they were sure to know something was occurring. Rifles and ammunition were carefully checked, and re-checked, between which activities the men wrote up their diaries, took some last minute photos, and wrote their letters home.

Turkish shelling also continued during the night, with special attention to the beach and communication areas. Considering the number of men landing, very few casualties were caused. Lieutenant

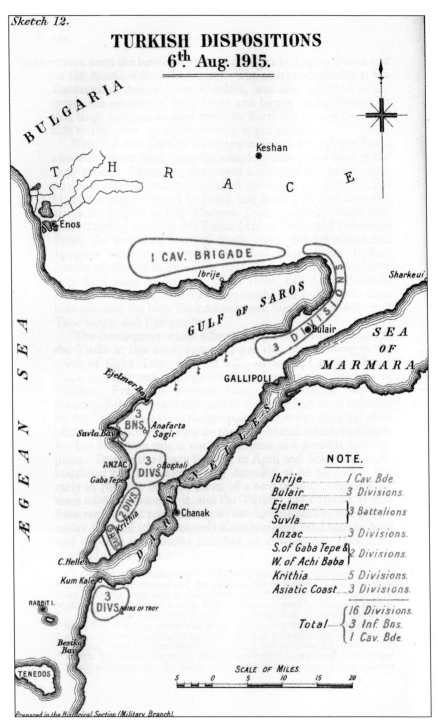

TURKISH DISPOSITIONS
6ᵗʰ Aug. 1915.

BULGARIA

THRACE

Keshan

Enos

I CAV. BRIGADE

Ibrije

GULF OF SAROS

Sharkeui

Bulair

3 DIVISIONS

SEA
OF
MARMARA

Ejelmer Bay

GALLIPOLI

3 BNS.

Anafarta Sagir

Savla Bay

Gaba Tepe

ANZAC

3 DIVS.

Boghali

2 DIVS.

Krithia

Chanak

DARDANELLES

C.Helles

Kum Kale

RABBIT I.

3 DIVS.

RUINS OF TROY

Besika Bay

TENEDOS

A E G E A N   S E A

NOTE.

Ibrije	1 Cav. Bde.
Bulair	3 Divisions.
Ejelmer	} 3 Battalions
Suvla	
Anzac	3 Divisions.
S. of Gaba Tepe & W. of Achi Baba	} 2 Divisions.
Krithia	5 Divisions.
Asiatic Coast	3 Divisions.
Total	{ 16 Divisions. 3 Inf. Bns. 1 Cav. Bde.

SCALE OF MILES.

5   0   5   10   15   20

Turkish Dispositions on 6th August (Official History).

Colonel Joseph Beeston, officer commanding Australian 4 Field Ambulance, recalled the occasion in his book, *Five Months At Anzac*:

Early in the morning the Gurkhas came ashore, but the Turks spotted them, and gave them a cordial welcome to Anzac. They are a small-sized set of men, very dark (almost black), with a Mongol type of face and very stolid. One was killed while landing. They were evidently not accustomed to shell-fire, and at first were rather scared, but soon reassured when we told them where to stand in safety. Each carried in addition to his rifle a Kukri, a heavy, sharp knife, shaped something like a reaping-hook, though with a curve not quite so pronounced. It was carried in a leather case, and was as keen as a razor. I believe the Gurkhas' particular delight is to use it in lopping off arms at the shoulder-joint. As events turned out we were to see a good deal of these little chaps, and to appreciate their fighting qualities.

During the night of 5 August both the British 29 Brigade and 29 (Indian) Brigade were smuggled ashore, out of sight of the Turks. With a further 4000 Anzac reinforcements, Birdwood's force stood at 37,000 men and 72 guns, facing 20,000 Turks and 76 guns. This would be the largest concentration of troops and guns that Anzac would ever see, but would it be enough to break out of the bridgehead and capture the heights?

Chapter Two

The Diversionary Assaults

This was a rotten place

Lone Pine

The offensive would begin with a series of head-on attacks by Major General Harold 'Hooky' Walker's 1st Australian Division at Lone Pine. These were designed primarily as diversionary, but if successful the plan allowed for further exploitation by driving a wedge into the enemy's main position. At 2.30 pm at Helles, preceding the Lone Pine attack, elements of the British 29th Division attacked towards a feature known as the Vineyard. This attack, like the one that would follow at Lone Pine, was aimed at focussing the Turkish attention to those areas, thus giving the best chance of success to the breakout.

The British attack at Helles failed, but at Lone Pine the outcome would be very different. Ambitious and risky yes, as all previous attacks of this nature had failed with enormous casualties, however this plan had the advantage of careful planning and cunning, which in previous efforts had been missing. The planned primary attack was against the southern lobe of 400 Plateau, a Turkish position known as Lone Pine. This was scheduled for the late afternoon of 6 August, and would be assaulted by 1 (Australian) Brigade, whilst at midnight, 6/AIF would attack further along the line at German Officer's Trench, just north of Johnston's Jolly.

Both positions were defended by Colonel Rüştü, *16th Division*, who had deployed *125 Regiment* on Johnston's Jolly, the northern lobe of 400 Plateau, and *47 Regiment* on Lone Pine. If the attack on Lone Pine proved successful, an attack on the front line trenches on Johnston's Jolly would then take place. Secondary to this phase, and only if the situation allowed, something that was rare during the fighting so far at Gallipoli, 1st Australian Division would then attack Gun Ridge to occupy its length from Scrubby Knoll to Gaba Tepe. There was nothing original in this, as it was one of the objectives of the covering force during the initial 25 April landings.

Lone Pine was a formidable fortification, positioned opposite the Australian salient known as The Pimple; less than a hundred metres of open, exposed ground separated the lines. The Turkish trenches, protected by barbed wire, were built up by a mix of sandbags and mud bricks, and in places were roofed over with heavy pine logs and earth. The pine log defence is of note as this was to take the Australians by surprise, a feature that had not been correctly identified in earlier aerial reconnaissances. Major Tevfik, commander of *47 Regiment*, had placed two battalions in the trenches, whilst his third battalion was close by in reserve to the north of Snipers' Ridge.

The frontage to be attacked by 1 (Australian) Brigade was just under 200 metres and consisted of flat scrubby ground, protected not only by the Turkish positions on Lone Pine but also by Johnston's Jolly to the north and the Turkish positions to the south by Cooee Gully. To reduce the time the attacking forces would be exposed to Turkish fire, the Australians had secretly dug shallow tunnels under No Man's Land, and designed exits to be opened up just prior to the attack; one such gallery, or Russian Sap, was dug within 25 metres of the Turkish line. Ingeniously the tunnels were to have another purpose; they could rapidly be converted into communication trenches to allow reinforcements, ammunition and other supplies to reach the captured positions, and to allow the wounded to be cleared.

Brigadier General Nevill Smyth VC's 1 (Australian) Brigade was to be used to make the assault, utilising the 2/AIF, 3/AIF and 4/AIF in the attack, whilst keeping 1/AIF in brigade reserve. There would be three waves, each wave consisting of 600 men, comprising about a company from each battalion.

The men would be lightly equipped with their rifle, bayonet, an iron ration (bully beef and biscuits), a full water bottle, two empty sandbags, a gas hood, their webbing equipment and a cotton bandolier, containing a total of 200 rounds of ammunition. Each man was instructed to sew on an artillery distinction white calico patch to their back and one on each arm to help identify the units during the advance.

The battalion bombing parties had a share of 1200 bombs that had been allocated to the brigade. The first wave would launch

Brigadier General Nevill Smyth VC, 1 (Australian) Brigade.

their attack from the secret underground positions, whilst the second would attack from The Pimple, the closest trench position to Lone Pine. The third wave would follow the second from The Pimple, but would be carrying, in addition to their fighting order, shovels and picks to consolidate the won positions.

The attack started at 4.30 pm with an hour's bombardment of the area. Twenty-eight guns could be mustered for this task whilst the Royal Navy supported the operation with HMS *Bacchante,* which sought targets in the valleys around the objective; and naval monitors provided counter battery aid on Turkish gun positions near Gaba Tepe and the Third Ridge.

Private William Quantrill (12/AIF) recalled the bombardment on Lone Pine:

On August 6 the bombardment by the British started just after dinner, by the howitzers, and about every half hour the field guns would join in with a perfect hail of shrapnel upon the Turkish trenches. The men at the guns were working at the double, infantry men helping to carry shells to the howitzers, so you can guess they were 'going some'. They had the range fine, and were spitting it right into the Turkish trenches. God knows how the Turks stuck to it, for their trenches were one cloud of smoke mid bursting shells, and while this was going on the boys were strapping their gear on, getting it nice and tight, and the good old bayonet securely fixed, everyone quivering with excitement. Of course, the Turkish guns were not sleeping; they gave us a

Lone Pine after the attack (*The War Illustrated*, 1915).

*hurricane of shells of all sizes, and did a lot of damage in the first
two or three minutes, but after that nothing much.*

*We were dead anxious for 5.30 to come, so that we could get
it over, for it is not a nice job, it is the waiting that kills, and seeing
the poor lads getting carried out of the trenches minus an arm or
leg, but all smiling and smoking the good old cigarette.*[2]

Observing the heavy allied bombardment, General Esat Pasha could
sense the impending attack. Even though the thick logs, that covered the
Turkish trenches, were good protection from shrapnel, when the high
explosive shells began to fall they had the effect of splintering the wood
to devastating effect on the occupants. The Turks had learned that
occupying the narrow communication trenches and saps provided the best
chance of survival, and then to reoccupy the front lines when the
bombardment had lifted. For now this bombardment was to continue.

For the 1800 Australians waiting for the whistle, the tension was
undoubtedly mounting, but morale was high. An unknown soldier
wrote:

*I was one of the mob that waited behind the parapets for the Lone
Pine attack. The signal was due any moment when Charlie Pearce
stuck a pin into Jackie Burns' rear. The attack was forgotten as
Jack threw himself at Charlie and within ten seconds both were
going hammer and tongs. "A minute to go," was heard as the
O.C. came along to stop the fight. "What the hell do you fellows
think you're doing," he roared. "I'm not quite certain sir, but I
think we're up to the last round," answered the dazed and
bleeding Jackie. With the screeching of whistles the hop-over
commenced. Within a minute Charlie and Jackie had gone to meet
their maker. Thus did fate turn Jackie's jest into stark tragedy.*[3]

Private Harry Clegg (3/AIF) described the moment the whistle was blown
and they charged towards the heart of Lone Pine:

*At 5.30 we charged with fixed bayonets. I can tell you we got a
warm time for a while. The moment we left our trench they opened
fire on us with machine guns, rifles, and shrapnel from their big
guns. Our boys were cut down like grass; but that did not stop us.
We charged straight on till we got to the first line of trenches. It
was our turn then. We very soon took possession of that, killing
every Turk that was in it. In about ten minutes we were over every
trench we could see. It was a splendid sight to see the boys*

31

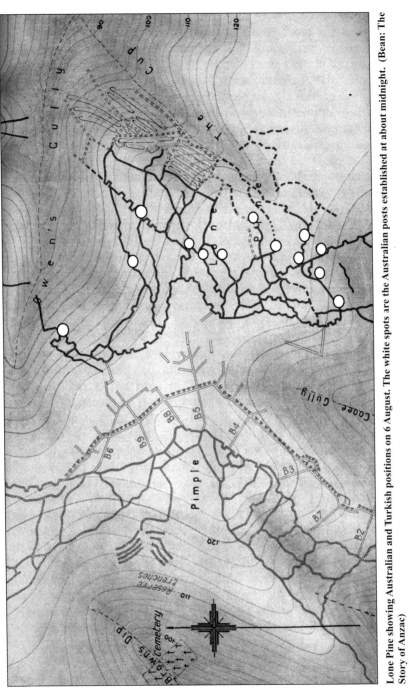

Lone Pine showing Australian and Turkish positions on 6 August. The white spots are the Australian posts established at about midnight. (Bean: The Story of Anzac)

standing on the edge of the trench, shooting down at the Turks. In less than no time we had them lying two or three deep in the bottom. All the time we were doing this their artillery was pounding away at us with shrapnel. It was when we jumped down into the trenches we had the real fun. We either shot, bayoneted, or knocked them on the heads with the butts of our rifles, whichever suited the purpose best. We scored a great victory, capturing every trench they had, and very few of their men got away. Those not killed were taken prisoners. We also got several machine guns and bomb mortars. Although I was hit at the start, I kept going till about 9pm. My leg got me beat then - it would not go to the ground, so I had to retire to a place of safety with the other wounded. The Turks counter attacked us with bombs during the night but although they did a bit of damage they could not drive us back an inch. The Australians are too much for them. It would do your eyes good to see our boys fight. They are frightened of nothing.[4]

Harry Clegg was out of the fight with shrapnel wound to his left leg; he was one of the lucky ones to come out of Lone Pine.

The three assaulting battalions went forward, two lines from the forward tunnels at only twenty five metres from the Turkish front line, the remainder from over the top of the Australian front line trenches. Because of the sudden and surprise advance there were few casualties crossing No Man's Land. What followed caused more of a surprise; an anxious moment was spent finding the front line trench that was covered in pine logs, all of which appeared untouched by the bombardment. Men, frustrated, fired through the loopholes and narrow gaps, whilst others sought ways into the Turkish trench system by finding large enough gaps, or forward saps to slip into the trench's dark interior. Others had to advance over the front line, where they found uncovered communication trenches to the rear, from where they could enter and then fight along the maze from the rear of the front line. Inside there was semi-darkness as a bitter struggle developed along the labyrinth of trenches and tunnels.

Lance Corporal Alfred Simpson (2/AIF) recalled the attack as his battalion went for the southern part of Lone Pine:

I got a good pair of wire cutters and a couple of bombs, and I was ready. Our company was in the front line, followed by C Company. We had a secret trench underground, thirty yards in front of our firing line, and this is where we got out from. The Turks must have thought us mushrooms the way we sprang up out of the ground - we seemed to come from nowhere We sat under the ground from 4.30 till 5.30 pm while a heavy bombardment went on. At 5.30 the order was given to charge. Then we got out and ran for their trenches. The artillery had blown their barbed wire away, but had not broken their trenches in, and when we reached the first trench, where we were supposed to have stopped, we found ourselves being slaughtered, and could not get into the trench, so simply had to go on. I shot a Turk here who was firing up through a hole in the ground, but not before he had done his damage.

I got down in the second trench. By this time the artillery was playing a big part, but what Turks were alive had flown. We found our way through communication trenches until the third trench was reached and we got the Turks with the bayonet. Although I did not get the pleasure of putting the bayonet through one, I accounted for four of them. Their artillery was simply terrible, and they shelled us out of that trench. I came back up the trench and the major saw me, and asked me to go with him to bomb some Turks out of the first trench. I lit one bomb and threw it in with them and the second one I threw on top, and when the dust cleared I poked my bayonet round the corner and had a look; one was dead another wounded in the heal and the other in the neck. I took them prisoners. I should have killed them, for they shot nine of our boys dead but I could not do it in cold blood.

We fought on all through the night with bombs and, my word, the way the Turks use them! They are the most deadly weapon of the lot. They throw them in twenty and thirty at a time all along the trench and knocked the men about terribly. They bombed us out of the trench twice, but we got them out with our own bombs. We fought for hours and I could only find one chap out of our company so the pair of us threw ourselves down amongst the supports and had about three hours sleep, then had to fight on again.[5]

Private Clarence Kirton (2/AIF) was in the second line of the attack. The battalion was caught in the open by both shrapnel and the Turks positioned on Snipers' Ridge, to the south, who were enfilading the advance with their machine guns.

Artist's impression of bombing at Lone Pine.

By this time the first line was well across the gully, and the enemy's artillery had opened a terrible shrapnel fire. The second line had shown their heads and were coming as rifle and machine gun fire grew thicker. I saw three men running, so up we jumped. I don't remember recognising anybody, but I know I got a bullet straight through my magazine, which fell out, hitting me on the toes. When we got in the Turks' first line a chap sang out that we would have to go to the second line. No sooner had we touched the ground then one of my mates got a bang on the side of the head. He was bleeding a good deal, and died before anyone could do anything for him.

We decided to push on a little with the third line of advance. The fire at this period had grown terrific (the third line coming) when bang! I thought someone had given my leg a sharp kick out of the way and looked and saw a hole in my puttee about two inches above my right foot. For a while it never gave me any pain, but as soon as I moved my foot the pain nearly drove me mad. Groans of agony are nothing here, I yelled at the top of my voice. I said to the one mate left out of five of us that I had stopped one in the leg. The third line was well on us now, and I made three attempts to get up, but my leg kept giving from under me. I was too weak, through loss of blood. My mate went on with a chap out of the third line but, poor chap, he stopped a bullet and I had to lie and watch him die. I was too weak to get him. The next thing was to get back to the sap. There were three more killed and two wounded there. One had his back broken, and was trying to roll down off the little crest he was on, when a machine gun caught him. It fairly riddled him. Anyhow, the poor fellow did not moan after. The fire and shells were so thick that the scrub behind us caught fire. A chap came and lay alongside me, holding in his right hand the arm-bone of his left, from which the hand had been blown off. I helped him to bandage it up, and he said he would wait with me till dark. He was an Australian to the backbone.

I never said my prayers so often and with such sincerity as I did those two hours or so, which seemed a week that we were lying there. It was just living hell. When darkness came I crawled and rolled back to the sap following the line as best I could. After a while I was in the sap getting my wound bandaged up and in six hours I was on the hospital ship. Well, Jim, you see we are not those six bob a day tourists that some people out there call us.[6]

An unknown lieutenant in 3/AIF, attacking the heart of Lone Pine, wrote of the attack later from a hospital bed, as he recovered from his wounds:

Our blood was up, and our only thought was 'Lone Pine must be ours'. It is a peculiar sort of 'don't care feeling'. You see your friends knocked out by your side, and you think, 'They're dead, and were as good as I am'. It is then that absolute contempt for death overtakes one. We got there, and were faced with a tough proposition. They had built their trenches with such perfection that the artillery did not do the damage we expected. Their

Turkish Soldier in marching order.

overhead cover made their trenches like tunnels—they had pine legs and cut timber laid closely together, and on top 2ft. to 3ft. of earth. Running out towards our lines were huge tunnels in which they sheltered during the artillery fire. We just simply had to draw them out. Dead and wounded were simply packed under these coverings. However, by 6.30 we were establishing a new firing line, building up one of their support trenches with sandbags, etc. Bombs—how I loathe the name—are only little things, about the size of a small jam tin, but they do the work of the devil. However, we hung on, and the position is still ours. I am certain if some of those who shirk could just set their eyes on some of those bodies, as they rot under the sun's rays, they would come along. By the periscope we could distinguish some of them, but for the most part they lay in a huddled mass. It is certain death to attempt to get to them to bury them, and so they lie there. If you could imagine fifty seven dead in about twenty yards of trench, and then lying there for three to four days, you will have an idea of what trench attacks are. We simply had to walk over them. Poor Meagers! His last words, after he was hit, about thirty yards from the Turkish trenches, were: 'Go on, boys; don't mind me'. He was hit in the stomach, and just turned over, and, I believe, died there. M'Gowan lay for fourteen hours outside the trenches with serious injuries. Young Vic Pinkstone was wounded and his brother Norman was attending to him, when a shell killed him in his arms. Norman got off without serious injury, but what an experience.[7]

Private Victor Pinkstone (3/AIF) is buried in Lone Pine Cemetery, and his brother Norman did survive both Lone Pine and the war. Lieutenant Hubert Meager (3/AIF) has no known grave, so his name is commemorated on the Lone Pine Memorial. Second Lieutenant Thomas McGowan, 3/AIF, was reported to have lain out between the second and third Turkish lines for thirty six hours, during which time he sustained fifteen different wounds. He recovered only to die from a severe attack of pneumonia in October 1915 and is buried on Lemnos.

By 5.40 pm the core of Lone Pine had been reached, and minutes later news was received that the position had been captured. A number of small post were quickly established deep within the heart of the Turkish position overlooking The Cup, to the north flank overlooking Owen's Gully, and the southern flank down the Cooee Gully spur.

It was unknown to the Anzacs at the time, but Major Tevfik, *47 Regiment*, had formed the routine of moving his men back from the front line trenches during a bombardment, leaving only a few sentries, so as not to suffer heavy losses. This undoubtedly helped the first waves establish positions in the Turkish trenches, as their advance was largely unopposed. When Tevfik realised that there was a follow-on attack, his men did not have enough time to come through the tunnels and reoccupy the abandoned line.

In amongst the bombarded trenches the Turks were in the thick of it and fighting a desperate hand-to-hand struggle for survival. An officer of *1/47 Regiment* wrote in a letter home about the Australian attack:

Major Tevfik Bey, *47 Regiment* (Gallipoli Through Turkish Eyes).

One day the enemy turned all their weapons against us. It was an extraordinary fire, and it lasted for about an hour. Once they had decided that there couldn't possibly be any survivors, they began to attack in waves as previously planned; one wave would collapse upon us like a wooden fence, and then a new wave would immediately appear, and in this way the enemy tried to advance.

Can you imagine our Mehmets letting them pass… unfortunately, the rifles in the hands of the soldiers overheated. The grease between the wooden and metal parts was sizzling and the mechanisms stopped working. The rifles had to cool, and our enemies profited from the situation. By then the battle was being waged hand to hand, and it was then that I was shot, and Sergeant Osman from Silifke carried me on his shoulders to the medical post. The active headcount of our battalion was down to thirty-three, no officers left; the second in command of the battalion from our company, Muhammed Ali the Arab, and the junior officer from the second company, Zahid from Tarsus, had prepared themselves. Then Muhammed Ali was killed at some point during this time. The adversaries took two of our trenches, but could not advance further; I was watching the fighting from the medical post. It was truly an apocalypse, an apocalypse indeed.[8]

Major Tevfik's men had been caught off guard, and those not already dead were now isolated within the Lone Pine fortress; bitter hand-to-hand struggles ensured. General Esat Pasha ordered Colonel Hans Kannengiesser's *9th Division* to position themselves nearby at Gaba Tepe, whilst he ordered *15 Regiment* to march directly to Lone Pine. By 7.00

Turkish soldiers in their bivouacs.

pm Esat ordered into reserve two battalions, *1/57 Regiment* and *2/13 Regiment,* in readiness for the counter attack. Major Zeki, commander of *1/57 Regiment*, was quickly on the scene but almost immediately came under fire from the Australians, who had gained a position overlooking The Cup:

> *The moment we turned into that valley we came under fire from the Australians at the head of it. Near there I met the commander of one of the battalions that had been holding the centre of the Lone Pine front. I asked, 'What has happened?' But he was clearly very shocked. He kept saying, 'We're lost; we're lost!'*[9]

Zeki reinforced the beleaguered Turkish garrison with his battalion and along with *2/13 Regiment* and *3/47 Regiment,* were organised together for a counter attack. At 11.00 pm the Turks attacked and, after fierce hand-to-hand fighting, began to force the Australians back. During this fighting the Turks loss two regimental commanders: Major Ibrahim Şükrü, *15 Regiment*, and later on Tevfik, both mortally wounded by bombs. Tevfik's last recorded words, spoken just before leading a counter attack, were, 'Well, I will take the troops myself and we'll do something whatever it costs'. Tevfik was held in such high regard by his regiment that he was buried near where he fell and a tomb was erected. In 1919, when Charles Bean visited the battlefield, he was guided by the very same Major Zeki who came to the aid of *47 Regiment*. He showed him the tomb of Tevfik, which today has been lost, but would have stood just outside the boundary of the present day Lone Pine CWGC Cemetery, close to the modern day road.

At 7.00 pm the Australian brigade reserve was sent forward into Lone Pine and for the next forty eight hours both sides dueled in one of the most severe bomb and bayonet battles ever to be witnessed. The Turks were desperate to regain their old positions but the Australians were not going to relinquish them without a fight.

Private George Talbot (12/AIF) was one of those sent to reinforce the hard pressed 1 Brigade:

> *... this was a rotten place. I was in charge of a section throwing bombs, and we got a pretty warm time of it. Two of them were killed, and three wounded, counting myself. This is a very large number out of eight, don't you think? I had three in one communication trench throwing bombs. One of them was killed, so not having another man available I went in his place. A few minutes later another man was wounded in the same place, so that only left two of us in the one place, one to throw bombs and one to put a sandbag over any Turkish bombs that might fall in our trench. We got on all right until three hand grenades fell in the trench at once. We got bags over two of them, but the third was too fast for us, and exploded before we could do anything with it. One*

Lone Pine, looking across The Cup from the newly captured positions onto the rear of Johnston's Jolly. (2013)

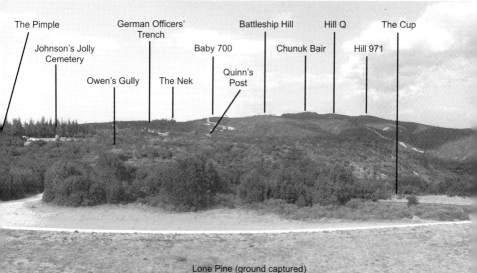

Lone Pine (ground captured)

piece hit me below the knee cap, but did not do much damage. I hung on till they got another man, and then went and got a bandage on it. I hobbled about for a couple of days, and was finally sent to hospital. This is the second time I have been sent to hospital since I landed. I would like to have been there all the time with our boys, but that I cannot is not my fault. I am just going to tell you something that will make your hair stand on an end. When we reinforced the 1st Brigade on Lone Pine ridge, dead Turks were stacked four high in the sides of the captured trenches. Some of these had been there four days, so you can guess what they would be like lying in the sun. Most of our dead were lying between the old trench and the captured one. We could not get out burying them, for the enemy's fire was too constant. In some places we had to walk over the dead. I never wish to see such a horrible sight again. Nor do I wish to smell such a horrible stench as we got from the dead bodies. We had to wear our respirators all the time we were in the trenches.[10]

The British Official History noted:

Throughout these days of incessant fighting the spirit of the Australian troops was beyond praise, and so great, and almost embarrassing, was the anxiety of the rank and file to take their share in this historic action that at one period the unique precaution had to be taken of posting piquets in the communication trenches leading to Lone Pine to prevent unauthorised men from going into the fight. Reserve troops would wait in long queues for a chance of pushing their way forward, and sums of five pounds and upwards were freely offered, and offered in vain, by employed men in rear to take the place of friends going up to the front line.

By the morning of 8 August the worst of the fighting at Lone Pine had ended, although the Turks would continue their attacks until 10 August. Both Australian and Turk were completely exhausted from the three days and four nights of constant bayonet and bomb fighting.

On 9 August Sergeant Major Paul Goldenstedt (3/AIF) thought that day would be his last.

The rifle, bomb and machine gun fire just after daybreak was something never to be forgotten. Our men were swept off the parapets like flies. General Smyth VC, who commanded the 1st

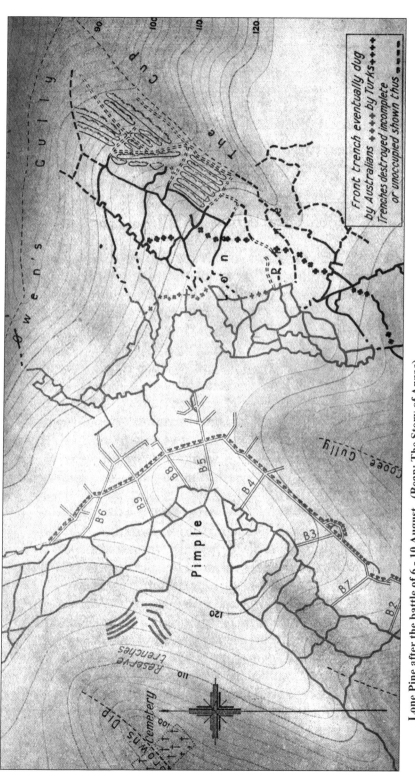

Lone Pine after the battle of 6 - 10 August. (Bean: The Story of Anzac)

Brigade, issued an order for every man to step down off the parapet and prepare to meet the Turk on the floor of the trench. I was then near Lieutenant Percy Woods - Percy and I had been sergeants together. He took out a pencil and wrote a few words to his wife on a field service post card. Having no wife and few relations that I could think of for the moment, I scribbled a few lines to her as well, and Percy fixed a bayonet to his rifle. I preferred my revolver. The feeling at that moment must be something like what a condemned man feels when the hangman is tying the rope. Anyhow, of a sudden there was a wild cheer and before we knew where we were the Turks had beat it for their trenches.[11]

This welcome comedown was followed by the battalion being relieved. For Goldenstedt and his men their ordeal was over, for at dusk the Turkish attacks petered out.

General Esat Pasha officially called the counter attacks off the following day, although sporadic fighting did continue for a few days longer. Turkish casualties had been heavy: 7164 men were either killed, wounded, missing or made prisoner. The 1st Australian Division's losses amounted to 2277, which included two commanding officers: Lieutenant Colonel R. Scobie (2/AIF) and Lieutenant Colonel E. S. Brown (3/AIF). It is of interest to note that the majority of the casualties suffered at Lone Pine were not by shellfire but from close hand-to-hand fighting with rifle, bayonet and bombs. With Australian and Turkish dead intermingled, Lone Pine became one big open mortuary, a charnel house, where the corpses lay under the feet of the living for some time to come..

Seven Victoria Crosses (Captain A. J. Shout and Private L. Keysor, 1/AIF, Private J. Hamilton, 3/AIF, Lieutenant W. J. Symons, Lieutenant F. H. Tubb, Corporal A. S. Burton and Corporal W. Dunstan, 7/AIF) were awarded to the Australians for gallantry at Lone Pine, the largest amount for any single action on Gallipoli. The legend of Lone Pine is remembered as a glorious but costly success of Australian arms; however, it had one unfortunate by-product that would have tragic consequences later. Lone Pine was the undoing of Birdwood's master plan, as its success convinced Esat Pasha that his southern flank would be the focus of the main British thrust. Because of this, he had over a division in the area. When they were no longer required, they were sent quickly to the northern flank when the New Zealanders stormed the heights. The success of the Australian attack at Lone Pine was therefore a significant factor in diminishing the chances of a New Zealand triumph at Chunuk Bair.

German Officers' Trench

As the Lone Pine fighting was raging, close-by, at midnight on 6 August, a lesser known attack was about to be launched. At Steele's Post the 6/AIF were to assault German Officers' Trench, so-called because two German officers had been observed there in early May. This position was of great tactical importance to the Turks, as it commanded the Australian positions in the area. This manoeuvre was therefore designed to remove the flanking threat that this strongpoint posed to the dawn attacks at The Nek, Turkish Quinn's and Dead Man's Ridge, which were to take place the following morning. Unfortunately the element of surprise had gone and, daring as the plan may have been, it was ill-conceived, as the Turks were on full alert and had drawn in many reserves towards the area as a consequence of the Lone Pine fighting. The only factor in the Australians' favour was the advantage of a night assault through secret tunnels that had been dug close to the Turkish lines. This had worked at Lone Pine, but would it work here?

Lieutenant Colonel Henry Gordon Bennett, commanding 6/AIF, reviewed the plans; his comments on the attack were published in *Reveille*, an ex-serviceman's magazine, in August 1932:

Three tunnels, 3-4 feet wide and 7 feet deep, had been dug, leading from our front line for a distance of about 30 yards. These were linked up by another tunnel, which was roughly parallel to our front line. A thin crust of earth, from 6 to 12 inches thick, was left as a roof to the tunnels. And from the forward tunnel a number of narrow saps were dug, leading to small posts, each capable of accommodating three or four men. These saps were just wide enough for a man to crawl through. The attack was to be launched by the 6th Battalion from these fire posts at midnight. The roofs were to be removed just after dark and the men were to charge across the intervening 20 yards to the enemy trench. The attack was to be preceded by three mine explosions: at 11 pm, 11.30 pm, and 11.40 pm. These mines, it was hoped, would destroy a portion of the enemy trench, with its garrison, and completely demoralise the rest of the troops holding that section of trench.

The assaulting troops did not dare occupy the forward tunnels from which the assault would be made until the last mine had been detonated in case the reverberations caused the tunnels to collapse all around them. Gordon Bennett was very tense in those final moments.

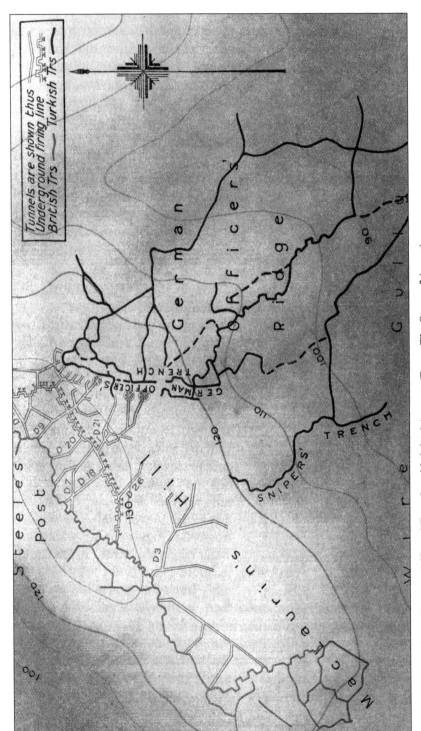

Tunnels are shown thus
Underground firing line
British Trs ━ Turkish Trs

6/AIF assault on German Officers' Trench, midnight 6 August. (Bean: The Story of Anzac)

As 11 o'clock approached everyone waited anxiously to see yards of the enemy trench go skywards. But instead there was a low muffled rumbling and a slight earth tremor. We peered over the parapet, expecting to see the flash of the explosion and tons of earth and a few Turks hurled into the air. But nothing happened. The mine was too deep to be effective. A minute or so later we were all crouching low hoping to dodge the shells the enemy poured on us in retaliation. Shell after shell landed in and around the trench, tearing great rents in the communication tunnels. At 11.30 the next mine was blown, with even less effect. This brought another hurricane of shells on Steele's Post. We were beginning to feel depressed. We realised that the enemy, instead of being destroyed or, at least, demoralised by them, had been made alert and ready. Then the third mine was blown at 11.40, with no better result.

Still, orders were orders and they would have to try their best. They moved down the tunnels to the underground front line, ready to break through the crust of earth and charge across the twenty metres to the Turkish front line at midnight. It soon became apparent that the Turkish counter-bombardment had been far more effective than the Australian mines. The Turkish bombardment fell onto the Australian positions, damaging their crowded trenches and blocking one of them. As reports came back, Gordon Bennett realised that his battalion was facing utter disaster.

The party moving by one tunnel groped its way forward in the pitch-black darkness, stumbling over the heaps of debris caused by the bombardment. Movement was difficult and slow. One tunnel was completely blocked and impassable, while another was almost as bad. The party that had been detailed to use one tunnel was forced to retrace its steps along the crowded trench and to find its way to its position by an unknown route. To make matters more difficult, commands could only be given in whispers and this made control almost impossible. Instead of reaching their position in ten minutes, as anticipated, it took almost an hour. The time for the attack was well passed and the troops had not arrived at their posts.

Brigade HQ were not happy with the delay and at 12.10 am ordered Bennett to move. At 12.30 am, still seeing no progress, they ordered him again to attack. At 12.35 am his men were finally in position, and the attack was launched. However, as they emerged almost in single file from the forward saps, they were met with withering fire from the defending *72 Regiment*, and almost to a man were cut down by their machine gun fire. The men fell back into the tunnels, blocking the exits. In the dark confusion reigned. It was an utter shambles. Finally, at 00.35 on 7 August, Gordon Bennett's men were in position and ready to attack. The signal for the assault was given - a blast of a whistle.

Men in the fire-posts jumped out and rushed forward. The moment they did, the enemy raked No Man's Land with machine guns, rifles and bombs. The thin line melted away. Men were hit before they left the posts. Those who followed fell back wounded, blocking the saps and preventing the rest of the attacking force from leaving the tunnel. The wounded crawled back out of the inferno into the safe refuge of the tunnel and before many minutes it was realised that the attack had failed.

The attacking troops were under a shattering fire, not just from German Officers' Trench immediately ahead of them but also from machine guns and rifle fire from the Turkish trenches at Quinn's Post on their left, Mortar Ridge to their front and Johnston's Jolly to their right. Seeing the hopelessness of the situation, Gordon Bennett reported back to brigade headquarters that the attack had been a total failure.

I telephoned Brigadier Forsyth telling him the result of the attack: the impossibility of attacking from the congested tunnels; the failure of our mines; with the result that the enemy trench was strongly held by an alert enemy. After consulting with the Divisional Commander, the Brigadier ordered another attempt to be made as soon as practicable.

Communications were bad and, despite Gordon Bennett's report, the brigade and divisional staff were not sure what was really happening. The capture of German Officers' Trench before dawn was essential to avoid the threat of devastating flanking fire into the southern flank of the planned morning attacks on The Nek, the Chessboard and Turkish Quinn's. Major General Walker and his Chief of Staff, Lieutenant Colonel Brudenell-White, believed that the attack was probably mishandled and ordered the attack to continue.

Gordon Bennett had no other choice than to clear the debris from the tunnels and reorganise his men for a second attempt. He knew what the outcome would be, but he would not willingly disobey a direct order.

The Australian view today from Steele's Post, overlooking the Turkish positions of German Officers' Trench and Wire Gully.

> *The tunnels were cleared of wounded; officers were given fresh orders for the attack and a commencement was made to reorganise the men ready for the charge. In the dark and crowded tunnels this took two hours to accomplish. But at last everything was ready. Everyone in those tunnels knew they were embarking on a forlorn hope. They knew the Turks were waiting to mow them down the moment they showed themselves. Still, they decided to give the best that was in them to make a success of the venture. The signal was given.*

It had taken a long time to clear the way for the second assault, but finally, at 3.55 am, the attack was renewed.

> *The enemy answered it with a hail of lead from the trench twenty yards away. Our men scrambled from the posts, only to be shot down. A few survived, to find themselves alone on reaching the enemy trench. As they essayed to return, they too were hit. For the second time the assault had failed, not because the men were unwilling to face the danger, but because it was physically impossible to succeed.*

The second attempt thus also failed, despite the bravery of the officers and men. Walker and Brudenell-White at divisional headquarters still refused to accept defeat, knowing the importance of taking this position to support the later attacks. He therefore ordered a third attempt. Bennett was furious and told Brigade HQ again how hopeless the situation was and said he would lead the attack himself. Bennett heard nothing back until about 8.00 am, by which time Walker, after consulting with Birdwood, stopped the assault. At this time there was no point in continuing, for the attacks at The Nek, the Chessboard and Turkish Quinn's were over.

Due to Bennett's efforts in stopping the attack, the casualties 6/AIF suffered were relatively small compared to the other assaults: eighty killed and sixty six wounded. This action was a classic example of those ordering the attack not fully understanding the situation on the ground, a common failing that would be repeated.

The Light Horse

There would be three attacks by the Australian Light Horse on 7 August; at The Nek, the Chessboard and Turkish Quinn's, with the principal objective of capturing Baby 700. The light horsemen were eager for a fight, as they had been at Gallipoli in a dismounted infantry role since May and, bar a few raids, this would be their first big chance to prove themselves. There is a painting by George Lambert, *The Charge of the 3rd Light Horse Brigade at The Nek*, which hangs in the Australian War Memorial that illustrates this action, but the popular perspective of The Nek comes from the Peter Weir film, *Gallipoli*. With its haunting soundtrack and cinematic beauty, it has helped make this action an Australian legend, despite its historical inaccuracies. Amongst other inaccuracies, the light horse were not providing a diversionary attack to help the British IX Corps come ashore at Suvla, and they were not sent to their deaths by British generals. As Lone Pine overshadows the assault on German Officers' Trench, so does The Nek overshadow the other attacks that day against the Chessboard and Turkish Quinn's.

The light horse attacks were planned as a spearhead to break out of the northern part of the old Anzac perimeter, and then to force a way north to meet up with Godley's men. His New Zealanders should have been on Chunuk Bair, advancing against the Turks on Battleship Hill from behind, whilst the light horse took Baby 700 with a frontal assault. These two converging attacks would then complete the capture of these hills. These attacks would have to be performed in conjunction with each other, thus giving the greatest possible chance of success. However, by dawn on 7 August it had become apparent that the capture of the heights was behind schedule and, in a reversal of roles, it was decided to allow the light horse attacks to continue in a hope that they would help take the pressure off the New Zealanders. Unknown to the light horse, the New Zealanders were resting, having breakfast, and had no plans to capture Chunuk Bair during the daylight hours.

Baby 700, which had been hotly contested since the original landings in April 1915, with follow up attacks in early May, remained in Turkish hands, as it would throughout the duration of the campaign. It had become a fortress, with several lines of trenches positioned on the forward slopes of the hill, overlooking the Anzac positions of Russell's Top and Monash Valley. For the Anzacs to get onto Baby 700 they would have to cross a narrow causeway, or neck, only thirty metres wide, either side falling away into steep slopes. Not only were there two strong Turkish trenches on The Nek itself, but the flat and open stretch of land was also protected by at least five known machine guns on inaccessible spurs on either flank.

The failure of the assaulting columns' night advance was known to Godley and Birdwood. With the New Zealanders just under a mile's steep climb short of their objectives, it was hoped that the lack of heavy opposition would allow them to take the heights at any time. However, it was also known that, with or without resistance, they would be nowhere near Baby 700 by 4.30 am, the time of the planned assault. The light horse attack was allowed to continue, as it was thought that focussing the Turks on the head of Monash Valley would give the New Zealanders the best chance of success.

The Nek

The attack on The Nek and Baby 700 on 7 August was to be conducted by 3 (Australian Light Horse) Brigade, under the command of Brigadier General Frederic Hughes. At Hughes' disposal were men from 8/LHR, 9/LHR, 10/LHR, along with two battalions from the 13th (Western) Division; 8/Cheshires, 8/Royal Welsh Fusiliers (RWF) along with 71/Field Company, Royal Engineers. For the initial assault Hughes chose to use the Victorian 8/LHR and the Western Australian 10/LHR, leaving 9/LHR and the Cheshires in reserve. The attack would be preceded by a thirty minute bombardment to soften the Turkish defences. Due to the narrow saddle of the ground at The Nek, approximately the size of three tennis courts, the charge would be formed of four waves, each of 150 men, two from each regiment. It was planned for the first wave to capture The Nek, the second to capture the front line trenches and saps on Baby 700, and the third the crest of this hill. The fourth would be held in reserve and advance with picks and shovels, closely followed by the Cheshires,

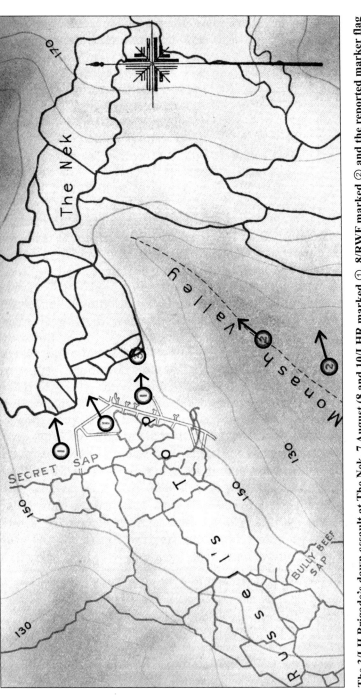

The 3/LH Brigade's dawn assault at The Nek, 7 August (8 and 10/LHR marked ①, 8/RWF marked ② and the reported marker flag ③ (Bean: The Story of Anzac).

who would help with consolidating the captured positions. Despite the strong defences, both Corps and Divisional command were confident of success.

Each man was dressed in their flannel shirts, shorts and puttees, and was to wear an identifying white calico patch. The men would carry a rifle, bayonet, an iron ration, a full water bottle, two empty sandbags, a gas hood, their webbing equipment and a cotton bandolier, containing a total of 200 rounds of ammunition. Bombers and bomb carriers would advance with each line, whilst others would carry scaling ladders and large wooden planks, to be used to cross over any barbed wire entanglements and for crossing the deep Turkish trenches. Each line would also carry four small red and yellow flags to mark the captured trenches to show progress. The assault would be using the bayonet only, with no round up the spout and the magazine empty. This should not be viewed as using out of date tactics more akin to the Napoleonic wars, but rather a method to prevent the attackers from becoming bogged down too quickly in a fire-fight. Utmost dash was the weapon of surprise, and it was the one hope that the Light Horse had in gaining their objective.

Lieutenant Colonel John Antill, the Brigade Major, issued his written orders:

> *One thing must be clearly understood and appreciated. We are out to stay; there is no coming back. The surest means are dash and determination. No time to waste on prisoners, no notice of tricks of the enemy such as 'cease fire', and there is no retire. Once out of the trenches, out for good, and the assault for all goes right home. The attack to succeed must be a surprise, carried out with a rush and without fire.*

The Nek, with Suvla off in the distance. The cemetery was built over No Man's Land, the area 3/ALH Brigade charged on 7 August 1915.

These words were actually Godley's; Antill echoed them in his orders. With or without surprise, the Turks would be waiting. The trenches, held by members of Mustafa Kemal's *19th Division*, would hear the crack of the rifle-fire coming from the north, probably wondering what was going on. Without distraction by other events, the Turkish position here was very strong, not only with several lines of terraced trenches that reached all the way up onto Baby 700, but there were also a multitude of saps and communication trenches for the Light Horse to fight their way through. In addition there were machine guns trained on this area, not only in front but also from the flanks on the Chessboard and from behind at German Officers' Trench. The Chessboard would be assaulted at the same time, however the Turks knew that 6/AIF's attack during the night had been a failure against the latter. With Baby 700 under no threat from behind, The Nek position remained as formidable as ever. The front line trenches at The Nek were manned by elements of *18* and *27 Regiments*, with *57 Regiment* and both *72* and *77 Arab Regiments* in reserve on Baby 700.

The thirty minute planned bombardment began on time at 4.00 am and, although noisy, achieved little damage to the Turkish positions. Then, as one witness wrote, the bombardment was *cut short as if by a knife*. For some unknown reason, possibly a mistake in synchronising watches, there was an unexplained seven minute gap from the last shell falling to the time of the assault. This left the light horsemen looking in astonishment. Was this a ruse to get the Turks back into their trenches for one final burst? With all the hope of the attack put on the element of surprise, this long pause did allow the Turks to man the trenches and prepare for the impending attack. There was no more shelling. To the right, sister regiments of light horsemen had begun their attacks against the Chessboard and Turkish Quinn's, but at The Nek they waited, confused and unsure what to do. Antill contacted Divisional Headquarters by telephone to ask if the attack was still to proceed, confused by what he thought was a premature stopping of the barrage; the response was the attack must proceed according to plan. At 4.28 am, or what was really 4.35 am due to the seven minute discrepancy, the Turks were observed manning the parapets and ranging the machine guns in readiness for the imminent attack. Not that the artillery had done much damage, as the bombardment being over a fairly large area including The Nek, Baby 700 and the Chessboard, was never going to be anywhere near as satisfactory as the infantry might have hoped.

At 4.30 am (4.37 am) the whistle was finally blown. With less than sixty metres of No Man's Land separating the trenches, the first wave of 150 Victorians, led personally by the popular Lieutenant Colonel Alexander White, commander 8/LHR, rose from their trenches to make their dash forward. White should not have gone with his men but, knowing what fate was waiting for them, he acted like a sportsman, not a soldier. The Turks opened a fusillade of concentrated rifle and machine gun fire into the on-coming first wave, and it was stopped almost dead in its tracks. Colonel White, along with all nine of his officers, became immediate casualties, and within seconds virtually every man in the first wave was either dead or wounded, most within twenty metres of their trench. Miraculously, a few Victorians survived who had stayed low to avoid the continuing machine gun fire that swept the ground in front. It was reported that three men managed to get into the Turkish trench, but were killed seconds after.

Artist's impression of the Australian Light Horse attack at The Nek.

At 4.32 am (4.39 am) the second Victorian wave followed and shared the same fate, adding to the pile of dead and wounded. If the machine guns were not bad enough, bombs were thrown towards the Australian lines, shortly to be joined by shrapnel fire from the Turkish artillery. It was about this time, through the dense cloud of dust that now shrouded the battlefield, that it was reported that an Australian red and yellow marker flag had been observed fluttering above the Turkish parapet to the right of the line, but within a few minutes it had disappeared. Hope that some men had actually gained a footing in the Turkish trenches saw the third wave line up and prepare for attack. Major Tom Todd, 10/LHR, who commanded the third wave, realising that the first two waves had failed and the futility of sending another, went to see the battalion commander, Lieutenant Colonel Noel Brazier. Brazier needed no convincing, knowing that any further attack would be insanity. Brazier went to Brigade Headquarters to see General Hughes, who had only just left to watch the attack from another vantage point. The Brigade Major, John Antill, knowing that a marker flag had been reported, insisted that the attack must continue. Brazier argued that no marker flag had been seen and to 'push on' would be 'murder'. After this furious row with Antill, who ordered Brazier to 'Push on!', he reluctantly left, but not before he said: 'Thanks, but don't forget I told you so'. Brazier returned to the waiting line and told Todd that the attack would proceed. He said to his men: 'I'm sorry lads but the order is to go'.

At 4.45 am (4.52 am), Trooper Harold Rush, 10/LHR, said to his friend 'Goodbye Cobber. God bless you', and then with the rest of the third wave went over the top to the waiting annihilation by the Turkish guns. In this wave was also Trooper Wilfred Harper, who was witnessed sprinting towards the Turkish trench, and this run was the inspiration for the last scene in the film *Gallipoli*. The characters in the film were loosely based on two brothers, Wilfred and Gresley Harper. Bean wrote of them:

With that regiment went the flower of the youth of Western Australia, sons of the old pioneering families, youngsters, in some cases two and three from the same home who had flocked to Perth at the outbreak of war with their own horses and saddlery to secure enlistment in a mounted regiment of the A.I.F. Men known and popular, the best loved leaders in sport and work in the West, then rushed straight to their death. Gresley Harper, and Wilfred, his younger brother... last seen running forward like a schoolboy in a foot race, with all the speed he could compass...

With the repeated carnage to the third line, Brazier raced back to confront Antill in an effort to prevent the fourth wave going. However, Antill once again told Brazier to 'Push on!' Furious, Brazier went off to find Hughes who, after listening to the facts, decided to suspend the attack. Tragically, the order did not reach the fourth line in time. At 5.15 am an officer asked why the line had not gone and, without the signal and in some confusion, part of the fourth line actually charged. Once again The Nek erupted into a deafening hail of Turkish rifle and machine gun fire, which culled the line and halted it in its tracks. The attack was now over. In just under an hour 8/LHR had 234 casualties, dead and wounded, from the 300 in the charge, whilst 10/LHR lost 138 men out of the 300 who charged. When the order was given for the survivors from the earlier waves to fall back, many were shot and killed in trying, so those who did not die in No Man's Land that day returned during the night.

Months after the attack the Australians, whilst sapping forward at The Nek, found the body of Lieutenant Colonel White, identified by a bullet damaged pocket watch:

The tunnel of the new firing line had been finished and cleaned out, and that night the crust collapsed and rapidly bagged up and built into a parapet. The enemy was suspicious all that night, but did not interfere much with the work. By morning the whole line

The steep slopes above Monash Valley that were assaulted by 8/RWF. The water tank in the foreground is original 1915 vintage. (2013)

was roughly complete and only needed deepening. As soon as dawn broke the enemy saw what had been done and shelled the trench furiously, so that most of the garrison had to be withdrawn. In opening this new line many of the bodies of the Light Horsemen in No Man's Land came within reach and were drawn in and suitably buried. Among them were those of a Colonel ... All of this unhappy band wore pith helmets and shorts, just as they had come from Egypt in. About five yards from the parapet of the post I first had on The Nek, one of them faced us on his hands and knees. He had evidently been wounded and started to crawl back to the trench when a second bullet killed him. A bush on one side had held him in that position, and a sentry on this post, while observing, had to look straight into his face. In the night time the only thing one could see was the faint smudge of the thin man's figure, and his face seemed always to be asking a question. Sentries could not stand the sight very long so we had to remove him. It was a hard job, as the Turk trench was almost within bayonet reach of him. Another man was found lying under a bush with his Prayer Book open in his hand and half of it ripped clean away as though cut by a knife.[12]

On the right flank of The Nek, two companies of 8/Royal Welsh Fusiliers (RWF) attempted their assault at 5.10 am. In the confusion they believed that the Australians had taken the first trench at The Nek, so advanced in support on their right flank, in an attempt to scale the steep slopes at the end of Monash Valley. The Welsh had initial problems advancing through the valley, which was not only thick with tall scrub but the sides were so steep, with much loose earth, that it made the footing difficult. Despite this, a company managed to get to the top, but was immediately engaged with machine gun fire and bombs. Further along to the right another platoon managed to get to the top, but were cut down by machine gun fire within seconds. With so much stacked against them, all they could do was withdraw. When news of the Welsh failure reached Hughes, he wanted his light horsemen to support them in the belief that progress could be made. Had he failed to grasp the situation? He must have realised by then that two of his regiments had been virtually annihilated just metres away? Eventually Hughes did halt the attack, although the Welsh had proven that this objective was as impossible as The Nek. The battalion had lost sixty five officers and men killed or wounded in the attack; the Turks reported no casualties.

Dead Man's Ridge

Immediate failure was not the case a little further along, where there was temporary success with the assault from Pope's Hill. Here two squadrons, comprising 200 New South Wales men from 1/LHR, under the command of Major Thomas Glasgow, and led by Major James Reid, attacked both Dead Man's Ridge and the Chessboard. The attack was timed to coincide with The Nek attack at 4.30 am, with the objective of taking the trenches at the Chessboard, from where the captured positions would command views over the Turkish communications up to Baby 700. This attack was therefore planned to augment the main assault at The Nek and Baby 700.

After a successful preliminary bombardment, Major Reid led a squadron from Pope's Hill, across the spoon shaped depression at the top of Waterfall Gully, towards the Turkish positions on the top of Dead Man's Ridge. To Reid's right flank, Major Glasgow led another squadron, but attacked up the steep slopes of this ridge by Bloody Angle, having climbed up into a jump-off position during the night. Both squadrons charged simultaneously at 4.30 am, taking the men of

Russell's Top Pope's Hill The Nek Dead Man's Ridge Bloody Angle Quinn's Post The Chessboard

Dead Man's Ridge today, which was assaulted by 1/LHR.

27 Regiment by complete surprise. Major Halis, commander of *3/27 Regiment*, described the moment the Australians broke into the trench:

> *Eight or ten of its men managed to penetrate a covered area of our trench number 21, from where they rained an uninterrupted salvo of bombs upon a trench, as a result of which this trench was emptied of its occupants, having all been killed, and taking this occasion they occupied a section of the trench equivalent to two squads, and threw stones to their rear to ask for reinforcements, but all the same very few of them, and of those who came to their aid, managed to escape, with the remainder being killed.*

The squadrons had captured three lines of trenches, but holding on to them would be the problem. Major Reid was wounded early on, and it was said that when he was shot in his right hand he changed his revolver to the left and carried on fighting. With casualties high, and bomb stocks low, efforts were now concentrated on holding on; but unsupported for over two hours and under constant showers of Turkish bombs, this was proving impossible. Glasgow realised now that their sister units' attacks at The Nek and Turkish Quinn's had failed and so, with no other choice, ordered the withdrawal. It was about this time that Reid, standing alongside fellow officer Lieutenant Burdett Nettleton, was killed by the same Turkish bomb; they were left behind in the trench for the Turks to bury.

Lieutenant Colonel Şefik Aker, commander of *27 Regiment*, wrote about the event in his memoirs:

> *The enemy was not successful. The Australians managed to capture only the small trench named 21 of the 27th Regiment, commanded by me, and that was only because all its defenders had either been killed or wounded. They planted their flag to indicate to their rear that they had taken the trench. However, following a brief counter attack, we took back the trench, including the Australian dead, who made up almost all the attackers, and their flag. These corpses were buried in a special location.*[13]

Şefik Aker mentions later the bodies of two Australian officers, as does Major Halis, who wrote:

> *... various weapons, digging utensils, two sacks of bombs and a map of the trenches, which had been abandoned by the enemy, were found. Two enemy officers, of whom one was a captain [sic], were buried. I submit also the information that the artillery fire towards our trenches, following the repulsion of the adversary, resulted in the partial destruction of our trenches and caused a great part of our fatal casualties.*[14]

The two Australian officers would have been Major Reid and Lieutenant Nettleton. Both bodies were lost in later fighting and today are commemorated on the Lone Pine Memorial.

Casualties were heavy for the Light Horsemen, with the loss of 154 officers and men, killed and wounded, out of 200, which is higher in percentage terms than the casualties suffered at The Nek. Glasgow was the only officer who came out unscathed. *27 Regiment* suffered 217 casualties, most of which were attributed to the Australian bombardment of the slopes following the withdrawal.

Turkish Quinn's

The Queenslanders from 2/LHR were also going to fail as they attacked Turkish Quinn's. Their plan was based on the basis that the New Zealanders would be attacking the Turks' rear, that German Officers' Trench would be captured and that the artillery would have thoroughly bombarded the opposing trenches. None of these had happened. After the explosion of a mine, the plan was for four waves, each of fifty men, due to the narrow frontage, to storm the Turkish positions opposite.

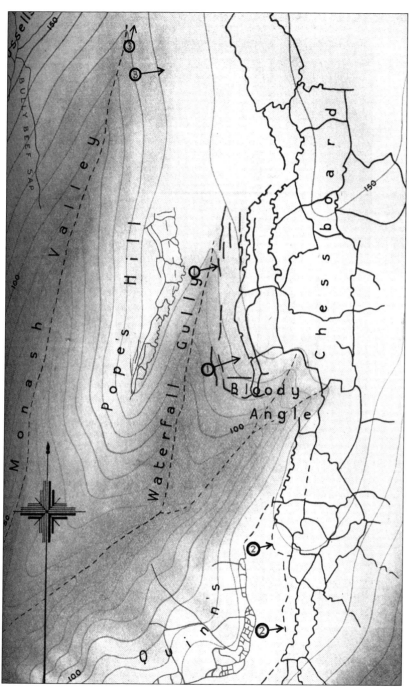

1 and 2/LHR dawn assaults on the Chessboard and Turkish Quinn's: 1/LHR assault on Dead Man's Ridge marked ①, 2/LHR on Turkish Quinn's marked ② and 8/RWF marked as ③. (Bean: The Story of Anzac)

From the start it all went wrong. At 4.30 am the mine failed to explode but, as ordered, the first line of Queenslanders, led by Major Logan, leapt from their trenches and an opened tunnel to rush the Turkish lines. Not surprisingly, they emerged into a wall of lead, as rifle and machine gun fire from the perfectly prepared Turks cut them down almost to a man. The Australian machine guns at Quinn's Post tried their best to suppress this fire, but to no effect. Major Logan was killed before he had gone more than five metres, and Lieutenant Burge was toppled before he had gone ten. With only one exception, every man in this wave became a casualty.

Corporal Percy Gooch (2/LHR) was a lucky survivor of the assault:

Lieutenant Burge was in our troop, and on the morning of August 7th, at 4 o'clock, the remainder of our line attacked, but I don't know how they got on. Our troop had to lead the way for our squadron, and we were split into four parties of seven. When the time came to charge we found that it was not possible to get more than eight men out of the trench at a time, so Sergeant Simpkins and I led the way, with three men each, Lieutenant Burge coming with us. Charlie Mowbray immediately followed with three others, and that is all of our troops who left the trench. We were all hit except two, one who was getting out and jumped back in again, and the other who was getting out and had to pull Sergeant Simpkins (who had been shot in the throat) into the trench again. Some of us arrived at the enemy's first trench, but could not get in owing to the bomb-proof cover, and the Turks were firing at us through chinks in the cover. Immediately behind this trench it was literally swarming with Turks, who were throwing bombs at us. On our crowd being ordered back to the trenches, there was a regular scramble back, leaving one of my party and myself to back Lieutenant Burge up. We dropped on our stomachs and wriggled behind an uprooted stump, but Lieutenant Burge and the other chap were hit and killed almost immediately. I fired until my magazine clogged, and then I couldn't do anything but lie still. I was in loose earth, and wriggled a bit of a hole for my body, but eventually reached the trench wounded.[15]

Tom Logan and Joe Burge are buried in Quinn's Post CWGC Cemetery.

The difference between the attack here and The Nek was that 2/LHR's commander, Major George Bourne, ordered the attack to stop as soon as he witnessed the complete failure of the first wave; within a minute this ill-fated attack was over.

Colonel Harry Chauvel, commanding 1/ALH Brigade, with Generals Godley (middle) and Birdwood (right).

By 6.30 am on 7 August the attacks inside Anzac had come to an end. These had all been in vain and provided no assistance to the New Zealanders, who at this time had not even begun their renewed advance on Chunuk Bair. Nevertheless, Birdwood let these diversionary attacks proceed against known enemy strongpoints, probably in the belief that they would, directly or indirectly, provide some support. It was the weakness of local command that turned the failed assaults on The Nek and German Officers' Trench into such a confused bloodbath. Brigade, in some misguided belief, carried on without finding out the cause of the failure and consequently did not adjust the plan but let it stand. Bean commented:

> *So ended the feints of August 7th. For sheer bravery, devoted loyalty, and that self-discipline which seldom failed in Australian soldiers, they stand alone in the annals of their country.*

Chapter Three

The Breakout

Like a long dark caterpillar

As soon as it turned dark on 6 August, Godley's hidden assaulting columns began to stir. As with the diversionary assaults, the men would be 'lightly' equipped. Designated bombers additionally carried haversacks full of bombs, both the jam-tin varieties and the official ball grenades. Each man also wore an artillery distinction white calico patch on his back and one on each arm to help identify the units during the advance. It was vital that no lights were shown and that silence was strictly maintained to give the best chance of surprising the Turks. It was at this stage of the operation that clockwork precision was required; if one force failed, the whole attack would be in jeopardy of collapse.

Two thousand men of Brigadier General Andrew Russell's Right Covering Force began to move from their hiding places as it grew dark. Clutha Mackenzie, a trooper in the Wellington Mounted Rifles and the son of New Zealand's High Commissioner in London, wrote in his book *The Tale of a Trooper*:

At last the sun sank behind the rugged islands in a glorious riot of colour, the high eastern hilltops which should be British by dawn gradually grew black against the appearing stars. The regiment, water bottles filled and in final trim, stood leaning on their rifles. Occasionally someone gave a hitch to his gear, others talked in subdued tones, or gazed solemnly

Brigadier General Andrew Russell, commanding the Right Covering Force.

out to sea where the black outlines of Imbros and Samothrace stood against the last glow of departing day. At this glorious hour there drifted up from the darkness in the ravine below such a sound as went deep to my heart. Rich in tone, perfect in key, unmarred by a single jarring note, to the accompaniment of battle sounds above, came the music of the soul, and I was awed. It was

*the chanting of five hundred Maoris and their prayer before this
their first great trial in modern warfare.*

*Then came the word to move, and the regiment, in single line,
filed down the slope and into the main sap to the north. It was
already full of troops filing to the attack, but, after many halts and
side-trackings, they reached the exit, which led to the ravine.
Here, at the parting of the ways, stood the fine old padre, and with
a "God bless you, my boy", I shook each by the hand as they
passed out to battle.*

It would be vital to the whole operation to capture the outposts quickly
and with maximum surprise so as not to alert the Turks in the surrounding
area. Russell's force consisted of the New Zealand Mounted Rifle
Brigade (Wellington, Auckland and Canterbury Mounted Rifles) along
with an additional regiment in the form of the Otago Mounted Rifles.
Also attached were two companies of the Maori Contingent and a field
troop of New Zealand engineers. The Wellington and Aucklanders were
to advance up Sazli Beit Dere to capture Old No. 3 Outpost, Destroyer
Hill and Table Top. The Canterbury and Otago men, along with the
Maoris, were to cross Chailak Dere, capture the Turkish outposts on
Bauchop's Hill, and then push the Turks back across Aghyl Dere.

Plans to take Old No. 3 Outpost had been in place for some time and,
with the help of the Royal Navy a long running ruse had been put in
effect. The navy had positioned a destroyer, HMS *Colne*, nearby, which
at 9.00 pm each night would turn its spotlights on to the Outpost and
open fire for thirty minutes. Punctually this went on for some weeks, so
the Turks had become accustomed to the routine, evacuating the post
during the nightly bombardment. Under the noise of the shelling and
away from the beam of the searchlights, the Aucklanders approached the
thorny southern slopes of the hill, avoiding the western slopes, which
they knew were heavily wired, in preparation to storm the trenches. At
9.30 pm, as the bombardment lifted and the searchlight was switched off,
the Aucklanders covered the last few metres and threw themselves into
the Turkish trenches to the Turks' complete surprise. The handful of
Turkish defenders were quickly overwhelmed and, whilst one squadron
set about securing the position, the other went off to engage those Turks
hiding in the surrounding scrub. With great cunning, and little loss of life,
the post had been captured. With this obstacle overcome, it was now the
turn of the Wellingtons to take the next one.

The Wellingtons and two attached Maori platoons, under the
command of Lieutenant Colonel William Meldrum, had different
objectives and were split up at this point. One squadron was tasked with

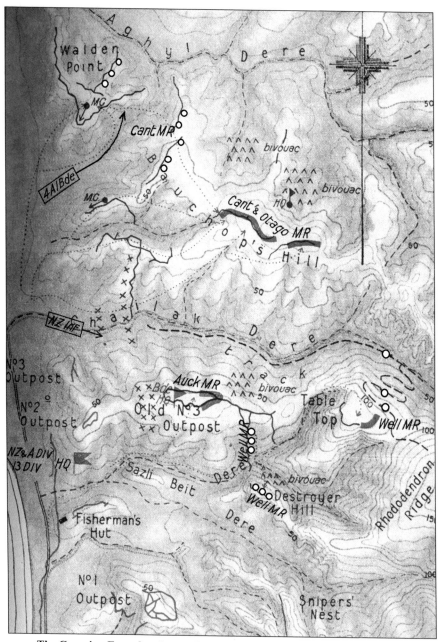

The Covering Force breakout. (Bean: The Story of Anzac)

capturing Destroyer Hill, whilst the remainder of the regiment would storm Table Top, which dominated Old No. 3 Outpost below. As with all the night assaults, the men's magazines were empty as the orders were for all the night work to be performed with the bayonet only.

Destroyer Hill would be the next to fall. Mackenzie wrote:

The forty silent figures crept up the sharp stony bottom for a short distance and then halted to await the critical moment of the attack. Then, while they waited, the long white beam from a man-o'-war at sea settled along the ridge on the left and showed the strong-wired entrenchments of the outpost. Whir-r-r went a shell overhead, and the

Lieutenant Colonel William Meldrum, Wellington Mounted Rifles.

first shot of the battle burst in an eruption of black smoke among the Turkish wire.

More followed in rapid succession; but the first shot had been the signal for the troop in the defile below to set off at a jog trot up its murky, twisty depths. They trotted along for five minutes, machine-gun bullets from high above sometimes hitting up small spurts of sand as they doubled round corners. Then, as they suddenly rounded a sharp ridge, a dozen or so rifles burst on them from fifteen paces distant. Some men went down in front of me, a cloud of dust sprang up and I stumbled over one of the prone forms. Instantly we were in among them, the terrified Turks shrieked, a few odd shots rang out, I killed two with my revolver, and then, with bloody bayonets, shadowy figures emerged from the murky depths of the trench, and passed on to explore the ground beyond. They pushed up through the thick scrub to beneath the outpost where a battle now raged, for the purpose of catching fugitives and preventing reinforcements. But none came, and the troop sat quietly in the scrub awaiting developments. The sound of musketry echoed beautifully across the ravines in the clear stillness of the night.

The other party of Wellingtons would go for Table Top, which was also being swept by the spotlights, and bombardment, of HMS *Colne*. In

HMS *Colne*.

support of her, land-based howitzers also joined the shelling, which would continue until 10.00 pm, the signal for the infantry assault on both positions. Their route to the top was troublesome, initially obstructed by a barbed-wired fence that they had to skirt around. They found the lower slopes of Table Top covered in thick, impenetrable scrub. This delayed the advance and by the time they had found a route up on the northern slopes of the hill the bombardment had finished and the spotlight was turned off. The party, led by Major James Elmslie, continued their climb to the top, unopposed, reaching the scrub covered plateau of Table Top just after 11.00 pm. Mackenzie noted:

The Turks were lighting fires in the stunted pine growth a short distance ahead, which lit with a red flickering light the overhanging clay cliffs of Table Top rising sharply at the farther side of the defile. Then the cold white glare of a searchlight settled on its flat top, and in a few minutes heavy howitzer, 18-pounder and naval shells shrieked overhead and burst, flashing and roaring, on the crest. The overhanging crag, her summit rent by an inferno of shell fire, her inaccessible escarpment lit by the lurid glow of scrub fires, and the fantastic smoke clouds eerily revealed by the searchlight, made altogether a wild night battle scene of weird glory. The bombardment ceased suddenly, the searchlight switched off, and part of the regiment, who had crawled through the scrub on the more accessible flank during the shelling, successfully rushed the Top.

Elmslie's men, supported by the Maoris, had captured an important part of the jigsaw. For the Maoris these two assaults were their first real action, and they:

> went into that splendid attack, their first battle with the bayonet, in a mood of savage determination and delight. This was their chance for fame. They went grimly for those Turks, bayoneted them in their lines, they burst into a tremendous haka when they had cleared the trenches – "Ka mate, ka mate, ka ora, ka ora!" – then silence as they pressed on to the next point.[16]

The Turks, from *2/14 Regiment*, were taken completely by surprise, which was illustrated later on during the night as several parties of Turks walked calmly onto Table Top without realizing its new occupants. By the morning the Wellingtons had taken just over 150 prisoners, here and on Destroyer Hill.

Whilst this was happening the Otago and Canterbury men, supported by some of the Maori Contingent, after following the beach north, had turned into Chailak Dere to attack Bauchop's Hill. The Otagos under Lieutenant Colonel Bauchop advanced directly across Chailak Dere and up onto one of the southern spurs of the hill. Advancing further north, Lieutenant Colonel Findley's Canterburys moved to capture the Turkish outpost and machine gun at Walden's Point, the seaward end of Bauchop's Hill. At Bauchop's it was not the steepness of the slopes that delayed its capture but the stoutness of the Turkish defence. The Turks, a company from *2/14 Regiment,* had positioned small groups on the forward spurs, with barbed wire obstacles, that broke up any organised advance. As soon as the Canterburys mopped up any resistance at Walden's Point, they advanced up the ridge, crossing Taylor's Gap, to meet up with the Otagos, who were having problems further up. It was here that Lieutenant Colonel Bauchop, with the support of the recently arrived Canterburys, charged the pocket of Turkish resistance further up the hill. The New Zealand initiative and spirited attack soon won through and, after capturing the hilltop by a bayonet charge, all remaining resistance disappeared into

Major James Elmslie, Wellington Mounted Rifles.

Table Top (2013).

Table Top being scaled by New Zealanders in 1915 (after the battle recreation).

the darkness. It was now 1.00 am; the timetable was already over two hours behind.

Casualties amongst the Right Covering Force were comparatively light, with 200 Turks killed and a similar number captured. The heaviest losses were amongst the Otagos, who lost their commanding officer, Lieutenant Colonel Arthur Bauchop, who was mortally wounded during the final bayonet charge. Lieutenant Colonel Findley was also wounded, but survived. Of the 400 men committed to the attack on Bauchop's Hill, twenty five percent had become casualties. The haul at Bauchop's Hill included a two-barreled Nordenfeldt gun, several old-fashioned bronze trench mortars, a hundred rifles and vast quantities of ammunition.

However, Russell's covering force had done well and although they were behind schedule this was not to have a direct effect on the rest of the plan. The path to Chunuk Bair had been successfully opened, and it was now the time of the Right Assaulting Column to complete the job and gain the heights by dawn. Before we move on to explain that action, let us describe what happened to the Left Covering Force in their attempt to open the path to Hill 971.

Brigadier General J. H. du B. Travers' Left Covering Force would lead off about thirty minutes after the Right, at 9.30 pm. Consisting of two New Army battalions; 4/South Wales Borderers and 5/Wiltshires, and half of 72/Field Company, Royal Engineers, they followed the coastal path north for about two miles. Leading the force was Lieutenant Colonel F. M. Gillespie and his 4/SWB. All began smoothly, despite a slight delay near Chailak Dere, when the force ran into some units of 4 (Australian) Brigade who, forming the Left Assaulting Column, had got ahead of schedule. Moving along a little further, several men

'The Spirit of his Fathers' – A patriotic cartoon depicting a Māori soldier charging two Turks. Behind him is a ghost of a warrior ancestor. (The Observer Christmas Annual, December 1915.)

71

were hit from firing coming from Table Top and Bauchop's Hill, where the New Zealand Mounted Rifles were clearing the slopes.

> *For a time the column had to halt and get what shelter it could in the prickly scrub along the shore, while the rear closed up. But it was soon moving on again, the 4th leading, though much delayed by the rugged ground, which was littered with boulders and covered with hollyoaks, a species of scrub standing about three feet high, with stiff and prickly leaves like a holly and bearing small acorns. The night was intensely dark, but the bursting shells and the naval searchlights playing on the hills, which formed the Turkish position, provided an intermittent illumination and made it possible to keep touch.*[17]

Brigadier General J. H. du B. Travers, commanding the Left Covering Force.

The force moved along the coast road and around Walden's Point, which was just about to be assaulted by the New Zealanders, and continued on, still undetected by the Turks. As they neared the mouth of Aghyl Dere, several men were hit by bullets coming from a trench the other side of the valley. This was quickly rushed and the Turks were successfully evicted. Several other groups of Turks in the area were also taken by surprise and by 1.30 am Damakjelik Spur had been fully captured. The 4/SWB and 5/Wiltshires then dug in to protect this flank from the expected Turkish counter attack. It was estimated that the Turkish garrison, all from *2/14 Regiment,* suffered some 200 casualties, killed, wounded or captured, whilst 4/SWB had suffered relatively lightly with twenty five casualties.

With both covering forces achieving their objectives successfully, and the area still in darkness, it was now the turn of the assaulting columns to achieve the goals of the heights before dawn broke on 7 August. It remained a tall order but, with the success of the earlier actions, it was looking hopeful for the allies.

The Right Assaulting Column, under the command of Brigadier General Francis Johnston, consisted of the New Zealand Infantry Brigade (Canterbury, Otago, Wellington, Auckland), the majority of the

26 (Jacob's) Indian Mountain Battery and No.1 Field Company, NZE. Johnston's objective was to reach Chunuk Bair an hour before dawn, by way of Rhododendron Spur. The Canterbury Battalion was to proceed along the left side of the Sazli Beit Dere, taking them past the northern side of Destroyer Hill, and then climb up the eastern side of Table Top to the saddle that joins Rhododendron Spur. The rest of Johnston's force would proceed along Chailak Dere, where they would ascend the northern face of Table Top, where they would join up with the Canterbury Battalion. From there the entire force would capture two minor Turkish trenches on the western shoulder of the spur, before proceeding the last kilometre onto Chunuk Bair.

Because of the fighting still going on at Bauchop's Hill, Johnston delayed the start of his column until 11.30 pm, when he decided that further delay would jeopardise the attack and ordered the advance. The main elements of Johnston's force, led by the Otago Battalion, made slow but steady progress up into Chailak Dere towards its first objective, Rhododendron Spur. It was now about 1.00 am, only three hours before daylight.

The scrub, the uncertain track, the darkness all hindered the advance. There would be a move forward of perhaps fifty yards, then a block in front, a crowding up behind, men standing wearily

A group of Otago Mounted Rifles before embarking for Gallipoli.

beneath their loads, expecting to move any second and not moving for five, ten or fifteen minutes. At last, tired of waiting, they would lie down, but no sooner had they done so than the file in front was moving, and they must race to join up again, and then, having done this, there was another halt. Nothing is harder than marching in this fashion at night, especially when men are loaded up with ammunition and weakened by privation and disease.[18]

It was not until reaching Table Top that they encountered a large body of Turks and their bivouac. Originally missed by Meldrum's mounted rifles, they were still in possession of parts of Table Top and so far had been left untouched. Seeing Major Frank Statham's Otago Battalion approaching them, they surrendered en masse but, even though they were captured without a fight, this action appeared to delay the column's advance until about 2.30 am; the schedule continued to slip. The moon had risen by about 2.00 am, which allowed some light into the deres, helping the column continue and increase pace and, with no further enemy encounters, some of the lost time was regained.

Major Arthur Temperley wrote:

It was a curious sensation to be marching along that valley in bright moonlight, far within the Turkish lines, without opposition of any kind. One Turk, who rushed out at the head of the advanced guard, I shot dead with my pistol. He was the only Turk seen that night.[19]

Prisoners were passed down the line when they were found, and every now and again within the scrub more Turks were found hiding. Statham continued past Table Top, crossing the narrow bridge of land that connects onto the Rhododendron Spur. Ahead, a forward party of the Otagos had reached the top of Rhododendron Spur, pushing a few fleeing Turks back beyond The Apex. It was about 4.00 am and would be getting light very soon. Further on, less than half a mile away, was Chunuk Bair, tantalizingly close. With no sign of the column to his left, Johnston halted here, despite Birdwood's and Godley's directive to push on regardless of delays. The New Zealanders were exhausted and its units had become fragmented along the approach to Chunuk Bair. Johnston did not want his column extending itself, piece-meal, any further into the dark, so he allowed time to reorganize and wait for the missing Canterbury Battalion to show up.

Lieutenant Colonel John Hughes' Canterburys, led by two mounted guides, had moved into Sazli Beit Dere but during the night had very soon become hopelessly lost. Initially they took the first fork of the dere, which led them to a dead-end at the cliff face near Table Top and then, retracing their tracks back to the junction, some took the next fork that took them near Destroyer Hill. Confused, about half the battalion and its machine guns went back to the starting point on Ocean Beach, where an angry Godley sent them back again. Eventually Hughes managed to orientate himself and eventually found his way onto Rhododendron Spur.

On the moonlit Cheshire Ridge, to the north, the Aucklanders under Lieutenant Colonel Robert Young and Wellingtons under Lieutenant Colonel William Malone were making their way along this steep-sided ridge towards The Apex. It was now

Lieutenant Colonel Arthur Bauchop, killed 6 August on the hill that bears his name.

about 4.30 am, and daylight. With two New Zealand battalions strung out along Cheshire Ridge and Chailak Dere below, whilst another two were stretched along the length of Rhododendron Spur, the chance of surprising the Turks on Chunuk Bair before light had now gone. As dawn broke the silhouette of Chunuk Bair could be seen less than a mile away. Falling off steeply from Table Top towards the north was a deep ravine, and thereafter ridge upon ridge as far as the eye could see. To the north-west, the dawn had opened the curtain on the overnight Suvla landing, with the fleet in the shelter of the bay, and a mass of men forming up around Lala Baba, to the west of the Salt Lake.

The Left Assaulting Column, under Major General Herbert Cox, had the most grueling mission ahead of them. The ground they had to cover was more complicated and bewildering in landscape, and the distance that needed traversing was twice as long than that of the New Zealanders. There had been no adequate reconnoitering. The only thing going for this route was the belief that there would be limited opposition.

Guiding this column was a New Zealander, Major Percy Overton from the Canterbury Mounted Rifles, who had first hand knowledge of some of this area, having scouted parts of it a few weeks before. Nevertheless, he had only ventured into a small percentage of it; the rest remained largely uncharted.

The column comprised Brigadier General John Monash's 4 (Australian) Brigade, Cox's own 29 (Indian) Brigade, the 21 (Kohat) Indian Mountain Battery and No.2 Field Company NZE. Led by 4

(Australian) Brigade, the column left in the dark along the northern stretch of Ocean Beach, past No.3 Outpost and then Walden's Point, before turning into Aghyl Dere. About a kilometre into the dere they would then cross Damakjelik Spur. With its left flank protected by the two New Army battalions of the covering force, two Australian battalions would continue towards Abdul Rahman Spur, piqueting the left flank. The rest of the column would then continue up Aghyl Dere to the head of the valley. From here 5 and 10/Gurkhas would ascend onto Chamchak Punar, a steep spur, to attack Hill Q, while 6/Gurkhas, 14/Sikhs and two remaining Australian battalions would continue north east into Asma Dere and ascend by way of Abdul Rahman Spur to attack Hill 971.

Brigadier General John Monash, commanding 4 (Australian) Brigade.

This all sounds straightforward on paper, but marching into unknown territory, in the dark and bearing in mind that dawn would be at 4.30 am, was to prove an impossible task. The expectation was that the units that were to attack Hill 971 would be forming up on Abdul Rahman Spur by 1.30 am, ready to capture the summit by 3.00 am. Marching a column of 5000 rifles would be a difficult feat in daylight, let alone at night, without adequate knowledge of this torturous ground or enemy disposition. This was madness! What must also be taken into account was the poor condition of the men, whose health had been wanting for some months. By August, the Anzacs were shadows of their former selves. Many were suffering from dysentery, old wounds and general fatigue brought on by the monotony of trench warfare. This was coupled with heavy loads of battle gear that they had to carry and which would make things no easier. Supplementing the veteran Anzacs who had been there since the landing was a large proportion of reinforcements. These were keen men, but they lacked battle experience. There were a high proportion of officers who did not know their men; and, likewise, the men did not know their officers.

So what caused the delays? Essentially, all went wrong near the start.

4 (Australian) Brigade, led by 13/AIF, left Reserve Gully at 9.15 pm and marched out on to Beach Road.

Like a long, dark caterpillar the column moved through the intense darkness and like a caterpillar it was silent, and wriggling. No one who took part in it will ever forget that march. To many it was a nightmare, to others intensely interesting, to all uncanny. The Aegean Sea could be dimly seen, rising up to the horizon as if to fall on us, and on it were the shapeless blotches of warships; overhead were stars in a cloudy sky, and on our right were cliffs illumined by a searchlight from the 'Colne' in order to blind the Turks who might be venturing to gaze beachwards in spite of the shells she was pouring into their lighted trenches ... The attack had already commenced on our Right and behind us, and we came in for a share of the 'overs', bullets causing several casualties in the column, and many shells screaming overhead into the sea. It was an eerie feeling to be marching in column over ground where by day no one could safely show his head.[20]

The column was stopped for about thirty minutes at No. 3 Outpost due partly to running into the British 40 Brigade, who were delayed getting forward due to the New Zealand Mounted Rifles falling behind the timetable slightly in clearing the foothills. Lieutenant Colonel Joseph Beeston, officer commanding Australian 4 Field Ambulance, recalled the area: 'as we passed what was known as our No. 3 Outpost, we came across evidences of the fight, dead men, dead mules, equipment, ammunition boxes and rifles lying all over the place.'

At 10.30 pm the firing reduced, which allowed 40 Brigade to continue. Half an hour later Monash then headed towards Taylor's Hollow, a depression just below Bauchop's Hill, about three kilometres from their starting point. Moving north along the beach, the column began well, but once it turned inland the real problems began, all due to the column taking a shortcut. This was believed by some to have been an accident at first; but it was not.

It was here, just before midnight, that Major Percy Overton was persuaded by a local guide to use a shortcut, a narrow gorge, which allowed passage into Aghyl Dere without the need to go around Walden's Point. Overton, wanting to make up time,

**Major Percy Overton,
Canterbury Mounted Rifles.**

77

made this last minute change to plans and directed the column into Taylor's Gap. However, what was a passable short cut for a man with his mule would not be suited for a heavily laden column of 3000 rifles in the pitch dark. This decision would prove disastrous. Subsequently known as Taylor's Gap, the 13/AIF continued to lead the way, but almost immediately they met some slight opposition, which halted the column whilst the bayonet men went onto the heights to suppress this fire. They advanced again but, getting barely a hundred metres into the gap, they stopped again due to heavier fire. A further company of men was dispatched to take care of this. Once again they continued, but then came to an area that narrowed into very heavy, overgrown, prickly scrub. Pioneers from the battalion were sent forward to cut their way through this, but still the advance was only in single file, all of this adding to the delay. The stop start affair caused its own problems amongst those at the end of the column. In the pitch black, with firing in the darkness ahead, at one stage a nervous medical orderly had ordered the retire, only to be challenged by a Gurkha officer.

Frustrated by the delay and lack of information, Brigadier General Monash asked permission of Major General Cox to proceed forward to try and find out what was happening, An officer he had dispatched earlier had failed to return, so Monash himself went through the gap and found the column halted just where the gap opens into Aghyl Dere. It was now 2.00 am, the time the column should have been on Adbul Rahman Spur, assembling for the assault on Hill 971. They were still waiting for a party of 13/AIF to return; they had earlier been sent across the dere in order to clear the lower parts of the Damakjelik Spur of snipers. What was not apparent was where exactly in Aghyl Dere they had exited. Overton thought that they were higher up the valley than they were; in fact they were still nearly half a mile short of where they thought they were. The original navigational plan based on a mix of compass bearings and paces was now redundant, and in the darkness none of the key features could be seen. Monash went forward with two platoons of the battalion but, reaching the stubble wheat field later to be known as Australia Valley, came under more Turkish fire. The moon had now risen, which made it easier for the Australians to see ahead, but also easier for the few Turkish riflemen to fire at the approaching column.

Lieutenant Colonel Leslie Tilney's 13/AIF soon found 5/Wiltshires, from the covering force, that had earlier set up a position on Damakjelik Spur. Knowing their position, 4 (Australian) Brigade could now place themselves into the line. Monash sent forward 14/AIF along with 13/AIF to clear the front and set up defensive outposts from Damakjelik

Turkish soldiers resting in their bivouacs.

Spur to Abdul Rahman Spur. Monash returned to Taylor's Gap and then ordered Lieutenant Colonel James Cannan's 15/AIF to advance along Aghyl Dere towards the heights, as per the original plan, to be followed by Lieutenant Colonel Pope's 16/AIF as soon as they exited the gap. Both experienced and proven commanders, these battalions were assigned the toughest task of spearheading the assault on Hill 971. Monash set up his headquarters in Australia Valley, soon to be joined by Major General Cox at sunrise.

15/AIF did not advance far before they came under fire, probably from *3/14 Regiment,* which Lieutenant Colonel Ali Rifat had ordered up to support his hard-pressed *2/14 Regiment.* Eventually they climbed up onto the spur to the east of Australia Valley, with views over Kaiajik Dere. From here, in small groups, the Australians pushed the Turks back and then dug themselves in, extending the line from the covering force on Damakjelik Spur. Both Cannan and Pope mistakenly believed themselves to be on Abdul Rahman Spur, and signalled back to Monash their position. In fact they were on another spur of the Damakjelik, overlooking Kaiajik Dere, still a ridge short of their objective. Throughout the morning the sound of rifle fire and sniping continued, but apart from that, no resistance from the Turks was experienced. Even if the Turkish resistance was negligible, the men of Cox's force were not

79

Turkish machine guns captured by the New Zealanders during the breakout.

only exhausted but had also become fragmented during the recent actions. Both generals agreed that a stop to allow time for the men to rest was needed.

Lieutenant Colonel Joseph Becston, officer commanding Australian 4 Field Ambulance, in his book, *Five Months at Anzac*, wrote of the main gully:

> *Aghyl Dere proved to be a fairly wide gully with steep hills on either side. A little distance, about three quarters of a mile up, we came to what had been the Turkish Brigade Headquarters. Here everything was as they had left it. The surprise had been complete, and we had given them very short notice to quit. Clothing, rifles, equipment, copper pans and boilers were in abundance, and it was evident that Abdul makes war with regard to every comfort. The men had comfortable bivouacs and plenty of bed-clothing of various patterns. The camp was situated in a hollow, round in shape and about a hundred yards in diametre, with dugouts in the surrounding hillsides; all was very clean, except for the fleas, of which a good assortment remained. The dugouts were roofed in with waterproof sheets, buttoned together and held up by pegs which fitted into one another. These sheets, with the poles, made handy bivouac shelters, easily pitched and struck. Altogether, their camp equipment was better than ours ... we annexed all the pans and boilers and made good use of them for our own Ambulance. Then, proceeding further up the gully, we found it*

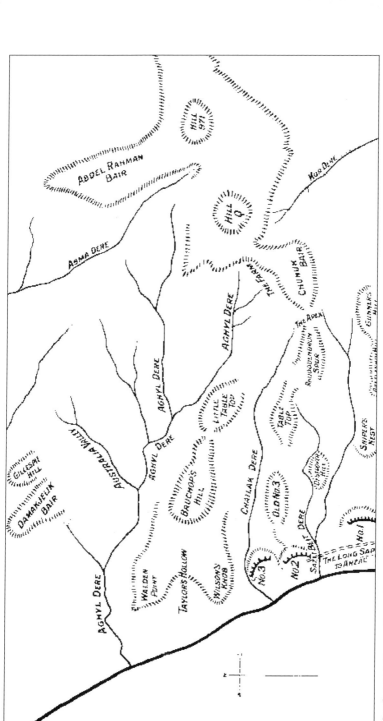

North Anzac's area formed a rough rectangle, 5,000 by 2,750 metres.

almost impassable by reason of dead Gurkhas and mules; a gun on a ridge had the range of this place to a nicety, and the ammunition train was held up for a time. I never saw such a mess of entangled mules; they were kicking and squealing, many of them were wounded, and through it all the Indian drivers were endeavouring to restore some kind of order. One had to keep close under the banks to escape the shells ... the shelling was far too heavy to let us pitch a dressing station anywhere here, so we retired to the beach to find a place more sheltered under the hills.

To the right flank, 29 (Indian) Brigade, who only exited Taylor's Gap at about 3.00 am, were directed by Major Overton further up Aghyl Dere, for their ascent towards Hill Q. It was about this time that Overton was shot and killed. Fighting their way slowly through the scrub, it became quickly apparent that for any of Cox's force to reach the main ridge before dawn was now impossible; it was fast approaching, and his Brigade had become separated amongst the broken spurs and gullies. Three companies of 5/Gurkhas had managed to establish themselves on the lower slopes of Chamchak Punar, the steep spur that leads up to Hill Q, whilst the other company, along with two companies of 10/Gurkhas, had become lost, having taken a wrong turn. They found themselves with the New Zealanders on Rhododendron Spur. By 9.00 am, 6/Gurkhas had reached Chamchak Punar with little resistance, whilst 14/Sikhs were in support of the Australians, to their immediate right. Cox was also of the belief that the Sikhs were on Abdul Rahman Spur with the Australians, and so ordered them to attack Hill 971 at 11.00 am.

Up to this time the casualties had been light, so the best part of two brigades were thought to be in good positions to continue the advance at daylight if the Turks would let them. The night march in some way was a success: the Turks had been surprised and the column had penetrated deep into enemy territory; but, on the other hand, the confusion caused during the night undid any initial success. The two brigades were now disorganised, deep in enemy territory and amongst some of the most tortuous and unforgiving ground in Gallipoli. They were in the foothills but still a long way from capturing the heights.

Chapter Four

7 August – Lost

Peace seemed to reign everywhere

Down in the lower Anzac valleys little had changed since dawn. The Australians, overlooking Kaiajik Dere, sent some scouts forward towards the undefended Kaiajik Aghala, later known as Hill 60.

> *We were now dead-beat, tired and thirsty ... some water which had been stored in tins for a long time was now issued. It was red with rust but was eagerly drunk. We also had a change of diet in the form of honey and mulberries obtained by parties fossicking near Susak Kuyu, gas-helmets being used to rob the hives, several making themselves sick with too much. It was not long before snipers sent the honey-seekers back into the Dere.*[21]

Some had wandered over a mile into Azmak Valley, towards Suvla, to fill water bottles at a farm, so Turkish resistance there was evidently negligible, although in other places any movement attracted sniper fire. One such position was on Hill 100, which prevented any further movement along the ridge. This position would prove a thorn for the

Men from 13/AIF part of Monash's 4 (Australian) Brigade.

Australia Valley today, with the Sari Bair ridge in the background. Monash placed his HQ here on 7 August 1915.

Australians in reaching Hill 971 as it would for those against Hill 60 later in the month.

Apart from a few scouts in advanced positions, both assaulting columns had come to a standstill by the morning. Major General Cox was aware of the urgency to commence the advance on Hill 971, but Monash's battalion commanders reported that their men were too exhausted to advance again during the day, so Monash halted the Brigade. Cox cancelled the order to attack at 11.00 am and with that any hope of reaching Hill 971 that day. Monash came under criticism later for what was seen as poor performance, a contrast to his later success as commander of the Australian Corps in 1918. The lack of his offensive action during 7 August, when his fellow Australians were heavily engaged at Lone Pine and The Nek, was not his finest hour. Cox then went in search of his own Indian Brigade to see if he could get them onto Hill Q, but he found them so scattered that hope of them reaching the heights was also dismissed. Higher up, on Rhododendron Spur, Johnston's men were also at a standstill. The night march appeared to have sucked the life out of all the brigades. The plan was in danger of failing and needed urgent action to restore energy and drive to it.

With no other option, Major General Godley decided he should use his reserve, 39 Brigade, under the temporary command of Brigadier General W De S Cayley, to bolster the Indian and New Zealand troops in a fresh effort to capture Hill Q and Chunuk Bair. It had been awaiting orders to consolidate the heights, but now they would be attacking them.

At 11.00 am Cayley received the orders to move, and went on ahead to reconnoitre the ground around Cheshire Ridge. Finding no room on Rhododendron Spur, as the New Zealand Brigade was still there, he decided to take his men straight along the bed of Aghyl Dere and up onto the Farm. The Farm was a flat area between Cheshire and Rhododendron Spur, and before the fighting had been a small square area of cultivated land. When Cayley returned to his battalions, by some miscommunication, they had started to move up Chailak Dere by mistake. When this was realised, runners were sent out to recall them, but it was too late for 7/Gloucesters who, leading the column, had joined up with the New Zealanders on Rhododendron Spur. It was not until dusk that the remainder of Cayley's brigade had returned to Aghyl Dere, a battalion short. What had been earlier in the day a fresh brigade was now so exhausted and suffering from acute thirst that they could not be committed to the battle. The whole day had been wasted, leaving Major General Cox with no fresh resource to attempt any advance on to, let alone consolidation of, the heights.

As dawn broke on Rhododendron Spur, the scene was quiet, apart from the noise of battle in the old Anzac area. Since the attack on Lone Pine the day before, the firing had not ceased and, more recently, the dawn attack at The Nek had only added to this sound of rifle and machine gun fire in the distance. Below, Johnston's men were not in a position to coordinate the attack with the Light Horse as they were still half a mile short of Chunuk Bair. Even after its capture, Battleship Hill would be another obstacle between them and the Turks on Baby 700.

All the New Zealanders could do now was watch. Mackenzie was on Table Top at this time, and would be a witness to this attack:

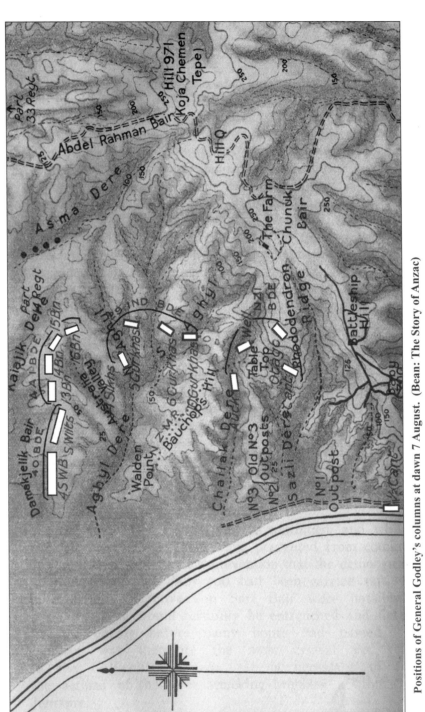

Positions of General Godley's columns at dawn 7 August. (Bean: The Story of Anzac)

Seized a few spare moments to watch an attack, half a mile to the south, which was being made by Light Horsemen from the main position on Russell's Top. Destroyers close in below sent high explosive shells whirring upwards to burst in a pall of black smoke and dust on the narrow neck between the Turkish and Australian lines. There was a tornado of machine-gun fire which reached my ears only as a high-pitched continuous note. The shelling lasted about ten minutes only, a hopelessly inadequate preparation on such positions. The storm of machine-guns rose to terrific violence, ripping and roaring. A grey fog of smoke and dust partially screened the scarred hill-tops, and shielded the melée from vision, but, knowing those tiers of Turkish trenches as I did, I was awed with the thought of what must be passing. For fifteen minutes it lasted in all its fury, then lulled slightly, to burst forth again for a few minutes only to diminish once more to a steady burr, which left nothing decided in my mind. What had happened I did not know, but when I turned my attention there later in the morning I gathered, from the fact that the machine-guns still rattled in the same locality as before, that ground had not been gained.

Blame was put on the physical condition of the troops who were already exhausted from the night breakout. Many of these men had been on Gallipoli since late April and were now physically weaker than the prime specimens that had landed sixteen weeks ago. Ailments like dysentery, as well as old wounds, had sapped health and energy from a good majority of them. Although many new drafts had been absorbed into the ranks, what these men gained in fitness was lost in lack of experience.

By 6.30 am the New Zealand column was preparing for the final drive on to Chunuk Bair. For this Lieutenant Colonel Young's Aucklanders would lead the way, supported by Lieutenant Colonel Malone's Wellingtons and two companies of 10/Gurkhas, who had arrived unexpectedly at the northern end of Rhododendron Spur during the night, having become separated from their column. The Otagos and

Lieutenant Colonel Robert Young, commanding the Auckland Battalion (photographed here later as a Brigadier General).

Canterburys were kept as reserve. The renewed New Zealand advance began an hour later, and within thirty minutes the Aucklanders had passed The Apex, a small rocky knoll where the Rhododendron and Cheshire ridges meet. Just eastward of this position is an open, narrow saddle that joined ninety metres further on to a similar hillock known as The Pinnacle. From The Pinnacle the ground rises up 250 metres onto the southern shoulder of Chunuk Bair. It was between here and Battleship Hill that the majority of the Turkish fire was coming from, soon to be followed by shelling. The Turks were now well aware of what was unfolding below them.

High above, on Chunuk Bair, Colonel Hans Kannengiesser was approaching some twenty sleeping Turks, the crew of two mountain guns. As early as 4.40 am Kannengiesser was made aware of the situation as General Esat Pasha knew it, and was instructed to move his *64* and *25 Regiment* to Hill Q to counter attack. Leading *64 Regiment*, he reached Chunuk Bair about 6.30 am to see for himself the enemy below.

Turkish infantry during the campaign.

> *Suddenly the enemy infantry actually appeared* [he probably saw the Auckland Regiment] *in front of us at about 500 yards range. The English approached slowly, in single file, splendidly equipped and with white bands on their left arms, apparently very tired, and were crossing a hill-side to our flank, emerging in continually increasing numbers from the valley below. I immediately sent an order to my infantry, this was the twenty man strong artillery covering platoon* [part of a two gun Turkish Mountain battery], *instantly to open fire. I received the answer: "We can only commence to fire when we receive the order of our battalion commander". This was too much for me altogether. I ran to the spot and threw myself among the troops who were lying in a small trench. What I said I cannot recollect, but they began to open fire and almost immediately the English lay down without answering our fire or apparently moving in any other way. They gave me the impression that they were glad to be spared further climbing.*[22]

The Aucklanders managed to find some shelter in a small hollow by The Apex. Taking this brief opportunity to eat breakfast, Lieutenant Colonel Young prepared his battalion for the final advance on Chunuk Bair. As the men bunched together, in what they thought was dead ground, a burst of machine gun and rifle fire from the direction of Battleship hill brought an abrupt conclusion to their morning meal, and with it removed any impetus to advance further. They were 350 metres short of the summit; however, above, the Turks were now being reinforced.

The attack at The Nek had already ended in an unnecessary massacre, whilst to the New Zealand left there was no sign of the Indian Brigade who were supposed to be closing on Hill Q, or 4 (Australian) Brigade, who should have been on the spur leading up to Hill 971. Off in the distance IX Corps were ashore at Suvla, but little could be seen of any fighting, just troops digging in. Major Temperley, who was on Johnston's staff, wrote, 'peace seemed to reign everywhere'. Because of this, Johnston called off any continuation of the advance for that day. It was hoped that when the Indian Troops and 4 (Australian) Brigade eventually reached his left flank that the advance could continue. Without knowing that these twenty rifles were the only defence between the New Zealanders and the most important key position to the Sari Bair range, the advance halted.

At 8.00 am, Brigadier General Johnston arrived at the forward position at The Apex, and with his battalion commanders began to plan the next course of action. Johnston wired Godley at his headquarters, recommending the delay. Godley was astounded when he heard this and, at 9.30 am, ordered Johnston to 'attack at once!' The operation was now five hours behind but, regardless, a renewal of the attack would be planned for 10.30 am. This was not a good time, as it would be in full daylight and the Turkish fire was already steadily increasing, but the opportunity of an earlier advance had been

Brigadier General Francis Johnston, commanding the Right Assaulting Column.

wasted; opportunity rarely offers itself twice. For a renewal of the attack Johnston organised a fifteen minute bombardment of the crest. Johnston and Temperley were not convinced of success but prepared for the assault nevertheless. Johnston now had four and a half battalions available. For this attack he chose to use the 10/Gurkhas and placed them on the Aucklanders' left flank. He now had five companies for the initial attack, three Auckland and two Gurkha; however there was no plans to use the machine guns in provide supporting fire.

Captain Jessie Wallingford, the Brigade Machine Gun officer, had requested permission to bring his machine guns up to support the Aucklanders attack, but Johnston shouted him down, furious by Wallingford's interference. In earshot of Johnston the Aucklanders second in command, Major Samuel Grant, pleaded with Wallingford to bring up his guns, only to be brushed off by Johnston. There would be no time for the guns even though Wallingford said he would only need twenty minutes to position them. Nothing would delay Johnston now. Lieutenant Colonel Young had been reconnoitring the ground ahead of The Apex and protested to Johnston that the attack should be delayed until nightfall. Johnston was furious, and would have none of it. This would turn out to be a costly mistake by him.

At 10.15 am the bombardment, a mix of field artillery and naval fire, commenced on Chunuk Bair. As this lifted the Aucklanders advanced in line, but were met with an immediately fusillade of rifle and reported machine gun fire. The first wave was cut down in its tracks but, due to persistence, the follow on elements of the battalion managed to reach The Pinnacle, less than a hundred metres from their jumping off point.

The moment came. The word was given. For an instant there was a deep intake of the breath, a tension, the hesitation as of one who nerves himself to leap into ice-cold water. From behind came an indescribable growl and murmur. Then Major Grant rushed out in

Private Joseph Jones, Otago Battalion, who died of wounds 7 August (New Zealand No. 2 Outpost Cemetery).

In Loving Memory

OF

Private JOSEPH JONES

Died of Wounds at Dardanelles,

AUGUST 7th, 1915.

Aged 27 Years.

90

front with waved arm and a call to follow on. The mass moved, Lieut. Dittmer's platoon of the Hauraki's leading. Twenty yards of dead ground, and then a hail of fire, fire from a thousand yards of Chunuk; fire from Battleship Hill; rifle fire and machine-gun fire from front and flank. Two hundred and fifty yards to go, and every yard of it raked with fire. There was no faltering; every man went straight forward, running up the hill as fast as he could go. Killed and wounded, they went down in heaps, but the survivors pressed on. The trench was reached, a small, narrow drain, and the foremost leaping in took what cover it afforded. It was soon too full to hold more, and the remainder lay down in rear. There was nothing to be done except wait and endure. The task was done, and at a great cost.

Johnston, who can only be described as being in a confused mental state, was standing in the open, cheering on his men before he was encouraged by wiser heads to get down. Actually the task was not done, and the battalion had barely advanced a hundred metres. The Auckland regimental history stated:

All the way back to the Apex the ground was a tangle of dead, dying and wounded. For most of them nothing could be done, as the ground was so terribly swept with fire. The men in front scraped a little cover, but it would have been impossible to dig in, even if picks and shovels had been available. No movement was safe, and to stand up meant certain death. An order to get into the trench was passed round, and more were killed while endeavouring to do this. In the blazing sun the torment of thirst became very great. Heat, thirst, and flies—the wounded suffered hellish tortures lying out on the slope. "God! Oh, God! When will it be night, and when will the stretcher-bearers come?"

Of the three companies committed, over 250 had become casualties, with very few getting much beyond The Apex. Those that did managed to man an old Turkish trench at a position later named The Pinnacle but, once there, they became pinned down. The Gurkhas advanced against the same fire, which forced them down the left of the ridge, towards the head of Chailak Dere.

Johnston quickly realised his mistake by not waiting for Wallingford's guns to be deployed. After another dispute Wallingford was finally permitted to 'help' Johnston and, bring his guns into action as he saw fit. At 12.30 pm Johnston then ordered the Wellingtons to prepare to attack over the same ground. Lieutenant Colonel Malone bluntly refused in front of several witnesses, saying he would not lead his men over this ground in daylight, and that he would do so it at night and take the hill. In his words, he was 'not going to send them over to commit suicide'. Johnston was furious. Under pressure from Godley to attack quickly, his senior battalion commander was being insubordinate, and this was on top of Young and Wallingford already openly questioning his judgement. Johnston now turned his attention to the Otago and Canterbury Battalions, however the opportunity of taking the heights in daylight had already gone.

Captain Jesse Wallingford, Brigade Machine Gun officer.

Kannengiesser had managed to stop the earlier New Zealander advance, with a skirmish line that stretched from Battleship Hill to Chunuk Bair. Further troops, in the form of two companies from the Turkish *1/72 Regiment* and the whole of *1/14 Regiment,* had also arrived to bolster the Turkish defence. These were sent by Mustafa Kemal, who had also spotted enemy movements in and around Rhododendron Spur, and immediately recognised the threat on Chunuk Bair, exactly as he had predicted months before. What was once a deserted crest line was now quite well defended. The Turks had the heights consolidated under

The Apex, looking along the narrow path to The Pinnacle, with Chunuk Bair in the treeline beyond. (2013)

A New Zealand Dressing Station near Rhododendron Spur.

Kannengiesser, although in the late morning his command would be cut short when he was wounded. Control was temporarily passed to his chief of staff, Major Hulusi, and then to Lieutenant Colonel Cemil, commander of the *4th Division*. For now the heights were secure in Turkish hands.

Below, however, the bloody advance was not the end of Johnston's New Zealand attack. In the late afternoon, in preparation for a renewed attack, he ordered forward the Otago and Canterbury battalions. The Otagos moved forward to the dead ground by The Apex without incident; however, when it was time for Lieutenant Colonel Hughes' Canterburys' to move it was a different story. The Canterburys' commander, completely unaware of the situation, assembled the battalion together on the open crest of the ridge, in full view of the Turks higher up on Battleship Hill. The most exposed company immediately attracted a devastating rifle and machine gun fire from the hill, whilst the remainder came under shrapnel as they tried to advance towards The Apex. Hughes was reported to have broken down in tears as the survivors from his battalion scattered; only thirty seven men got as far as The Apex. The Otago Battalion whilst digging in then began to suffer casualties. This resulted in both battalions having become disorganised and requiring time to reform; this only left the Wellingtons intact.

Johnston, who had earlier seemed only too pleased to report back to Godley that the attack was the failure he had predicted, now got a reply from Godley who, seeing the futility of the daylight attack, ordered him to wait until nightfall to continue his operation. The Auckland regimental history described the scene:

The stillness of the night was broken by the cries of the stricken in their agony. Carrying parties and stretcher-bearers toiled up and down with their heavy loads, the scrub breaking and crackling beneath their feet. The bursts from the Turkish machine-guns whizzed venomously overhead. Bullets fell everywhere, with the sound of heavy, slow drops before a thunderstorm. The night was full of noise, yet within a small space it was very still and quiet.

During the night of 7 August, Cemil, the newly appointed commander of the Turkish *9th Division* and Chunuk Bair's defence, began to plan a counter attack to push the New Zealanders off Rhododendron Spur. However, Lieutenant Colonel Servet, commander of *64 Regiment,* spoke against the attack as any charge on the open slopes of this ridge would have to take place under the fire of the British land and sea based artillery. It would be very costly and, if it failed, it would leave the gates to Chunuk Bair open for the New Zealanders to take the advantage.

Whilst the Turks considered their next move, Godley was already planning a renewed general assault at dawn along the whole line. This would be launched on the heights at 4.15 am, proceeded by a forty five minute artillery bombardment. He ordered Brigadier General Johnston to renew the attack on Chunuk Bair, and for this the New Zealand Brigade's numbers were bolstered by 7/Gloucesters, 8/Welsh Regiment (Pioneers), the Auckland Mounted Rifles and two companies of the Maori contingent. To Johnston's left flank, Major General Cox would assault the ridge by Hill Q with the Indian Brigade and Hill 971 with 4 (Australian) Brigade; additional support, in the form of Cayley's 39 Brigade (6/South Lancs would take the place of the 7/Gloucesters) and the 6/King's Own, was sent from 38 Brigade to support Monash. The orders, drafted at 6.00 pm and summarised to the brigades by 7.00 pm, were officially despatched at 8.30 pm. The night would be spent preparing for the dawn assault, with hope that the Sari Bair ridge would be carried after first light.

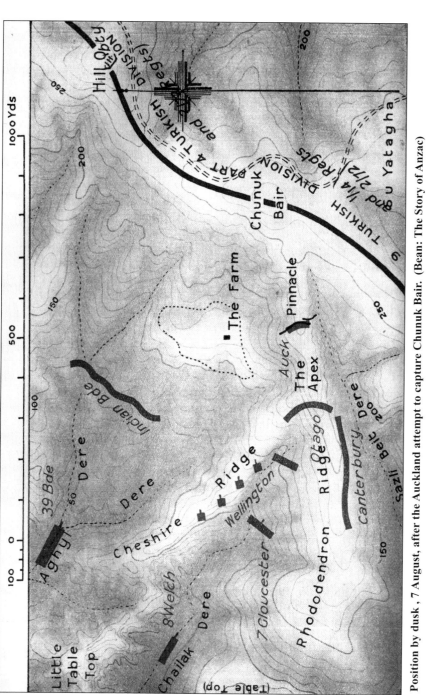

Position by dusk, 7 August, after the Auckland attempt to capture Chunuk Bair. (Bean: The Story of Anzac)

Chapter Five

8 August – Chunuk Bair

By Jove! They are our men

By dawn, Cox was still not yet in a position to attack. With the exception of 4 (Australian) Brigade, his other units remained scattered or, in the case of 39 Brigade, still missing. His own staff only consisted of a brigade-major and a staff captain. He attempted to organize his troops into four columns, which would be the responsibility of the column commanders to gather and position themselves ready for the assault at 4.15 am. The battalions were now organised in a 'column' according to where Cox believed them to be located. Confused and tired already, this reshuffle was a risky decision that would have dire consequences later.

Lieutenant Colonel F.G.H. Sutton and No.1 Column would attack the northern slopes of Chunuk Bair. This column comprised 6/South Lancs (38 Brigade), 9/Warwicks (39 Brigade) and Sutton's own 10/Gurkhas (Indian Brigade). Lieutenant Colonel T.A. Andrus would command No. 2 Column with the objective of the southern peak of Hill Q. It comprised 7/North Staffs (39 Brigade), 9/Worcesters (39 Brigade) and 6/Gurkhas (Indian Brigade). Lieutenant Colonel P.C. Palin would command No. 3 Column and attack the northern peak of Hill Q, leading 14/Sikhs and 5/Gurkhas (Indian Brigade). Lastly, Brigadier General Monash would lead No. 4 Column, with the objective of Abdul Rahman Spur and Hill 971. His forces comprised his Australian brigade and the attached 6/King's Own (38 Brigade). Brigadier General Cayley would not command in the assault, but would be in command of the ridge as soon as it had been captured.

Lieutenant Colonel Thomas Andrus ordered his men forward just after dark, bringing 7/North Staffs and 9/Worcesters up towards 6/Gurkhas on the slopes below Hill Q. Unfortunately, the two New Army battalions struggled to get onto the scrubby high ground and become fragmented in the twisting gullies below. By dawn, when they should have been advancing on Hill Q, they were still strung out deep below, in Aghyl Dere. Major Allanson's 6/Gurkhas were still very much on their own, having climbed to the lower slopes of Chamchak Punar the previous day, lodging themselves about 450 metres below the crest of

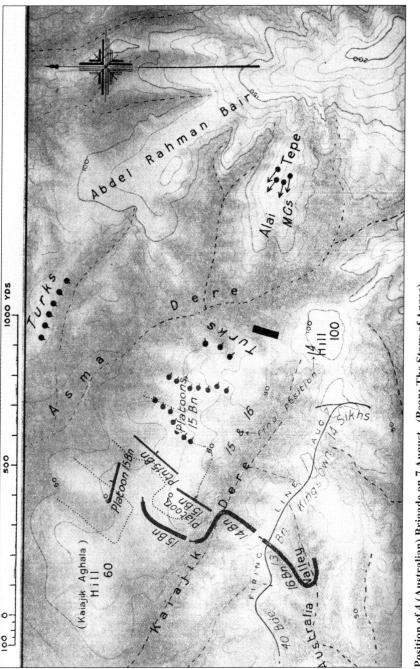

Position of 4 (Australian) Brigade on 7 August. (Bean: The Story of Anzac)

Hill Q. Allanson had waited all day and night for signs of the other battalions, so on 8 August he decided to advance without them. The Gurkhas continued their climb, but this time encountered increasing opposition and suffered more casualties. They eventually reached a spot on Chamchak Punar, within 180 metres of Hill Q's crest. In a deep nullah below his position Allanson spotted parties of men from the 6/South Lancs and 7/North Staffs. After dark he gathered a company of the South Lancs and forced his way up another fifty metres despite the enemy fire and thick scrub. Here he called a halt until dusk.

Allanson wrote in his diary:

Further movement was impossible; it was now 9.30 am, blazing hot; I lay there without movement till 6 pm with every conceivable shot flying in the air about one; shrapnel, our own maxims, rifles, and our own high explosive bursting extremely close, which told me how near we were to the top. I lay between two British soldiers; the man on my left had a Bible, and read it the whole day; the man on my right I found was a corpse.

During the night the Gurkhas and the party of 6/South Lancs edged themselves even closer. They then prepared themselves for the final dawn assault. A young second lieutenant named William Slim shared a small packet of raisins with Allanson that night. Slim was hit by machine gun fire later, the bullet going through his shoulder, through his lungs and narrowly missing his spine. He was one of the lucky ones who managed to get down from the slopes and, surviving his wounds, was temporarily invalided out of the army. Slim would become Field Marshal William 'Bill' Slim, 1st Viscount Slim, the famed British military commander in Burma in the Second World War and the thirteenth Governor-General of Australia. For any chance of success, Allanson desperately needed reinforcements, but looking down into the valleys below there was no sign of life.

So what happened to the other columns? In preparation for the attack on 8 August, Monash had moved forward 14, 15 and 16/AIF before dawn, leaving 13/AIF and 6/King's Own in the vacated positions to protect the Damakjelik Spur flank. During the night the Australian battalions descended from their positions on Damakjelik and into a valley they thought was Asma Dere. In fact it was Chailak Dere, a narrow valley that separated the two spurs of the same ridge. They then climbed onto what they thought was Abdul Rahman Spur, but in fact it was just the northern lobe of Damakjelik, known to the Turks as Yauan Tepe. Still not realizing the earlier navigational error, they walked blindly up the same spur whence they had come, thus the Australian advance had no hope of reaching Hill 971 before dawn.

It was not long into the advance that the leading platoons of Lieutenant Colonel Cannan's 15/AIF began to run into heavy machine gun fire. This began as they climbed onto Yauan Tepe and were caught in the open whilst crossing a cultivated oatfield. 14/AIF were met with similarly heavy fire, but this came from further up the spur at a place known as Hill 100, and beyond it from Alay Tepe, a high point on Abdul Rahman Spur. About this time, Monash realized that his brigade was on the wrong spur. Some of the Australians attempted to cross Asma Dere to get onto the lower slopes of Abdul Rahman Spur, but here they found the spur already heavily defended by not only two battalions of *14 Regiment*, but also Major Willmer's *1/32 Regiment* and a machine gun company of *11 Regiment*. Lieutenant Colonel Pope's 16/AIF avoided the oatfield by using the length of Kaiajik Dere as cover, but as soon as they climbed up onto Yauan Tepe they came under fire from Turks further up the spur on Hill 100. As with their sister battalions, they were stopped in their tracks. Monash, who remained in the Brigade HQ in Australia Valley, soon realized that any further daylight advance would be suicidal and reported back to Major General Cox. There was nothing for it but to withdraw; the forward lines the Australian had reached were so thinly held that any concerted Turkish counter attack could seriously

Some of Lieutenant Colonel Cannan's 15/AIF.

threaten this flank. Even if they held on, their positions on this spur would remain enfiladed by the Turks, now reinforced by Major Hulusi's *1/33 Regiment*, who were deploying on the Abdul Rahman Spur. Monash's men therefore withdrew from Yauan Tepe, crossed back over Kaiajik Dere and back to their starting point of that morning; it was 8.30 am. They had barely made it more than a quarter of the way to Hill 971 and now, back in their original trenches, all they could do was to count the cost. 15/AIF had lost 400 men and nearly all of its officers, including Cannan's brother, Major Douglas Cannan; 14/AIF had lost eight officers and 250 men. Many of the wounded in forward positions had to be left to their fates, the lucky ones becoming prisoners of war. It had been a costly morning for Monash's men, who had suffered in excess of a thousand casualties.

The other two columns became hopelessly tangled, but nevertheless managed some success. Lieutenant Colonel Sutton's 6/South Lancs and 9/Warwicks managed to get close to Hill Q, with forward elements of the South Lancs actually joining up with 6/Gurkhas. 10/Gurkhas had become separated, with two companies ending up near the Farm and joining with the New Zealanders. Close by, 9/Worcesters had also arrived close to the Farm, and began to climb up fairly close to Allanson's position. The 14/Sikhs and 5/Gurkhas from Lieutenant Colonel Palin's Column, to the right of Monash's flank, had tried to

9/Warwicks - Officers and Sergeants just prior to landing at Gallipoli.

advance but found themselves unable to make any progress through the terrain; when the Australians pulled back they made no further effort that day. Unknown to Allanson, Generals Birdwood and Godley had met during the afternoon. Realizing that neither column had any chance of achieving their objectives that day, the assaults had been postponed until dawn on 9 August.

With a mix of units forced together under commanders who were unfamiliar with their men, let along trying to move in confusing terrain, it should be no surprise that little was achieved. There was no significant reconnaissance that day, and even in the areas where the commanders thought they knew where they were, this knowledge was complicated by poor communications, enemy fire and the generally poor condition of the troops. Even the fresh British troops pushed into the attack from reserve were suffering from dysentery, lack of water and sheer exhaustion in this unforgiving climate.

The Capture of Chunuk Bair

Brigadier General Johnston had a distinct advantage over the other assaults; his brigade was only 350 metres short of its objective. Sutton's column to his left flank was nowhere to be seen, but the attack would go ahead as planned. Preceded by what was at that time considered a heavy artillery bombardment, Johnston's assault would be led by the Wellingtons with the British New Army battalions of 7/Gloucesters on the left and 8/Welsh on the right. The Auckland Mounted Rifles and Maori Contingent would be in support. Half the Canterbury Battalion (represented by only four officers and fifty men) was ordered to support the attack if required, and moved to The Apex in readiness. The Otagos would hold The Apex.

Just before 4.00 am the leading elements of the Wellington battalion began to move forward, crossing the narrow saddle between The Apex and The Pinnacle. It was dark. Where the Aucklanders had suffered so heavily crossing this ground in the daylight, this movement forward resulted in no casualties. Zero hour was 4.15 am, which would be proceeded by a 45-minute artillery barrage, as well as support from twelve of Captain Wallingford's Maxims. From The Pinnacle, the Wellingtons continued and, expecting a volley of fire to meet them at any moment, ascended the last couple of hundred metres to their objective. Surprisingly, there was no enemy fire and, upon reaching the top the Wellington's fanned out, gaining the southwestern slopes and crest of the main knoll of Chunuk Bair. The Turks had been scattered by the bombardment, and all that remained was a sheltering machine gun crew and a few sentries. Within minutes two companies, led by Lieutenant

Colonel William Malone, had disappeared out of sight and, up on the crest, began to dig in, whilst two platoons were pushed out as a screening force onto the forward southern slopes and towards the landward eastern slopes, where empty gun pits were found and occupied by the New Zealanders. On the reverse slope, above The Pinnacle, Malone ordered a support trench to be dug.

Lieutenant Colonel Richard Jordan's 7/Gloucesters followed on the heels of the Wellingtons; however the Turks were now alert so, as with the Aucklanders the previous day, they walked into machine gun and rifle fire from the northern part of the ridge, held by *25 Regiment*. The Gloucesters carried on, about half the battalion eventually making it to the left of the Wellingtons' firing line, on the northern crest of Chunuk Bair and

Lieutenant Walter Evans, 8/Welsh Regiment.

overlooking Hill Q. Without any trenches to occupy, the Gloucesters were forced to lie down in the open. The party of 8/Welsh, led by Major Peel Yates, fared worst, and suffered from the full force of the awoken Turks. Lieutenant Walter Evans, 8/Welsh, described what happened:

> *The Wellingtons went over in the dark and lost very few in the attack itself. The Gloucesters hung back and lost heavily through this. We, going up in the light, lost very heavily before we even reached the top of the hill. When we got on to the top of the ridge we found many of the Gloucesters lying down there. We pressed on through them and so became disorganised as some men got through faster than others and some stayed behind. When we were through, Captain Gwyer and myself, went to the right and got down into the Sari Bair. I then had with me about 20 men of my platoon and about 30 others belonging to different companies and some of the Gloucesters. We advanced up the Sari Beit and then wheeled to the right. Captain Gwyer was killed by a shell when quite close to me. I went on and we lay down at the top and covered the right flank as well as we could. I had been hit in the leg going up and sometime after was hit in the shoulder.*

Miraculously, about seventy Welshmen managed to reach the top and went into the line on the Wellingtons' southern, right, flank. Captain

7/Gloucesters moving up to Chunuk Bair, morning of 8th August.

The same slopes today.

Wallingford then sent four machine guns with crews to the top in support, and although three eventually made it, the guns were so badly damaged that they had to be cannibalized to make one working weapon. This gun, along with a captured Turkish maxim, were the only machine guns Malone had on the summit and, because of the exposed positions on top, they would soon be out of action.

Malone's New Zealanders, the Gloucesters and Welsh could now gaze at the distant prize of the Dardanelles straits and the rear of the Turkish line. Was this 'Victory'? Where were the Turks? Chunuk Bair would become one of the campaign's fiercest battles, as desperate fighting for its summit would go on for two days. Because it was deemed so close to being a 'victory', it would also be written as one of the greatest tragedies of the Gallipoli campaign. In reality, even if the whole of the Sari Bair ridge could have been captured and retained, it would arguably offer no more of a tactical advantage to the allies than any other position at Anzac. Possession of Sari Bair would only be a stepping-stone; this path of dreams was far away from anything close to being a 'Victory'.

The 13th (Western) Division commander, Major General Frederick Shaw, was watching the attack:

> *There is an observation post here and from it one can see a large portion of the country over which we are operating. To that post about 4.15 went a procession of sleepy generals and staff carrying glasses, telescopes and anxiously awaiting the dawn, to show the success or otherwise of the troops. It began to get gradually lighter and all glasses were turned on the summit of Chunuk Bair, which was the only point of attack which could matter. Still it got lighter, and then someone said "I see men on Chunuk Bair", "They are our men", said another, and then "By Jove! They are our men", and so they were. We had reached the summit, but should we hold it and should we progress?*[23]

It was now light and the Turks along the ridge now observed Malone's men on Chunuk Bair. Colonel Mustafa Kemal's was headquartered with his *19th Division* on Battleship Hill, so could clearly see the crisis unfolding. He despatched his aide-de-camp to Chunuk Bair to report. This aide was shot on the way, so Mustafa Kemal next sent his chief of staff, who confirmed the critical situation and that the British had established a position on the ridge.

Confusion amongst the Turks started to reign. No one knew who was in command, what the intentions of the Anzacs were, all exacerbated by some units being unfamiliar with the ground. Major Nuri, *24 Regiment,* telephoned HQ for more information but received a blunt reply,

> *At the Corps Headquarters they told me to attack on Chunuk Bair but I did not know the ground and asked for details. When I asked for the details, Esat Pasha and his chief of staff said angrily, 'There is no point in talking, just go'. Tell me, who is the commander there?" Mustafa Kemal said, Go to Chunuk Bair immediately and the time and circumstances will decide who is the commander there.*

Originally the German, Kannengiesser, was in command locally but he was wounded earlier in the day, and when his chief of staff took command this was only briefly, as he too was wounded. Lieutenant Colonel Cemil was then appointed as the new commander, but when the Turkish *8th Division* arrived, Colonel Ali Reza became the commander. To make matters even more confusing, Liman von Sanders then appointed another German officer, Pötrih, as the commander of the Turkish *9th Division*. The spilt in army group responsibility has been mentioned previously, with Hill 971 coming under Suvla command, whilst Chunuk Bair was the responsibility of the Turkish *3rd Army Group*.

Lieutenant Colonel Cemil Conk, commanding the Chunuk Bair Turkish forces.

There were sufficient Turkish troops in the area to counter attack both north and south of Chunuk Bair, however they lacked direction and control. This was no different to the situation of the Anzac and British forces, who at the same time had sufficient troops to take the Sari Bair ridge but had the same leadership issues as the Turks. Unknown to the Anzacs, a two-day window of opportunity that could have been crucial to success was now rapidly closing.

With no real threat elsewhere at Anzac, or Suvla, the Turks could concentrate their attention on Chunuk Bair. Mustafa Kemal immediately ordered Lieutenant Colonel Kemal to take two battalions of *10 Regiment* to counter attack Malone. Many did not get far; the exposed slopes of Battleship Hill were a prize target for the Anzac artillery, who brought the initial counter attack to a standstill.

Major William Cunningham, Wellington Battalion, takes up what happened next:

> *For the best part of an hour the Wellington Battalion was unmolested in its digging operations, but owing to the hard and stony nature of the soil, and the fact that the majority of the men had only entrenching tools, progress was very slow, and the trenches were not more than two feet deep when the Turkish counter-attack started. Preceded by showers of bombs, the Turks worked their way up until they were able to fire into the gun-pits where our advanced covering parties had been placed. These pits soon became untenable and the survivors of the covering parties returned to their companies in the new front line.*

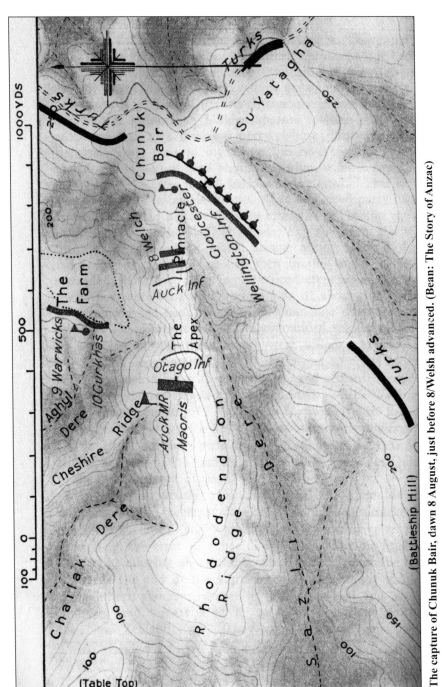

The capture of Chunuk Bair, dawn 8 August, just before 8/Welsh advanced. (Bean: The Story of Anzac)

Only a few survivors made it back from the forward slopes near Su Yatagha and the gun pits, leaving behind the dead and a few wounded who were made prisoner. Meanwhile the Gloucesters, failing to dig into the rock-hard ground and openly exposed to Turkish fire from Hill Q and Hill 971, were forced to pull back to the shelter of the reverse slope by the Wellingtons. Cunningham continued his account:

By now all digging had ceased and the front line companies, taking what cover their shallow trench line afforded, were engaged in a deadly musketry duel with the Turks, who were crowding up from the valley to recapture the hill. Enfilade machine gun fire from the old Anzac position made matters most unpleasant and soon the shallow front line trenches were filled with the killed and wounded. No longer able to hold the forward line, a few unwounded men were able to dash in safety to the reverse or seaward slope of the hill.

During the initial Turkish attacks, Malone held the trench on the crest, this being an old Turkish trench, almost straight and about two foot deep. The continued onslaught of bombing attacks by *64 Regiment* soon drove out this garrison and, with no further reinforcements, a withdrawal to the support line on the reverse slope was ordered. In these shallow trenches, about fifteen metres from the crest, there was little ground separating them from the saucer shaped hollow that crowned Sazli Beit Dere. Malone was criticised later for digging in on the reverse slope, where the field of fire was poor and with no observation on what was happening the other side of the crest, allowing the Turks to edge forward. But staying there was proven to have been suicidal, as it was also for any Turk trying to occupy the same crest. This area became a No Man's Land. In the rock hard soil, under fire from virtually all sides, in reality he had no other choice.

Odd Turks began to work into a position from which they could fire into the reverse slope of the hill. When the forward trenches had been abandoned the Turks crept up close enough to the crest line to hurl showers of egg bombs among the men on the reverse slope. These had long fuses and were promptly thrown back before they exploded. Bolder and bolder, the Turks essayed a bayonet charge, but were promptly stopped by a few well directed volleys at point-blank range. Several times the Turks gallantly repeated their attempts to charge over the top, but always with the same result.

Some of Wallingford's New Zealand machine gunners at The Apex.

Due to the other columns failing to capture Hill 971 and Hill Q, the Turks could concentrate their energies against Chunuk Bair. The savage fighting continued here, with each Turkish attack forced back by Malone's own bayonet charges, the only thing that kept the crest free. It quickly became a scene from hell. Due to the loss of officers and lowering morale, the flanks were under threat of giving way, the wounded were lying everywhere with little hope of aid or rescue, ammunition was running low and water was all but gone. Both machine guns were soon put out of action, whilst the lightly wounded helped to load rifles and gather ammunition and water from the dead and wounded, if they were reachable. The situation was becoming desperate. In between these head on charges, Malone's men clawed desperately at the hardened ground to make the trench deeper, hindered by the rock that lay across much of the surface and by Turkish shelling and small arms fire.

Lieutenant Colonel William Malone.

What had happened to the supporting Auckland Mounted Rifles and Maori Contingent? At 9.00 am two companies from the Maori contingent were sent forward but, after passing The Apex, they came under heavy fire from the direction of Battleship Hill, forcing them to take cover down in Chailak Dere.

The Maoris were in the thick of it here and, in common with their pakeha comrades, lost heavily. It was the most deadly yet the most glorious day of their campaign, glorious because of the countless deeds of valour and self-sacrifice that attended the splendid lost-endeavour. The episode of the Maori machine-gun taken up the ridge is worthy of record on canvas by some great artist; it is a subject for an understanding battle painter like the artist of 'Rorke's Drift' and 'The Roll Call'. Lieut. Waldren [who was actually Private C. Warden, and not an officer], *a pakeha officer of the Contingent, had a machine-gun taken up the hill with great difficulty. When it was set up a heavy fire was concentrated on it by the Turks, higher up the range, and one after another of the crew was shot down. Lieut. Waldren was shot dead while working the gun. Corporal Ferris* [identified as Private D. Ferris] *took his place and he also was shot down. A bullet was the certain fate of any man who attempted to use the gun, and Maori after Maori was hit until seven men were wounded. Then anyone operating the machine-gun had to crawl cautiously up and work it lying down. At last the gun, the only one on this flank, had to be withdrawn.*[24]

The Maoris did not get onto Chunuk Bair and played no further part in direct support of Malone, although they did later join up with Cox's forces near the Farm.

The two squadrons of the Auckland Mounted Rifles also tried to get up to Chunuk Bair, but only made it as far as The Pinnacle. About 2.00 pm, after urgent calls for support, a few Aucklanders managed to fight their way up and, in small groups, finally reached Malone's beleaguered men. It was quickly becoming apparent that is was almost impossible to reinforce Malone's position with men in sufficient numbers, let alone supply the garrison with ammunition, bombs, food and water.

Communications from Chunuk Bair to Johnston's HQ had originally relied on runners, although all of these were soon wounded or killed; due to the time delay it took to get through, it often meant that the message was out of date when received in any case. Soon two New Zealand signal parties were sent up onto Chunuk Bair to make contact with Malone, with the intention of setting up two separate telephone lines. Unfortunately this would not prove possible, as the wire cable was found to be too short. Corporal Cyril Bassett, who was in charge of one of the parties, decided to use one line to extend the first, and thus a field telephone connection now linked Malone's command post to Brigade HQ at The Apex.

This was short lived as within thirty minutes the cable was severed. Bassett sent back one of his signalers with an urgent message from Malone, whilst he and Sapper William Birkett went back down from Chunuk Bair, all the time under constant fire and shelling, to locate and repair the broken wire. It was miraculous that these men survived this trip on a section of ground that was so exposed to Turkish fire that it prevented any daytime reinforcements getting to Malone's position. Even more astounding was this did not happen just the once. They worked up and down Chunuk Bair and Rhododendron Spur tirelessly for three days. Bassett narrowly escaped being killed or wounded on several occasions; once two bullets had ripped his clothing; one went straight through his collar and the other tearing off his right-hand pocket. Unpretentiously Bassett later said: '*It was just that I was so short the bullets passed over me*'.

His citation for the Victoria Cross reads:

For most conspicuous bravery and devotion to duty on the Chunuk Bair Ridge, in the Gallipoli Peninsula, on 7th August, 1915 [sic]. *After the New Zealand Infantry Brigade had attacked and established itself on the ridge, Corporal Bassett, in full daylight and under a continuous and heavy fire,*

WILLS'S CIGARETTES

**Corporal Cyril Royston
Guyton Bassett VC,
Divisional Signals, NZ
Engineers.**

**An artists' impression of
Bassett's VC action.**

*succeeded in laying a telephone line from the old position to the
new one on Chunuk Bair. He has subsequently been brought to
notice for further excellent and most gallant work connected
with the repair of telephone lines by day and night under heavy
fire.*

Bassett was the only New Zealander to be awarded the Victoria Cross
at Gallipoli, although there were numerous other acts equally worthy.
Official recognition, in terms of the Victoria Cross, were to embitter
New Zealand soldiers at Gallipoli, who thought that they were neglected
in comparison to the Australians. Blame was directed at their
commander, Major General Alexander Godley, who was rumoured at

the time to have quashed numerous VC recommendations, posthumously or otherwise, for the belief that his men were merely doing their jobs. Bassett, during an interview some fifty years later, stated: *All my mates ever got were wooden crosses.*[25]

After the few reinforcements had arrived from the Auckland Mounted Rifles, the Turks began to shell Malone's position, followed by another Turkish bayonet charge, again repulsed. The Anzac artillery and Royal Navy then began to drop shells onto Chunuk Bair, a few of which fell close to Malone's position. It was either this, or the Turks artillery, that killed Malone and wounding several others.

Towards 5 pm, the shelling seemed to have ceased and Lieutenant Colonel Malone and Major Schofield stood up together in the trench with the idea of looking over the ground and deciding the dispositions of the troops to be maintained during the night and where the men of the Auckland Regiment might most profitably be employed. Just at this moment, the Turk fired his last salvo and the gallant Colonel fell with a ball through the head while Colonel [sic] Schofield received a ball through the lung. Throughout that long and arduous day, Lieutenant Colonel Malone had fought with his men and none knew better what a magnificent fight they had put up. Armed only with an entrenching tool, he had, time after time, dashed in among the firing lines when the Turks threatened to break through, encouraging his men with his words and example. He was firmly resolved that the Regiment would rather perish than yield the hill.[26]

Major William Cunningham took command and as soon as the shelling stopped so did the Turkish counter attacks. As darkness fell the Wellington Mounted Rifles and the Otago Infantry Battalion were ordered up onto Chunuk Bair to reinforce what was left of Malone's men. Lieutenant Colonel William Meldrum, commanding the Wellington Mounted Rifles wrote:

The men we relieved were the Wellington infantry and mounted men, under Colonel Malone. They had been cut about pretty badly, especially the mounted men, who had lost about 190 out of 240 odd. We realised we had no soft thing, and dug in, improving and adding to the trenches till daylight. Several threats were made by the Turks, who were just on the brow in front of us, but no attack was made before dawn.

Malone positioned the trenches along the seaward side of this slope.

Clutha Mackenzie, one of Meldrum's troopers, made his way up to Chunuk Bair by following the telephone wire that Bassett had laid earlier:

From above came the incessant roar of bursting bombs and shells and rattle of musketry. At dawn the summit had been gained, but just how good or bad our position was I had not the vaguest idea. I had not heard of, nor had I seen, any progress except the taking of this summit, since Saturday morning, and had no idea as to whether the battle was progressing favourably or otherwise. What was expected of them up there to-night none knew. Each carried a pick or a shovel and two bombs. They passed the dressing-stations, perched on either side on the steep slope, where hundreds of wounded lay, then over a ridge where the track stopped and out into the pitch black open. The bullets zipped past or thudded into the ground. The troop lay down while they got their bearings. A fellow close by me gave a yell and was dead. A few wounded men, limping or crawling back, passed them. Then, in extended order, they went forward again, guided by a telephone wire, keeping touch with difficulty in the scrub and the darkness. Frequently there would come from the blackness in front of their feet a warning 'Keep clear of me, cobber, I'm wounded,' or groans

113

and the gleam of a white bandage, and sometimes they stumbled over prone, still forms. Slowly they picked their way forward, making towards the centre of the firing, which was in a semicircle round them, the whistling bullets came from both sides as well as from in front, and the din grew fiercer. They reached at length a hollow full of wounded, then went slowly up a slope littered with equipment and dead, and, at last, topping the rise, they came upon a scene so weird and infernal that I instantly stopped and stared with awe.

Lit fantastically by flickering flames, which were licking slowly through the scrub, was a small, ghastly, battle-rent piece of ground, not one hundred yards in width and rising slightly. Beyond and close on either side, it was bounded by the starry heavens, and seemed a strange, detached dreamland where men had gone mad. The Turks lined the far edge, their ghostly faces appearing and vanishing in the eerie light, as they poured a point-blank fusillade at the shattered series of shallow holes where the remnants of the New Zealanders were fighting gallantly. Sweeping round to the left was the flashing semicircle of the enemy line, bombs exploded with a lurid glare, their murky pall drifting slowly back towards me. Shells came whirring up from the black depths behind, and burst beyond the further lip. Everywhere lay dead and dying men, mostly the former, Turkish and British. Equipment and rifles were strewn in the greatest confusion over the torn earth, and all the time the creeping flames cast weird lights upon the passing drama.

As soon as the light faded on Chunuk Bair, the darkness enabled the mounted rifles to reach the top by about 10.00 pm, with only a few casualties. Water, food, bombs and ammunition was also now taken up to the beleaguered defenders. Just after 11.00 pm the shattered remnants of the Wellingtons, just seventy unwounded remained out of nearly

Company Sergeant Major John Aitken, Wellington's, who was killed on 8 August. (Commemorated on the Chunuk Bair Memorial)

114

Sari Bair on 8 August : ① 4(Australian) Brigade -② British & Indian near Hill Q - ③ British at The Farm -④ The Apex - ⑤ The Pinnacle -⑥ Chunuk Bair -⑦ Lone Pine. (Bean: The Story of Anzac)

800 who had originally occupied the crest, slowly made their way down. With them were the battered, and now battle hardened, New Army men from 7/Gloucesters and 8/Welsh. The Gloucesters had lost all their officers, including Lieutenant Colonel Jordan, who was wounded in the face and leg, as well as all of their sergeants and 350 men, the 8/Welsh had lost seventeen officers and 400 men, killed, wounded or missing. On the arrival of the reinforcements, the remnants of these battalions withdrew, having erroneously assumed that they were relieved instead of merely being reinforced, and returned to The Apex.

Behind the scenes, the Turks were steadily being reinforced. The *8th Division* had arrived from Helles during the afternoon of 8 August with a plan to send it into the Lone Pine fight, but instead it was directed towards Chunuk Bair. The whole Sari Bair ridge and down along Abdul Rahman Spur, a frontage of nearly five kilometres, was now defended by some 5000 Turkish rifles, with machine guns and artillery support. Any surprise from the initial attack had long gone, and any movement forward for Godley would now be a real fight.

As dawn broke on 9 August, Chunuk Bair was being held on to by the finest margins. Turkish attacks at Suvla the previous day had finally eliminated the danger of the British IX Corps capturing the Tekke Tepe range. With Suvla now contained, Mustafa Kemal arrived at Anzac during the evening and, after surveying the situation, planned a general attack for the following morning.

115

Chapter Six

9 August – Fight for the Heights

We had held victory in our grasp

The capture of Chunuk Bair had been the only real allied success during the last twenty four hours, leaving Godley's other columns no closer to their objectives than the first day. In full daylight on 9 August, it looked like Johnston's Brigade would be isolated for yet another day.

With 4 (Australian) Brigade now almost out of the picture and unable to advance, Godley decided that the capture of Hill 971 would be put on hold. Monash's brigade was not going to have a quiet time, as Colonel Halil's *7th Division* was filtered into the open ground between Suvla and Anzac, and engaged the Australians and the British 4/SWB and 6/King's Own, further along the Damakjelik Spur. This went on all night, but the Turkish onslaught was held back.

Again all day we dug under a blazing sun, with no water, a few at a time managing to get a few hours' sleep, most having had none for 80 hours. All night again fresh hordes of Turks amassed in Kaiajik Aghala, their patrols and ours scrapping among the bushes in the Dere. Just after midnight great masses of them assembled in battle formation within 50 yards of us. We watched into the gloom with our fingers on our triggers until 2.00 am, when they rose and rushed, several reaching our trench, to die there, however. Within a moment a hundred hand-to-hand fights were taking place, those not using their bayonets pouring bullets into the second and third waves rushing up the slope. Men just fired without sighting in the gloom. It was a grim, voiceless struggle – no orders, invitations or callings on Allah from the combatants. Day dawned, and still the fight raged, but with the light the Turks had no chance of sending reinforcements. By 6 it was all over.[27]

Turkish casualties were heavy. Both *20 Regiment* and *21 Regiment* lost their commanders, and all of their officers were either killed or wounded. The total casualties for these two regiments for 9 August was 978 officers and men. The Turks could not throw back the Australians and 40 Brigade,

116

and likewise Monash could not get forward. Pinned down and with little hope of renewing the advance on Hill 971, Godley had to alter the plan. Godley now wanted a concentrated effort to capture the ground from Chunuk Bair north to Hill Q. For this he would use a composite Brigade under Brigadier General Anthony Baldwin. It comprised 6/East Lancs, 5/Wiltshires, who would be withdrawn from the end of Damakjelik Spur, and the last of Birdwood's Corps reserve: 10/Hampshires and 6/Royal Irish Rifles. All Baldwin's original battalions were in the line elsewhere.

Lieutenant David Campbell, 6/Royal Irish Rifles, wrote:

Brigadier General A.H. Baldwin, commanding 38 Brigade. Killed 10 August. (Commemorated on the Helles Memorial.)

During the afternoon we received our orders. They were, 'Make good hill "Q" at dawn. Farm "B" is already in our hands!' That was all. Now that I have been through quite a few properly organised attacks, I realise how totally inadequate they [the orders] *were.*

Godley also wanted Cox's 39 Brigade and 29 (Indian) Brigade, both of which had not been engaged or suffered that badly, to renew the attack on Hill Q. Whilst Cox was assigned to Hill Q's capture, Johnston was instructed to extend the right flank from the southern lobe of Chunuk Bair down towards Battleship Hill. Preceding this attack would be a bombardment that would begin at 4.30 am and forty five minutes later the infantry would launch themselves as one onto their respective objectives.

A plan so simple overlooked one main factor: allowing adequate time to get the assaulting troops in position, a problem that had plagued many of the earlier attacks. Godley advised that the best route for Baldwin to use was the Rhododendron Spur as the path to the top, as Chunuk Bair was already protected by Johnston's men; and then from the top to reach Hill Q by the northern lobe of Chunuk Bair. Johnston was not convinced about this and when Godley left the decision to the two brigadiers to agree, Johnston advised Baldwin that this route would be too exposed once he had reached The Apex, which had obviously been the problem during daylight hours. This Baldwin accepted, not knowing the ground, and took his advice to use the Chailak Dere route to Cheshire Ridge, and from there to drop into Aghyl Dere to reach Hill Q by way of the Farm.

117

Chailak Dere – the narrow, twisting and mule choked gully.

However, Johnston had failed to consider that movement by night masked them from Turkish fire and this was how both the Otago Battalion and Wellington Mounted Rifles had moved forward from The

Apex. If Baldwin had gone via The Apex the story might have been different, but he did not, and the way Johnston directed him would prove a complete disaster. Johnston had made several poor decisions and in such a key role, his incoherent and confused orders were the undoing of much of the operation.

Baldwin set off about 3.00 pm along Chailak Dere with his four battalions, the headquarters of both 38 and 29 Brigades and with Brigadier General Richard Cooper in tow. The march did not begin well, and even though they started their advance about half way up the dere, they soon found continuing difficulties due to the narrow, twisting bottom of this dry river bed. This was further impaired by Turkish shelling, gullies still choked with wounded from two days of fighting and lines of

Brigadier General 'Ricco' Cooper, commanding 29 Brigade. Wounded during the advance.

sweating men and animals trying to make their way along this narrow 'highway'. Mules laden with ammunition and water, the transport of Johnston's brigade, were also in Chailak Dere, all of these factors causing delay and lack of cohesion for Baldwin. It was after midnight when the head of the column found themselves at a dead end towards the head of Chailak Dere.

Lieutenant David Campbell described the night march:

It was the most wearying, the most trying, the most nerve-racking I have ever been through. We set out about an hour after dusk; we were still on the move at dawn. All night we blundered forward, now halting, now moving at a snail's pace, now struggling forward as fast as we might over the uneven ground. As the night wore on the halts became more and more distressing. The men slept in their tracks. To rouse them to keep the column from braking was indeed a most difficult and heartbreaking task. More than once, I myself dozed off for a few moments. Once I awoke to find the column moving past me. I rushed forward, fear gripping at my heart, and was relieved to find I was only a few paces from the head of my platoon.

Johnston sent Baldwin some New Zealander guides to take the brigade over Cheshire Ridge and into Aghyl Dere; however, they became lost in the dark and confused spurs and ended up in a narrow gorge that ended at an unscalable cliff face. Baldwin ordered the column back which, due to the narrowness of the gorge, only exacerbated the problems. Backtracking, Baldwin found a way over Cheshire Ridge and into Aghyl Dere, but by then it was dawn and the noise of the bombardment was already drowning the area.

Baldwin's column was strung out all over Aghyl Dere with little hope of reaching the Farm, let alone Hill Q, in time. When the 6/East Lancs and 10/Hampshires finally arrived at the Farm, it was about 4.00 am, with no hope of reaching a position to attack the ridge line. At around 8.00 am, headed by the Maoris, the leading elements of Baldwin's column began to climb up from Aghyl Dere to the Farm plateau. Soon after the Turks, who were now fully aware of the movement below, fired down onto the advancing troops. Turkish artillery then began to shower the whole of Aghyl Dere in shrapnel, stalling the advance. In full daylight, under the direct observation of the Turks and still with more than 300 metres to climb, Baldwin was forced to order a halt and, deploying his brigade along the edge of the plateau, began to dig in.

Without Baldwin's brigade in the centre any chance of a coordinated advance using the three brigades had gone. However, Cox was still on the left and Johnston on the right. Cox had the 6/Gurkhas and a detachment from the 6/South Lancs ready to advance on Hill Q, with the 10/Gurkhas and 9/Warwicks in positions close by. Supporting Cox's two attacks were the other two battalions of 39 Brigade (9/Worcesters and 7/North Staffs), who were ordered to wait for Baldwin and then move from their line. Likewise, Johnston's attack was coordinated on the supposition of Baldwin being in position so, when this did not occur, the awaiting lines remained in situ and when it became light it was too late.

On Chunuk Bair the desperate struggle to hold back the Turks continued, as Ali Reza, commander of *8th Division*, pressed on with counter attacking the New

Lieutenant Colonel A. Moore, Otago Regiment, wounded during the night of 8/9 August.

120

Zealanders that morning. Lieutenant Colonel Athelston Moore of the Otago Regiment was soon wounded and passed command to Lieutenant Colonel Meldrum of the Wellington Mounted Rifles. Meldrum had about 170 of his own troopers, about 400 men from the Otagos and a few men from the Canterburys. As he crammed these 600 men into this small area, attrition continued to take its toll:

> *Just after 4 am they* [the Turks] *began developing for an attack. Our artillery and the warships got going at them, but we could not tell how much damage they did. About 4.15 they came on, starting with a bomb attack, supported with rifle, machine gun, and shrapnel. Our boys replied vigorously with rifle fire, but the bombs began to get in the trenches, and a good many men were hit. Captains Hastings and James both had broken legs (from bombs) within a few minutes.*

At about 5.00 pm, at the height of the Turkish assault, disaster struck the New Zealand positions again. Probably thinking that the front line trench had been overrun, the navy and Anzac artillery began dropping shells onto the New Zealander defenders. Meldrum recalls that moment:

> *Unfortunately, some of our own high explosive shells fell in our trenches. Major Elmslie fell wounded on the edge of the trench, and Captain Kelsall was killed by a bomb immediately after. A flag was sent up in the trenches to show the artillery we held them, and everybody set himself to beat back the attack. For about an hour the Turks kept it up with varying intensity, but our boys kept their heads, and put in a heavy rifle fire, which ultimately told its tale.*[28]

Lieutenant Colonel W. Meldrum, Wellington Mounted Rifles (shown after promotion to Brigadier General).

Major Elmslie's last words were 'I'm afraid I can't help you much further boys, but you're doing well, keep on'. Major Frank Statham and his brother, along with Sergeant Major Alexander Porteous and several others were also killed by this friendly fire. Many others were wounded. Trooper Cluthna Mackenzie, Wellington Mounted Rifles, was another of those who was witness to this dreadful episode:

The battleships were concealed by a thick pall of brown smoke through which spurted the flashes of their batteries, field guns of all sizes barked from ravines and ridges; the shells roared and shrieked up towards the summit, and burst in a continual shattering crash on those few hundred square yards of deadly battlefield, or passed aimlessly beyond the ridge and exploded harmlessly far over enemy territory. The Turks, being mostly under the farther lip of the small plateau, suffered little from the bombardment except on the knob which protruded into the line to the left. It was torn constantly by high explosive, and Turkish bodies were flung high in the air, in whole or in part. Equipment, earth and sandbags mixed with the sickly, murky green smoke, which drifted in a choking cloud across the line. Rapidly fresh Turks filled the places of their dead, and they in turn were blasted by the bombardment.

But many of the shells were falling short; or maybe they were not falling short, rather it was a position which should never have been bombarded in this fashion. The artillery was directed upon a hill high above it, lying between it and the breaking day. On its crest, separated by only a few yards, were both the defenders and the attackers. Few of the shells were likely to hit the enemy, for the majority must either spend themselves in the air beyond the crest or else fall among our own men on the crest itself; so they fell thickly along the line, and thus to the danger of an enemy on three sides was added the tragedy of our own artillery on the fourth. Helpless they were to shield themselves or to stop this mad destruction. They had red and yellow flags to mark their positions, and these they waved violently, but it could be of no avail in the dawn light, the dust and the smoke ... One after another those shells burst with a yellow glare and a fountain of black smoke, sending men, some alive, and many dead, flying upwards; and when I could see again there would be a space in the line where one, two or more of the troop had taken the long trail. They rained faster, bursting incessantly on that narrow strip between them and the edge of the cliff, often falling behind and always odd ones and twos dropping into the trench itself.

Mackenzie was suddenly blinded by *an awful lurid flash*, as one of the shells exploded. He then:

... crawled along the shattered trench to the left, feeling my way past the legs of the one or two men who were left. They paid no

Aerial photograph of Chunuk Bair (the majority of trenches shown were dug after 10 August).

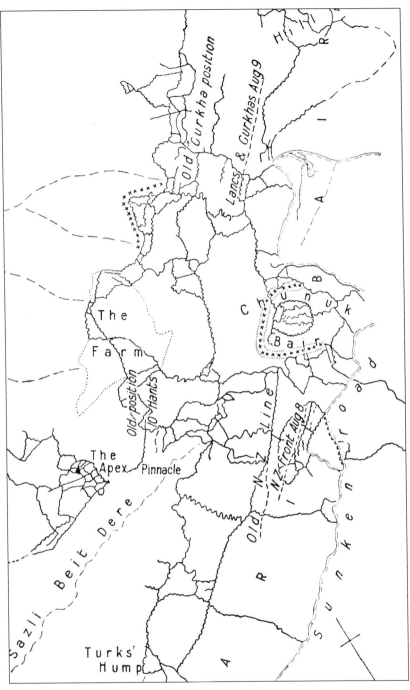

**Associated Trench Map of Chunuk Bair, showing the British positions before
their loss on 10 August.**

attention to me, being too busy with the enemy to be concerned with other matters. I felt my way along on my hands and knees, down into holes, over dead bodies, avoiding wounded, across the open ground, until I came to where I thought the communication trench ought to be and turned to the left. There seemed to be little of it remaining. It had never been much of a thing, and was now blown about and full of wounded and dead. I was finding many difficulties getting past some wounded men, when someone came out from the second line and led me in.

One of the boys took charge of me, and I stumbled off through the little piece of trench into the open, across which, from both sides, the bullets fled whistling and zipping. Jogging awkwardly short distances over the rough ground, then lying in hollows for brief rests, we covered at length that exposed slope of about one hundred and fifty yards which separated the trench from the shallow head of a ravine, wherein lay hundreds of wounded and dead. The trooper guided me carefully over a space where bodies lay thick, and made me lie down on a sloping clay bank, took my field dressing from my pocket and bandaged my head.

I lay there through the whole of that long terrible day, a day of strange unearthliness, when I seemed to float away into a weird dreamland and at times into nightmare, and yet it was not a day of unmixed suffering. The sun glared down pitilessly through the hot hours, the tormenting flies swarmed in their millions, the dead lay thick around, already blackening in the heat, the dying raved in delirium for water which never came, and the battle raged on with unceasing violence. Lying uncomfortably on a slope, propped against a dead Turk, I scarcely seemed to feel the burning heat of the sun, the irritation of the flies, the torturing thirst nor the pain of my wound, for his spirit lay soothed in a strange restfulness, in the satisfaction of peace, in a manner like the weary wishing for nothing but sleep after a day of honest work. For me the fight was over.

Cluthna Mackenzie was blinded, but survived Gallipoli. He spent some time in the NZ Hospital at Walton on Thames before returning to New Zealand in 1919, where he married Doris Sawyer, a nurse who had looked after him in England. Mackenzie left the army in 1920, and began what would be his life's work - service for the blind. He was appointed Director for the Institute for the Blind in Auckland in 1923. The New Zealand soldier on the Anzac Memorial in Port Said is modelled on Mackenzie, along with Bess, the only horse that went out with the NZEF that returned.

When the bombardment lifted at 5.15 am there was little movement. The Otagos and Wellingtons remained under fire from the Turks, who were now rolling bombs down the hill. To their left flank there was no sign of Baldwin's men, whilst Cox's men also remained in position, awaiting Baldwin's arrival. No one came and no one sought to take the initiative, apart from one. On the left, Major Cecil Allanson, 6/Gurkhas, decided that when the bombardment lifted, with or without Baldwin, he would take the opportunity to capture Hill Q. Already within assaulting distance, Allanson was only fifty metres from the saddle that joined Hill Q with Chunuk Bair and under cover of the bombardment was edging closer to the top. In immediate support were two companies of 6/South Lancs and a company of 9/Warwicks. When the thirty minute bombardment lifted at 5.15 am, they rose up and reaching the top of the ridge unhindered, surprising a few Turks who were returning to their positions after sheltering from the bombardment. In Allanson's own words:

Major Cecil Allanson, commanding 6/Gurkha Rifles.

At the top we met the Turks; Le Marchand[29] went down, a bayonet through the heart. I got one through the leg, and then, for about ten minutes, we fought hand to hand, we bit and fisted, and used rifles and pistols as clubs; blood was flying like spray from a hair wash bottle. And the Turks turned and fled, and I felt a very proud man; the key of the whole peninsula was ours, and our losses had not been so very great for such a result. Below I saw the Straits, motors and wheeled transport on the roads leading to Achi Baba.

After a bitter ten minute hand to hand melée, the few remaining Turks of the recently arrived *24 Regiment* were routed, and this small but important part of the ridge was in British hands; unfortunately this would only be for too brief a period.

General Sir Ian Hamilton wrote of the incident:

Not only did this battalion, as well as some of the 6th South Lancashire Regiment, reach the crest, but they began to attack down the far side of it, firing as they went at the fast retreating enemy. But the fortune of war was against us. At this supreme moment Baldwin's column was still a long way from our trenches on the crest of Chunuk Bair, whence they should even now have been sweeping out towards Q along the whole ridge of the mountain. And instead of Baldwin's support came suddenly a salvo of heavy shells. These falling so unexpectedly among the stormers, threw them into terrible confusion. The Turkish commander saw his chance; instantly his troops were rallied and brought back in a counter-charge, and the South Lancashires and Gurkhas, who had seen the promised land and had seemed for a moment to have held victory in their grasp, were forced backwards over the crest and on to the lower slopes whence they had first started.

Allanson was wounded, and the last remaining Gurkha officer, Lieutenant John Le Marchand, was killed. Every other British officer in 6/Gurkhas had been killed or wounded, except for the Medical Officer, Captain Phipson. Subadar Major Gambirsing Pun, with the help of Phipson, who translated for the non-English speaking Gambirsing, carried out the withdrawal of the battalion in good order. Total casualties amounted to all of the British officers, sixty per cent of Gurkha officers and fifty two per cent other ranks. Allanson and Phipson were awarded the Distinguished Service Order, and Gambirsing the Military Cross.[30]

Hill Q (left) and Hill 971 (right), photographed from Chunuk Bair. (2013)

In Allanson's words:

> *And so ended the great battle of Chunuk Bair; we had held victory in our grasp, and had the whole operation been a success, nothing would have been too good for us; as it was we must suffer with the failure; it is galling to think of how many of one's own battalion are no longer alive, through whose example and death we gained the objective, only to be given up because others could not reach us or support us.*

It is still disputed today as to whom shelled Allanson off his position within minutes of capture. Whether this was the Royal Navy, a New Zealand battery or Turkish artillery, suddenly they came under a rain of shells. This second bombardment of Hill Q caused mass confusion and casualties as the Gurkhas and South Lancs were caught on the open forward crest and slopes that led down towards Maidos. The bombardment forced the tiny band of survivors back up to the ridgeline and, in such an exposed position, they withdrew back down the way they had come. The saddle remained unoccupied for the remainder of the day, with the Turks sheltering on one side, and the British on the other.

The origin of the shells that fell so devastatingly among Allanson's Gurkhas has always been a subject of controversy. Allanson, Phipson and others blamed the navy, thinking the shells were coming from HMS

HMS *Bacchante.*

Bacchante, stating that the yellow staining on the casualties was caused by a high explosive filling. However, according to Roger Keyes, no ships were firing on the ridge after the initial bombardment lifted. The historians Bean and Rhodes James point the finger at an Anzac howitzer battery. The latter are probably correct as the howitzers were ordered to shell the reverse slopes at zero hour, the time the Gurkhas were approaching that side of the hill. To support this view, the trajectory of the naval guns would have been too flat to hit the reverse slope; however a howitzer could. It is certain that eye-witnesses did see naval fire around that time, but almost certainly it was not to blame for the destruction that fell upon the Gurkhas. All of this is immaterial however, as a large number of Turkish reinforcements in the area would have pushed Allanson off if he had stayed. Even if the shells had not fallen upon them, the unsupported Allanson would have had to withdraw in face of such heavy opposition.

By the end of the day, the New Zealanders still retained a precarious foothold on Chunuk Bair, which gave Godley and Birdwood encouragement to plan a fourth attack. Johnston's men had been fighting up there for almost three days and nights without sleep and with little food and water. Godley's third assault on Sari Bair had clearly failed and any further window of opportunity had, in fact, firmly gone. If Chunuk Bair was to be held any longer, relief would be needed soon.

During the night of 9 August arrangements had been made to relieve the New Zealanders on Chunuk Bair and The Pinnacle, but strangely Godley did not choose the reserve battalions that were the nearest and most rested. These were two British battalions; 6/Loyal North Lancs, who had been in reserve at The Apex all day, and 6/Leinsters, who had been brought up from Chailak Dere during the early afternoon. The battalion chosen was 5/Wiltshires, who were both the furthest away in Agyhl Dere and the most exhausted.

Chunuk Bair was now put entirely in the hands of the New Army battalions and under the command of Major General Shaw, commander of the British 13th Division. Shaw instructed Lieutenant Colonel Henry Levinge's 6/Loyal North Lancs and Lieutenant Colonel John Carden's 5/Wiltshires to relieve Meldrum's New Zealanders up on Chunuk Bair. The relief began at about 8.00 pm on 9 August, though the Wiltshires were still some distance away and did not arrive until about 2.00 am the following morning. Godley had advised Shaw not to use his only fresh battalion, the 6/Leinsters, who were now at The Apex so, when Johnston heard that the Wiltshires would be late, he suggested sending up the Leinsters to support the Loyals. This request was denied, leaving only the Loyals on Chunuk Bair. Although it was realised that two battalions would be required to hold Chunuk Bair, Shaw only chose to position one at the top.

Levinge was briefed by Meldrum with the information that his last patrol had detected large bodies of Turks forming up the other side of the crest for an attack. He told Levinge to dig in and await the inevitable and then Meldrum took the remainder of the New Zealanders from the slopes of Chunuk Bair and The Pinnacle. Instead of digging in, the Loyals appeared to settle down for a rest, with many of them going to sleep. Because of the lack of room, they were also spread out, holding not only the slopes of Chunuk Bair but also the ground down to The Pinnacle. As already proven, riflemen in great numbers was the only defence against any determined attack. The departing Wellington Mounted Rifles and Otago Regiment were in a bad state. The Wellingtons had lost two-thirds of their number and the Otagos over half, as well as seventeen

Lieutenant Colonel H. G. Levinge, 6/Loyal North Lancs, killed 10 August (Commemorated on the Helles Memorial).

officers. The Aucklanders at The Pinnacle had lost a similar number.

When the first companies of 5/Wiltshires arrived in the early morning, they were directed to the head of Sazli Beit Dere, which was in a cup-shaped hollow on the lower slopes of Chunuk Bair, behind the front line. After a consultation between Levinge and Carden, it was decided that there was not enough room for the Wiltshires in the shallow trenches on the upper slopes as well as the Loyals, and those behind were still full of wounded. The Wiltshires settled down behind the Loyals in the 'safety' of this protected hollow, to await the remainder of the battalion to arrive. What the Wiltshires did not know was that on the other side of the ridge the Turks were massing for a dawn attack.

Liman von Sanders had received the news of the landing at Suvla and breakout at Anzac during the early morning on 7 August. As soon as it became clear that Bulair was not threatened and, sharing the fear amongst his Turkish commanders that the British would break through soon, he ordered both Turkish *7th* and *12th Divisions*, under the command of Colonel Feyzi *(XVI Corps)* to the south. Ahead of these battle hardened units was a punishing thirty mile forced march, which they began soon after receiving the order to move at 6.30 am on 7 August. This force would be needed urgently for von Sanders to launch a counter attack, which he wanted to happen as early as possible on 8 August. He directed the *7th Division* to go into the line north of the Sari Bair ridge, where the Anzac offensive was threatening the line, whilst directing the *12th Division* against Suvla. With the high ground around Suvla secured, Mustafa Kemal could then focus on the threat to Sari Bair ridge, where he knew the main attack was taking place. By 8 August the British were only three miles away from their goal at Suvla, and less than a mile at Anzac; the Turks thirty miles!

The leading elements of Feyzi's reinforcements had begun to arrive, near Büyükanafarta, a little earlier than anyone expected, during the night of 7 August. However, the bulk of the troops did not make an appearance until the morning of 8 August. The Turks were as exhausted as the British, as this was one of the hottest days of the summer and the men had been forced to march over thirty miles in an oppressive heat. Feyzi asked for time to rest his men, but von Sanders wanted them to counter attack immediately. Feyzi objected, because his men were tired and there was no available artillery support; however this did him no good. Von Sanders immediately removed him from command, and replaced him with Colonel Mustafa Kemal, commander of the *19th Division*. By 9.45 pm on 8 August Kemal was now responsible for the

Suvla sector as well as Sari Bair. Kemal had a great advantage over Feyzi as he knew this area intimately, having fought in the Anzac area since 25 April. He rode out that night to view the situation for himself and to examine the condition of Feyzi's men. He came to the same conclusion: that the troops were completely exhausted and suspended the attack until the morning of 9 August.

As we know, Chunuk Bair itself posed a problem for the Turkish command as it rested between two different army groups, one controlling Chunuk Bair the other Hill 971. The position needed to be

Major General F. C. Shaw, commanding the British 13th Division.

131

recaptured, but by whom? Confusion and disarray reigned amongst the Turks just as much as it did with Godley's men. After an unsuccessful attack by *2/33 Regiment* during the day, the *8th Division* commander, Lieutenant Colonel Ali Reza, ordered Major Nuri's *24 Regiment* to retake the hill during the evening, regardless of which group had command, whilst he kept *23 Regiment* in reserve. To add further weight to the attack, German Lieutenant Colonel Pötrih was appointed commander of *9th Division*, as Kannengiesser had been wounded; however his units were badly mixed up and he needed time to reorganize them. The attack was temporarily postponed by *Third Army* headquarters, not because of this, but because there would be a new commander.

As the commander of the newly formed *Anafartalar Group*, Mustafa Kemal now had responsibility for both Suvla and the Sari Bair heights. He appointed Lieutenant Colonel Şefik to command of his own *19th Division*, whilst he went in person to the *8th Division* to review Ali Reza's plans for the next counter attack on Chunuk Bair. He found the crest a No Man's Land, dividing the British and Turkish trenches; neither side could hold the summit. Kemal went to the *64 Regiment's* headquarters in a gully just behind the Su Yatagha ridge. Men from the *24* and *10 Regiments* were still holding the front line trenches on Chunuk Bair. Just behind them were the men from the *23 Regiment*, who were the freshest of the units available, all part of *8th Division*. Still in the area were the battered *9th Division*, now under the command of Pötrih, but they were still scatted and mixed up with other units. Further right, men from the *4th Division* were deployed from Hill 971 and down Abdul Rahman Spur.

Kemal and Ali Reza finalised the attack plans during the night. Spearheading the attack on Chunuk Bair would be *23 Regiment*, along with *28 Regiment,* which had just arrived from Helles, which would attack towards Rhododendron Spur. In total, over 6000 men were allocated to the attack. When Mustafa Kemal explained his intention to attack Chunuk Bair , *8th Division's* chief of staff, Galip voiced concern: *We have been attacking for two days but all the attacks have been futile and there may be another disaster*. Galip was talking from experience, but Mustafa Kemal believed that a surprise bayonet charge and without the forewarning of a bombardment would succeed.

Mustafa Kemal spent the night of 9/10 August at the *8th Division's* HQ on Su Yatagha:

I had an uneasy and sleepless night. I didn't get a minute's rest because on one hand throughout the night I was receiving reports

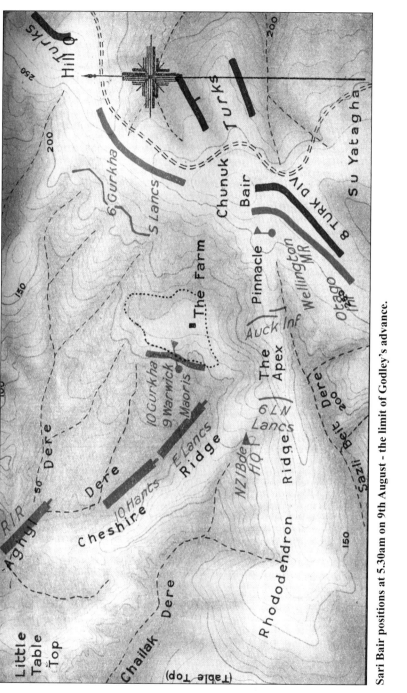

Sari Bair positions at 5.30am on 9th August - the limit of Godley's advance.

which were deliberately misleading and inaccurate, yet none the less were important to interpret. These reports came from the Anafartalar sector. On the other hand I was being constantly solicited in my headquarters by officers who had lost their units and superiors. I sent out some of these officers again to check the activities and dispositions of the 8th Division. Of these officers, Captain Hidayet of the General Staff had done an outstanding job in controlling preparations for the attack.

The 41st Regiment did not arrive till the moment of the attack. They went to the wrong location and could only join us later; on the other hand the 8th Division was ready for action. The 23rd Regiment was ready to attack towards Chunuk Bair, with two battalions up at the front line, one in reserve. The 28th was equally ready to attack towards Falcon's [Rhododendron] Ridge. It was almost daybreak ... I stepped out of my tent. I could see the soldiers from the units that would make the attack. Here I waited for the moment to launch the attack.

For the British the end was near.

Chapter Seven

10 August – Turkish Counter Attack

They stormed forward, crying in the name of God

Just after 3.30 am Turkish bombers began to work their way forward towards the British lines from Chunuk Bair and north along the saddle to Hill Q. Below, the forward elements of Baldwin's and Cox's brigades (9/Worcesters, 6/South Lancs, 6/Gurkhas and 9/Warwicks), who were strung out along the upper slopes, began to come under increasing bomb and rifle fire from the top of the ridge. This was nothing unusual, and at this time no one knew what would soon be unleashed upon them.

Closely packed into whatever cover the slopes around Su Yatagha could offer, the Turks were able to place over a division of men, its ranks so thick that it was likened to ants swarming their nest. Kemal wrote:

It was early in the morning, on 10 August, the dawn was about to break. I was standing in front of my tent, and I could see all the men. The time was 4.30 am. I was worried about my men waiting in densely packed infantry lines. If the enemy opened fire on these lines it would be disaster. I immediately ran to the front to greet and inspect the men and said, ' Soldiers! I am sure that you will defeat the enemy, you do not hurry, let me go first, when you see my whip go up, you all go together.' Then they walked with the commanding officers. All the men were in attack position, one step forward, rifles with fixed bayonets, officers with revolvers or swords in hand, watching for my signal.

At 4.30 am, as the frail morning light had begun to lighten the shadows, Mustafa Kemal gave the signal. Five thousand men, in several lines, bayonet charged the British lines, shouting "*Allah ... Allah ... Allah*". Many of the British defenders did not have time to return fire, as the overwhelming numbers of men swept over the forward positions. The British troops were wildly scattered, many running in panic back down the slopes. The Turkish *23* and *24 Regiments* regained the lines at Chunuk Bair, whilst *28 Regiment* charged down the slopes and recaptured The

135

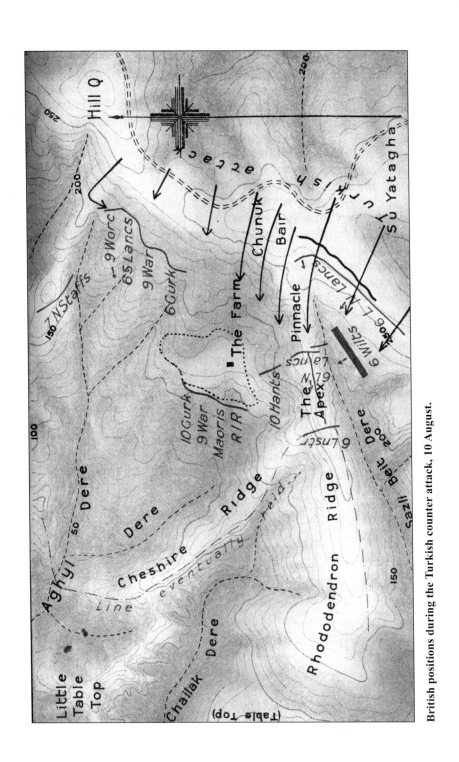

British positions during the Turkish counter attack, 10 August.

Pinnacle. The Auckland's history described this action:

Turkish troops in bivouacs.

All night they were massing behind Sari Bair, and on the morning of the 10th the whole mass was in motion, moving with the power of an avalanche and the speed of a landslide. The English battalions in front broke and were swept away. The Turks came on. The hillside was brown with their charging battalions. On toward the 'Farm', and the Deres below, and the margin of the sea! It was a bold stroke, executed with determination and courage. For a moment it seemed that no power on earth could stop the moving mass, but the target they made was a good one. Aucklanders on Cheshire Ridge were firing—firing as fast as they could load and fire—and with them now were the Fifth Reinforcements. The Turks came on, three hundred men in a line, and twenty lines, following at a little space one behind the other. They stormed forward, crying on the name of God, calling aloud the proclamation of their faith; for them it was victory or the fields of Paradise. If fanatical valour, if contempt of death could win, then surely the host of the Turks would break through.

Wallingford had ten machine-guns in action, six of them well forward, two of the six being Auckland guns. They were trained across the line of the Turkish advance. The men behind, cool and resolute, set up a zone of death. The first line of Turks charged into it and went down to a man. The next line melted away on the same spot. But still they came on, line after line, and the leaden sweep reaped them in swathes. No hesitation; no faltering; the last line charged on with the same high courage. They also fell. Now the artillery has picked up the range, and the great heap of death and agony is torn and blasted by the bursting shells. The wounded Turks who were able to crawl back were unmolested, so full of admiration were the machine-gunners for the charge they had made.

Lieutenant Colonel Levinge's Loyals, although not as prepared as they should have been, were able to hold the first wave back but, without bombs and artillery, the front line trench was quickly overwhelmed by the superior numbers. From below little could be seen apart from the

137

fusillade of British rifle fire and then a stream of survivors silhouetted against the rising sun as they fled the massacre above. Within minutes the Turks had overrun Chunuk Bair and The Pinnacle, crushing the defenders. The next to give way were 5/Wiltshires, who were shocked to see four or five lines of Turkish infantry charging towards their camp. The battalion had arrived only an hour or so before the attack, had not slept for about seventy hours and had had very little water and no food since Friday evening; they were exhausted. It was reported that they took off their equipment, piled their arms and made no attempt to dig in, falling asleep dog tired. Few of the Wiltshires had time to put up a stand and, with their rifles still piled, many ran down the hill side in panic, into Sazli Beit gully

Lance Corporal William Thomas Parker, 5/Wilts, killed 10 August. (Commemorated on the Helles Memorial).

below. Those who neared the bottom were then exposed to further Turkish machine gun fire, so their escape route was cut off. Some remained and took the Turks head-on, but were quickly overrun and killed.

In total it was estimated that there were twenty two lines, each of 300 Turks, pouring down from the heights, enveloping Chunuk Bair and the whole saddle along to Hill Q. The Apex was next in line and was under threat of imminent loss, along with the possible collapse of the whole front line. Wallingford's New Zealand machine guns, positioned at The Apex and strategic points on both Rhododendron and Cheshire ridges, ripped into the advancing masses. Unfortunately there was no time to distinguish between the Turks and the 300 or so New Army troops in front; both Turk and British fell together; but, at the loss of friendly lives, the Turkish onslaught had been halted within a desperate hour of fighting. The Royal Navy, witnessing the line collapsing, was firing salvo after salvo onto the seaward slopes with high explosives, completely blanketing them with smoke, earth and debris as the shells smashed into the hillside and advancing Turks. On the inland slopes the Anzac artillery began to join the dawn chorus by dropping shells onto the crest and forward slopes, catching the Turkish troops still being fed into the charge. One piece of shrapnel hit Mustafa Kemal's pocket watch,[31] smashing the casing, but saving his life.

The Loyals and Wiltshires who had not been killed were trapped between the lines and endured their fate. Lieutenant Walter Evans, 8/Welsh, wrote: *They were obliged to abandon all their wounded and that is why there are so many missing. The wounded in the gully remained there all day, many dying, and in the evening, when it was dark, all who were able ran back over the hill to where our bivouac was on Saturday night.* Some fled off the spur and into the valleys below but were trapped, later being made prisoner, whilst others were sniped, or died through lack of water or from their wounds. A few did manage to make it back to friendly lines. Behind the Wiltshires, 6/Leinsters and the Auckland battalion stood firm at The Apex, spared by not being under the full

Mustafa Kemal.

force of the Turkish onslaught. At the point of the bayonet, the few who managed to break through fought a furious hand to hand battle. Hard pressed, the men, in whatever dress they had been sleeping in, eventually stemmed the flow of the Turkish attack.

Major Temperley wrote in the *Reveille* journal of April 1938:

We had tempted fate too long. As dawn was breaking, I heard the brigade machine-guns in action at The Apex and, as I went to them, I saw the whole of the slopes of Chunuk Bair alive with Turks. At the same time a few fugitives arrived to say that we had lost the hill. The execution done by the enfilade fire of the machine guns was immense. A few minutes later the naval guns joined in the chorus, shooting directly over their sights. The Turks pressed on with superb gallantry right up to the Farm and along Rhododendron Spur to The Apex. Few of those who came over the crest can have returned. The situation at The Apex was critical, and it seemed to me we had reached the end. I collected a few signallers and odd men and, with fixed bayonets, we awaited what I expected to be the full weight of the counter-attack, but for some reason it never came. A certain number charged right up to us and were dealt with by rifle & revolver. I remember Major Wallingford, the champion shot[32], rushing out and accounting for one or two with his pistol.

The surviving Wiltshires, with a few other men from the Loyals, were cut off. Some tried to rush past the machine gun fire in Sazli Beit, but virtually all were killed or wounded in attempting that path. Others tried

139

The Mustafa Kemal memorial which is placed near the site that he was wounded.

to climb up the sides of the gully, but few succeeded. This drove most to stay still and hide in the gully until nightfall, after which small groups eventually found their way to safety. In one account it is probable that a group of Wiltshires who were trying to make a run for it were actually shot by men from 8/LHR, who witnessed a body of Turks in the valley approaching the British lines. They fired and the 'Turks' ran back. It was noted that these men had no weapons, so were almost certainly survivors trying to make their way back. In another account it was noted that several men were rescued from the gully having hidden out there for sixteen days, gathering water from a small spring and food from the haversacks of the dead. These men reported that there were originally many more wounded with them, but that they died of their wounds or simply of exhaustion and lack of water.

One of the Wiltshire men, Private W. J. Head, won the DCM.

For conspicuous bravery and resource. Private Head was one of a party of seven, who became separated from their regiment during the fighting on the 10th August 1915 at Chunuk Bair and who remained within the enemy's lines for over fifteen days. Although wounded three times between 10th and 26th of August, he collected food for his wounded comrades from the bodies of the dead, this being the sole and very slender supply. He displayed the finest qualities of endurance and leadership in keeping up the spirits of the survivors in most trying conditions.

All that could be mustered from this battalion was about 340 men. Their commanding officer, Lieutenant Colonel John Carden, was killed, along with nine other officers. None of their bodies could be identified after the war, so they are commemorated on the Helles Memorial.

Further along from Rhododendron Spur, the Farm simultaneously felt the full force of the sudden Turkish attack. The Turks were cut down in swathes as they stormed down the slopes towards the Farm's plateau,

The Farm and plateau, photographed in 1915 from Rhododendron Spur.

but the attack was at such a rapid pace that the Turks were soon upon the British positions in large numbers, frenzied and triumphant with pushing the enemy from the heights. Small groups of men from 5/Wiltshires, 10/Hampshires and Irish were still clinging on precariously to the surrounding slopes but their positions soon became untenable. Further north, the Gurkhas, South Lancs, Worcesters and Warwicks, despite some brave last stands, were either overwhelmed or pushed back. The 9/Warwicks, commanded by Major William Gordon, had originally been held in divisional reserve. During 8 August they advanced up Aghyl Dere amidst the confusion of that day to reach a position during the night by 6/South Lancs and 6/Gurkhas, on a ledge between Hill Q and Chunuk Bair. Gordon was soon wounded and handed command to Major A. G. Sharp, who was killed during the counter attack. When the battalion was eventually withdrawn they had no officers and only

Major W. A. Gordon and Major A. G. Sharp, 9/Warwicks: Sharp is Commemorated on the Helles Memorial.

248 men left, although about forty one missing rejoined the battalion the following day. With battalions losing all their officers like this, it goes a long way to explaining why few, if any, records survive to tell the story of this fighting, with many acts of bravery going unrecorded. The battalion history does try to fill this gap from a story of an unnamed New Zealander, an old Birmingham man himself, who bore witness to their exploits.

They had immense difficulties to overcome. They were led the wrong way, and had to retrace their steps; they had to attack in full view of the enemy; their left was exposed to enfilading fire and, in spite of all, they reached the Rhododendron Spur, and some the very ridge of 971. They held on like grim death, held on when first one and then another unit retired. They asked for reinforcements, but were told none were available, and still they stayed. They were now by themselves, and it was only when every officer save one was killed or wounded that three companies slowly retired. The fourth company, with its gallant major, [Major

Robert Shuttleworth] *held on to the farm near the ridge till all were killed. With their ranks terribly thinned they came back as from parade, parched and hungry, but still undaunted. I was close by to their dressing-station, where a padre, Leighton* [The Rev. F. Leighton MC], *and a medical officer, O'Brien, and later the padre alone, worked night and day. Gurkhas, Maoris and Colonials, as well as their own men, were treated there with a cheerfulness and nerve that was amazing. As the last officer of the Warwickshire was badly wounded next day, deeds that should be known may not have hitherto found record. They are as noble as any of our own at Lone Pine. I saw a Warwickshire officer, I think Baker* [Captain H. S. Baker] *was his name, dressed for wounds three times in one day and, despite the medical officer's advice he went back to the firing-line, I saw the Padre Leighton go out to a wounded engineer lying out under fire, bandage him up and place him in safety, and then, finding a wounded Gurkha, he hoisted him on his back and carried him to the Indian hospital halfway down the Aghyl Dere. This man was a sport in all conscience, and became a friend to all our boys in the gully. I saw him later wade through machine-gun fire to attend a man of the Connaughts, who lay mortally wounded. Then there was a lance-corporal, Guillaume, of the machine-gun section, who stayed up near the Rhododendron Spur for six hours after all had retired, fired four thousand rounds, and then, burying the tripod of his gun, walked back with the rest under his arm. I saw a quiet-mannered orderly bring his officer down the gully, and heard the latter telling how his man had seen him fall on the hill and, dashing up under heavy fire, had carried and slid with him to safety. I saw the same poor fellow a few days later lying in the padre's dug-out mortally wounded—Greenway was his name. I saw men tended there from this regiment who smiled at death, just because they had been to the top of the hill and seen the Maidos road. A war correspondent has kindly spoken of our deeds as epic. Well, there was an epic*

Major R. G. Shuttleworth, 9/Warwicks.
Killed on the slopes near The Farm.
(Commemorated on the Helles Memorial)

143

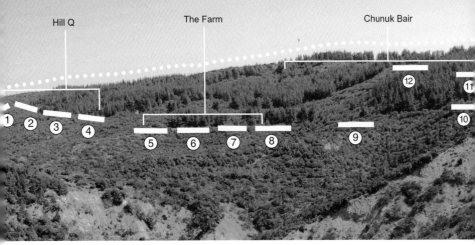

Looking up to the area where the main Turkish counter attack fell. The dotted line represents the Turkish positions on the crest before the counter attack. (1) 9/Worcesters, (2) 6/South Lancs, (3) 9/Warwicks, (4) 6/Gurkhas, (5) 10/Gurkhas, (6) 9/Warwicks, (7) Maoris, (8) Royal Irish Rifles, (9) 10/Hants, (10) 6/Leinsters, (11) 6/Wilts, (12) 6/Loyals.

here. As an eye-witness, I wish to testify to the work of these men from England, whose deeds made us proud to be counted their comrades.

Mention has been made of the missing who returned; especially distressing to their loved ones were the missing who did not return. Many deaths could not be confirmed until much later due to the lack of eye-witnesses or recovery of a body. Hope that they had become prisoners was common, and newspaper columns often had requests from relatives about the fate of their loved ones. In the case of Private William Cowley, a West Bromwich lad, the anguish of the parents is imaginable. A statement, forwarded by the British Red Cross, by Private Frank Davies, 9/Warwicks, stated:

On August 10th 1915 at Sari Bair (Hill 971) I was in a trench with Bill Cowley and he was shot at about 7.30 in the morning. He died instantly and I was one who helped to bury his body. Davies later wrote to Cowley's parents with further information of his tragic death: I much regret to say that I was with your son on August 10th at Sari Bair when Bill was killed. He lay in the trench dead, shot through the mouth. Afterwards the battalion retired, not being strong enough to check the attack. Bill was covered in with the parapet from the Turk's shells. That is how we could not get

144

anything of Bill's small book (i.e. pay book) and property. There were four or five of the type of Bill buried in the trench. He was a battalion sniper and did fine work before his end. We lost a good fellow in him for we were not very strong after we came out of action.[33]

At the Farm Brigadier General Baldwin was killed and his headquarters was overrun, and a considerable amount of equipment and many rifles and machine-guns were lost to the enemy. Those encamped at the Farm had little time to react and many just ran away as the front line collapsed. Command of the brigade temporarily passed to Lieutenant Colonel Bewsher, 10/Hampshires, until he was wounded. At around 10.30 am, officer-less units were falling back. In one incident, Captain Norman Street, a 39 Brigade Staff Captain, led forward a group of retiring men back to hold the Farm. When Street was killed the troops withdrew again, ending up near Cayley's headquarters near the easternmost fork of the Aghyl Dere. Birdwood sent Cayley his last reserve, 5/Connaughts, but by the time they arrived at the Farm at around midday the situation was just about irreversible. Chunuk Bair had been lost, the Turks had recaptured The Pinnacle and from that position were threatening the British troops at the Farm. At dusk the Farm was evacuated, leaving behind about a thousand British and Dominion dead.

At 12.15 pm, after eight hours of fighting, Mustafa Kemal ordered Ali Reza to stop the attack. In a report Kemal sent to the Turkish *Fifth Army* Headquarters, he wrote: *I think they are done and the British cannot launch another serious attack on Gallipoli.* This was true. Kemal's counter attack, although ferocious and with a devastating 9000 Turkish casualties, had succeeded in pushing the British off Chunuk Bair. Birdwood's plan was in shatters and his army had been fought to a standstill with no hope of renewing the attack. The window of opportunity had not only passed, but was now shuttered close. Lieutenant Walter

Private John Williams, one of Shuttleworth's men, who was killed on 10 August. (Commemorated on the Helles Memorial.)

Evans, 8/Welsh, wrote that, *there was a lack of generalship and orders and it was foolish to attack Chunuk Bair and leave Battleship Hill alone; it was a miracle that anybody came out of it alive. Still we can't tell what was in Hamilton's mind so we will not criticise, but the whole thing was a box up and the men never really had a chance.* Evans was not alone with this conclusion. The lack of generalship and the misinterpretation of the geography were elements that cannot be ignored, but these were but two of multiple reasons for failure. We must also take into account the flaws in the preparation and planning, the shortage of materials, the inadequacies of the logistical support, the poor physical condition and lack of experience of the men, and also, importantly, the continued underestimation of the Turks. All contributed to the failings of the August Offensive to deliver the desired breakout and expected victory.

Turkish commanders photographed in July 1915. These include Major Izettin Çalişlar, Colonel Fahrettin Altay, Major Kemal Ohri, Major Wilhelm Willmer, Colonel Hans Kannengiesser, Colonel Rüstü, Colonel Mustafa Kemal, General Esat Pasha, Major Haydar Alganer, Major Mehmet Nazim and Colonel Hulusi.

The casualties for the Anzac attack on the Sari Bair ridge had been heavy. In five days of fighting the British and Dominion forces had lost a third of their force; 12,500 men out of a total of 37,000 deployed. The British 13th (Western) Division had lost 5500 men, whilst the 1st Australian and NZ&A Division lost 2,500 and 3,300 respectively. The two attached infantry brigades: 29 Brigade and 29 (Indian) Brigade lost 1200 men. For an offensive that has become popularly associated with the Anzacs, it should be remembered also for the sacrifices of the British and Indian armies, the former in particular bore the brunt of much of the fighting and suffered many of the casualties. When the offensive at Anzac came to an end on 10 August, at Suvla the British were already planning another attack. At Anzac itself it would not be quiet for long, as many of the same units involved in the earlier offensive would be thrown again into battle.

Chapter Eight

Hill 60 – The Last Battle

We just blazed away until the rifles glowed red-hot

On 17 August Sir Ian Hamilton notified Lord Kitchener that the August offensive had failed. He had not given up on the campaign, though, and immediately requested 45,000 reinforcements to bring up to strength the formations already on Gallipoli, and a further 50,000 to add weight for a future offensive. Hamilton was now planning a joint attack at North Anzac and Suvla. At Suvla, IX Corps would attack the W Hills; part of this attack would involve the re-taking of Scimitar Hill. At Anzac, the focus was on capturing a small, indistinct knoll, named Hill 60, and some nearby wells. These attacks would enable both battlefronts to be securely linked and the vital paths of communication masked from the eyes of the Turks.

Brigadier General A. Russell, commanding the New Zealand Mounted Rifles Brigade.

At Suvla the attack was yet another disaster; with over 5000 British casualties, it became no more than a charnel house. For details of this attack read *Suvla: August Offensive*. At Hill 60 it was little different. Formed at the juncture between the Anzac and Suvla sectors, it was referred to by Brigadier General Andrew Russell, commander of the New Zealand Mounted Rifles Brigade, as *an abominable little hill*; and most certainly it was. Tactically the hill had a commanding position over the Anafarta Sagir valley, which the Anzacs wanted to deny the Turks. The hill also had command of two groups of wells, Susak and Kabak Kuyu, which the Anzacs wanted. Water was strictly rationed and, as the temperatures soared in August, the want was ever greater: *there was, indeed, no object for which any man in the rank and file would more willingly fight in Gallipoli in August than a well.*[34] The historian and author Robert Rhodes James wrote: *For connoisseurs of military futility, valour, incompetence and determination, the attacks on Hill 60 are in a class of their own.*

147

The hill was first observed, but not occupied, by the forward elements of Monash's Australian 4 Brigade during the morning of 7 August. Some of these scouts even went foraging by Hill 60 and along the bridle track that goes past it, gathering honey from beehives they found in the area. Why did they not, or 40 Brigade, capture the hill? It was not an objective, the goal being the high ground of Sari Bair and not an insignificant feature in the middle of what was then nowhere. When the Turkish 7*th*Division came into the area on 9 August they began to occupy the hill, so when 9/Worcesters tried to seize the Kabak Kuyu wells, between Damakjelik and Hill 60, on 12 August, they failed. The Turks were already fortifying this scrub-covered hill by digging a network of trenches to defend the hill and wells. The defences on Hill 60 were connected by a kilometre long trench with Hill 100, another formidable Turkish position further

Major General H. V. Cox, commanding the British and Anzac composite force.

along the spur at the head of Kaiajik Dere. It was believed that there were only two Turkish companies holding the hill, supported by two machine guns, but in reality there was over a regiment defending the position. On the hill were *2/21* and *3/21 Regiments*, whilst close-by were both *1/33* and *2/33 Regiments*, all from the *7th Division*. It would not be an easy fight.

For the attack on 21 August, a composite force of Anzac and British troops under the command of Major General Cox were used. Why a composite force? Because this was all that Birdwood could scrape together from units that were either not in the line elsewhere, or had not ceased to exist as a fighting unit during the Sari Bair fighting. Even those within this force had all been in action and were not their former selves. The force comprised the seriously weakened New Zealand Mounted Rifles (Otago and Canterbury), the shattered 4 (Australian) Brigade along with 4/SWB. Two battalions from the British 29 Brigade were also allocated: 5/Connaught Rangers and 10/Hampshires; and three Gurkha battalions from Cox's own 29 (Indian) Brigade: 5, 6 and 10/Gurkhas.

The objective was Kaiajik Aghala, as Hill 60 was originally known, and the nearby wells. Once captured, the line would be extended towards Dervish Ali Kuyu to link up with the British IX Corps at Suvla. He would use the Gurkhas on the left to cross the open plain from Kavlar Chair to capture the Susak Kuyu well, north of Hill 60, whilst to their right the 5/Connaughts would capture Kabak Kuyu. With the wells captured, 5/Connaughts, about 700 strong, would advance to the left of the Otago and Canterbury Mounted Rifles, who were only 400 rifles strong, across Kaiajik Dere and capture Hill 60 itself. To the New Zealanders' right, 500 men from 4 (Australian) Brigade, supported by 335 men from 10/Hampshires, would take the Turkish communication trench on the scrub covered spur that led up from Hill 60. This was in fact another branch of the Damakjelik Spur that ran up to Hill 100 and the Sari Bair ridge beyond, but for this attack the immediate spur would be taken in order to join up with the rest of the Australian 4 Brigade's positions.

The supporting artillery comprised of only thirty two guns and howitzers, with a limited allocation of ammunition, so the bombardment was to be far from heavy. The 5-inch howitzers of 69 Brigade RFA had limited ammunition available and were under orders to conserve their supply, whilst the larger 60-pounders of 10 (Heavy) Battery RGA had mechanical failures with some of the guns. If this was not bad enough, this artillery was ordered to bombard the Turkish positions in support of the British attack on the W Hills first. This not only depleted the supply of shells available for the Hill 60 attack, but it also forced the infantry assault to be delayed by thirty minutes to allow the bombardment to be switched back. When the bombardment eventually fell on Hill 60, all it really achieved was to prompt the Turks of the opening of the inevitable attack. With the Turks warned, and the Hill 60 attack now made in

69 Brigade, D Battery, with a 5-inch howitzer firing at Hill 60. (Alexander Turnbull Library, Wellington, New Zealand.)

isolation of the originally planned general attack, its chances of success were narrowing.

At 3.30 pm, in the brilliant afternoon sunlight, the attack began. The Gurkhas advanced across the open ground and, despite being heavily opposed, they reached and captured Susak Kuyu, to the north of Hill 60. Simultaneously, the New Zealanders and Australians began their advance. Their jump off positions were almost a quarter of a mile away and involved crossing two small ridges. These had the effect of helping to shield the advance from the eyes of the Turks, resulting in few casualties. As the Australians approached the most exposed position, overlooked by the Turkish redoubt on Hill 100, they advanced at the double, which also reduced casualties. By 3.45 pm, the leading New Zealand elements had crossed the grassy Kaiajik Dere and were making their way up the lower slopes of Hill 60 to capture the first trench. They had a few problems with enfilade fire from Hill 100 when crossing the Kaiajik, which forced them to veer off to the left of the hill, out of the line of fire. With the first trench cleared the New Zealanders continued up the slope and into a Turkish communication trench that led towards the summit.

To the New Zealanders' right was a steep re-entrant that led from Kaiajik Dere to the summit; this physically separated their attack from the Australians, who were trying to get onto the flat spur to the right. On the corner of the spur an oak tree provided a navigation mark for the Australians, behind which lay their objective. Before this spur was the narrow, grassy valley of Kaiajik Dere where; at its head, marked by Hill 100, the Turks had positioned a machine gun. A few Australians managed to cross this valley but there were heavy casualties, which littered this narrow stretch of grassland. Those that reached the other side then had enormous problems trying to fight their way through the thick scrub; thus far they had not seen a single Turk. Pinned down on both sides of the valley, the Australian assault had nowhere to go.

Newton Wanliss, the historian of the 14/AIF, wrote:

At 3.30 pm, the bombardment ceased and the first wave, consisting of 150 men of the 13th Battalion under Lieutenant Ford, charged. Suffering heavy casualties crossing the Dere, they drew up at the foot of the hill just at the top of the other side of the Dere. A few minutes later came the turn of the 14th Battalion, the second wave of 150 men under Major Dare. A whistle blew, and down the hill they raced like madmen. The Turks were by this time thoroughly aroused and alert and the moment the crest was passed by our men, artillery, machine-guns and rifles vomited death in their faces. Forty per cent

Hill 60 and the grass covered Kaiajik Dere to the right. (2013)

became casualties in that short, wild, frenzied charge. Lieutenant Crabbe and Duffield were killed. Major Dare, Lieutenant D. R. Macdermid, and Sergeant Ernie Hill got through unwounded. The survivors joined up with the 13th Battalion men who had stopped at the foot of the hill. It was impossible to complete the attack on the trench without artillery support, so Major Dare (who assumed command of the survivors of both waves) ordered the position to be consolidated. Fortunately, though it was impossible either to advance or retreat, the position was immune from the Turkish frontal fire, being tucked away in the front of the hill. It now became the duty of the third wave of 200 men (consisting of a hundred men each from the 13th and 14th Battalions) to repeat the attack made by the first two waves. It, however, proved impracticable. The Turkish machine-gun fire had now become so hot as to block all advance, and when the third wave attempted to charge it was brought to a standstill, with the exception of Sergeant Bertram Edmonstone and a handful of men, who charged through and survived the deadly fusillade. Many were hit immediately they appeared on the crest and fell straight back into the gully. Some managed a few yards and were then wounded, or had to lie down in the scrub, the machine-gun bullets just grazing them. The fourth wave, consisting of a Hampshire battalion, had a similar experience. Scores were shot down and it, too, failed to support the two leading waves, now isolated, and with no means of communication with their own lines, except over the fearful bullet-swept slope behind.[35]

Pinned down, the situation was to become worse for the Australians and the Hampshire survivors. Just as it had at Suvla, Turkish artillery fire set the tinder-dry scrub alight:

To add to the horrors of the day, an enemy shell set fire to the scrub on the hill just crossed by the attacking waves. As the fire spread, it ignited the bombs carried by some of the dead lying scattered in the scrub, which, exploding, increasing the area of fire. The plight of the hapless wounded was appalling. Some who tried to escape from the flames were shot down by the enemy's snipers. Little assistance could be rendered in daylight on the bullet-swept hill, though under cover of the smoke several wounded men were dragged away by the stretcher-bearers.

Helping the stretcher bearers was a Scottish-born Presbyterian minister, Reverend Andrew Gillison. Gillison, who was attached to the Australian brigade, went out under the cover of the smoke with Corporal Robert Pittendrigh, 13/AIF, who was a Methodist minister from Lithgow, NSW and also Captain Henry Loughran, 14/AIF's medical officer. They helped to drag the wounded from the flames as the stretcher bearers made the mad dash across the open ground back to safety. The dead had to be left and when the flames eventually reached them it was not uncommon to hear the sound of cartridges from their pouches and bombs in their pockets exploding. The following morning the luck of both ministers would run out. During a burial Gillison heard a soldier, later discovered to be a man from the Hampshire Regiment, groaning amongst the scrub. He called for help from Pittendrigh and one other, all knowing the dangers of going out in daylight. As soon as they reached the man, having crawled across the open ground, they were hit by machine gun fire. Both Gillison and Pittendrigh continued to drag the wounded man back to the trench, where Gillison succumbed to his wounds. Pittendrigh, although hit multiple times, looked as though he would survive, but died of his wounds upon a hospital ship a week later.

Corporal Robert Pittendrigh, 13/AIF (The Sydney Morning Herald).

Chaplain The Reverend Andrew Gillison.

On the left, the Connaughts were the next to go, at 3.40 pm, and made their cold steel bayonet charge to capture Kabak Kuyu.

The leading platoon dashed forward with a yell like hounds breaking cover. Advancing they were met with a roar of rifle fire, coming not only from the trench attacked, but also from Hill 60, and from snipers concealed in the scattered bushes. Not a man stopped to return it; all dashed on with leveled bayonets across the four hundred yards of open country, each man striving to be the first into the enemy's trench.

The first to get there was Second Lieutenant Thomas Johnson, who killed six Turks. He shot two more and narrowly missed killing another. The stream bed, used by the Turks as a communication trench, was quickly cleared by Johnson and the well captured. The Connaughts then made their way along the bridle track that led past the western side of Hill 60. Sunken in places, which provided some cover, it did not prevent further casualties when the Turks laid down a barrage on this position. Johnson was a pre-war Irish International footballer and medical doctor, who had already been mentioned for gallantry at Lone Pine during the actions of 8/9 August. Now he was holding an advanced trench against Turkish counter attacks and using his medical skills to tend the wounded. For his bravery at Kabak Kuyu and previously at Lone Pine, Johnson was awarded the Military Cross and, although severely wounded, went on to survive both the campaign and war.

The Connaughts were later joined by 5/Gurkhas in the sunken lane, which extended the line north towards Susak Kuyu. Although sheltered in places from Turkish fire, it was not safe from shelling. Lieutenant Colonel Henry Jourdain, commanding 5/Connaughts, wrote:

The sunken lane: Hill 60 is to the right, with the W Hills in the background.

I was sitting on a stone in the sunken road, endeavouring to write a dispatch for the Brigadier, the enemy began to shell us heavily, and one member after another of my staff was taken from me. One of my two runners, the faithful Michael Judge, had been shot through the face by a Turk, who lay ensconced in a bush only some five yards away, but although his face was covered with blood, and the bullet had gone through from cheek to cheek, he said that he was sorry he had to leave, but he was glad they had hit him and not me. My Adjutant was severely wounded almost at my side, and the Senior Major also; the Sergeant Major had been wounded, and I had only one orderly left.[36]

With little more than a toehold on the hill's forward slopes, these small gains needed exploiting quickly. The Connaughts' reserve company came forward and in the confusion was followed by the rest of the battalion, who then bayonet charged the hill. The sudden charge was successful and cleared the seaward side of the hill of Turks, from the sunken lane to almost as far as the present day Hill 60 cemetery. At this location the Turkish fire was so concentrated that the Connaughts' charge was stopped, with the survivors falling back to the New Zealand line. The attacks petered out as dusk fell: for now at least there was a respite in the fighting.

With no more reinforcements available to follow up the attack in the morning, Godley reluctantly had to allow 5 (Australian) Brigade to be thrust into the battle. This brigade had only just landed on Gallipoli, coming ashore during the morning of 20 August; although the Australians were fresh and strong, they were not battle ready or tested. Lieutenant Colonel Alfred Chapman's 18/AIF battalion was selected to capture the remainder of the hill. The battalion was moved from the Ari Burnu area during the night, but became lost and only reached Damakjelik Spur just before dawn. Thinking that he was just taking over part of the line, Chapman then learned that he would be attacking Hill 60 with bombs and bayonets only. When he remarked that he had no bombs, he was told to do his best without them. With Hill 60 pointed out to them in the dim light of dawn, the men fixed bayonets ready for the attack.

The first wave, under Captain Sydney Goodsell 18/AIF, made a dash across the open to the left of the Connaughts. With speed they managed successfully to gain a footing in the Turkish trench, but not without significant casualties. Many from this wave were caught in the open by Turkish machine gun fire from the top of Hill 60, the battalion's objective. However, with this footing established, more men were sent

The view from Hill 100 down into Kaiajik Dere, the valley the Australians had to cross.

forward to exploit the captured ground and more carnage ensued as the advancing line simply disintegrated under the weight of the Turkish fire. One of those men was Corporal George Garland who wrote:

> *I went through a terrible experience, the bayonet charge I shall never forget, nor the terrible din of the rifles, machine guns, bombs, and bursting shells. I was only at Gallipoli a week, but was more or less under fire the whole time. Just imagine our company in the grey dawn going through the saps, from which the Turks had been driven out the day before, the bodies of many still lying on the ground, and the air heavy with their unearthly odour, in an endeavour to get as close to the enemy as possible, then suddenly forming line on the left under a terrific fire, then a series of short, wild rushes with fixed bayonets, our numbers growing less at every moment; and then, when only a few yards from the Turks, not a man left to make the final rush that would have carried us into their trenches. Though I was struck on the clothing several times during the charge, I remained unhurt until the last rush, when I came within full view of a machine gun manned by Germans, not more than 20 yards off, and what seemed to me several others, and lined away to the right and left hundreds of Turks with fixed bayonets, and all firing away for all they were worth. We received the full blast of machine guns and rifle fire, and, strange to say, though my haversack was shot through, I only*

155

received a slight wound in the shoulder. I saw a man standing up in the trench and urging the others on. I fired at his stomach, and he fell over the parapet of the trench. Instantly machine guns and rifles were turned on me, and, bless my soul, if I did not escape again. A trick that I learned in South Africa saved me, I lay flat on the ground with arms spread out, and the side of my face pressed on the earth, and as still as a mouse. The bullets fairly rained around me, and several knocked the dust into my eyes. Some of the bullets, striking the ground, broke up, and the fragments stuck in my head, but they caused me no hurt. After that lot, as I was the only man left who was able to move, I tried to join Captain Morris, who was on the right, but I had not squirmed ten yards when I received another dose from the Turkish trench, and one got me in the head. When I regained my senses I discovered that I was between the fire of our own and the enemy's, and, worse still, shells were exploding very close to me. I thought I would go mad, for I was unable to move. I tried to get up, but I could not, and, oh, the terrible thirst, I shall never forget it; my tongue seemed too big for my mouth. I had water in my bottle, but I could not get it to my mouth. At last I got it clear, and drank the contents of the bottle, which was full. I do not know how long I lay there, but a shell must have burst close at hand, and the shock sent me unconscious, and, as I discovered afterwards, paralysed the optic nerve. When I regained consciousness a man told me to hold onto his boot, which I did, and we crawled along, pulling me after him. It turned out that he had been wounded in the thigh. His name is Private Tuckwell. He saved my life by his unselfish devotion, and many a man has been decorated for far less than what he did. God bless him. I have not seen him since I regained my sight. Though my sight is damaged and my head scarred, I am not downhearted, and will cross bayonets again with my enemies. I admire the Turk, because he is a sport.[37]

Private Stanley Tuckwell, although wounded himself in the hip, survived to be evacuated from Gallipoli. During the night the survivors of the Australian assault were steadily bombed out of the trench they had captured and forced back to the line held by the New Zealanders. Goodsell's men held onto about forty metres of newly captured trench throughout 22 August, until they were finally relieved. Out of 205 men in his company, 149 were killed, wounded or missing. The 18/AIF went into the charge with 750 men and lost 383 officers and men in total. They had certainly received their baptism of fire.

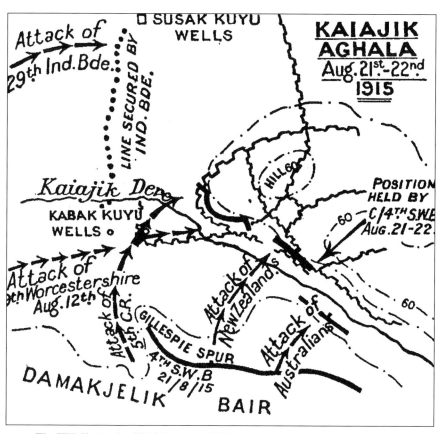

The Hill 60 attack of 21-22 August 1915.

At the end of 22 August, Cox and Russell's men bravely held onto their gains, but this toehold was still far from the summit of Hill 60. Of nearly 4000 men who attacked Hill 60 during these two days, over a third were now casualties.

The general advance on the Suvla front may have ended in dismal failure, but at Hill 60 the attack was far from over. On 23 August, in a cable to Kitchener, Hamilton was unusually pessimistic. He wrote: 'Naturally, I shall keep on trying to harry the Turks by local attacks and thus keep alive the offensive spirit but it must be stated plainly that no decisive success is to be looked for until reinforcements can be sent'. Without any hope of fresh reinforcements, but in the 'offensive spirit', he permitted Birdwood 'to harry the Turks' with another assault on Hill 60. This time the whole hill must be taken. The problem he had was lack of troops, whilst those that he had were either sick or already wounded. A renewed attack planned for 25 August had to be delayed due to lack of troops. Eventually a composite force of about a thousand men was collected together and another attack was planned for 27 August. This force consisted of the survivors from several different battalions from the first assault; the Connaughts (250 rifles) would attack on the left; the New Zealanders (Auckland, Canterbury, Otago and Wellington Mounted Rifles, including support from the Maori Contingent) and 18/AIF (400 rifles) would assault the centre, whilst elements from Australian 4 and 5 Brigade (350 rifles) would attack from the right.

A meagre bombardment that began at 4.00 pm was not dissimilar to that supporting the attack on 21 August; lasting only an hour, the few shells available did little to soften the Turkish defences. At 5.00 pm the guns ceased and one continuous line of men rose for the charge. Captain Bryan Cooper, 5/Connaughts, described this attack:

At four the bombardment began. Ships, howitzers, mountain-guns, all combined to create a babble which, if less intense than that of the previous week, was nevertheless sufficiently formidable. The trenches were so close to one another that our troops waiting to advance were covered with dust from the high explosives, but no injury was done. At last, at five, the bombardment ceased and the stormers, led by Lieutenant S. H. Lewis, went over the top. They went into the Turkish trenches almost before the enemy were aware of their coming and forced their way along them with bayonet and bomb. The supporting parties, however, were not so fortunate. The range to the parapet from whence they started was accurately known to the enemy, and from every part of the trench which was not actually under assault violent machine-gun and rifle fire opened. Man after man as he climbed over the parapet fell back into the trench dead, yet the next calmly stepped forward to take his place. Now, too, the enemy's artillery opened and as, un-menaced elsewhere, they were able to concentrate all their forces on the defence of Hill 60, their fire was terrific. Incessant salvoes of shrapnel burst overhead, while the parapet of the trench from which the advance

Private Gerald Coffey, 5/Connaught Rangers, who was wounded in nine places during the attack, dying of his wounds in the UK two weeks later.

158

was taking place was blown in by high explosive. Yet, still, the
men went on over the parapet and gradually a few succeeded in
struggling through the barrage and in reinforcing their comrades
in the captured trench.

The surviving Connaughts managed to reach the communication trench, later known as D-C Trench, that ran up the hill. In here they were hampered by the amount of Turkish dead and debris in the trench; in some places it was reported that the dead were up to six deep and elsewhere never less than two. At 5.57 pm the Connaughts signaled back that the whole of D-C Trench had been captured, and again they were within touching distance of the crest. However, this success could not be long lived without support. After dark the Turks began to counter attack and with their bombs began pushing the Irishmen back.

Cooper's narrative continued:

Again and again, the Turks attacked, mad with fanaticism,
shrieking at the top of their voices and calling on Allah. The
merciless bombing continued and the trenches slowly became
encumbered with dead. At last, about 10.30 pm, after the fight had
lasted five hours, a crowd of Turks succeeded in entering the
Rangers' trench near its northern extremity. This northern end
was held by a small party of men who died where they stood. The
remainder of the trench was, however, blocked and further
progress by the enemy arrested. Still the fight raged and bombs
and ammunition were running short, while the losses became so
heavy. Fresh Turkish attacks kept coming on, and for every
assailant that was struck down, two more sprang up in his place.
It was clear that soon the defenders would be swept away by force
of numbers.

Sergeant John McIlwain, 5/Connaughts, wrote in his diary:

Not long there when Turks bomb us from front and left flank, also
snipe us along the trench from left. My men with few exceptions
panic-stricken. By rapid musketry we keep down the bombing. My
rifle almost red with firing. By using greatcoats we save ourselves
from bombs. Turks but ten yards away drive us back foot by foot.
I have extraordinary escapes. Two men killed beside me following
me in the narrow trench and I am covered head to foot in blood.
Casualties alarming and we should have fought to the very end
but for the 18th Australian Battalion, a party of whom jumped in

amongst us and held the position until reinforced. When able to look about me I found but two Rangers left with me. The rest killed, wounded, or ran away before or after the Anzacs had come. Struggling all night: consolidating, firing, and looking out. Anzacs abusive for Rangers having lost trench. The most awful night of my life.[38]

The Connaughts had lost 152 out of their 250 remaining men. Elsewhere the New Zealanders had some success, but similar casualties. Lieutenant Colonel William Meldrum, commanding officer of the Wellington Mounted Rifles, wrote:

In the centre our men rushed forward to the minute and, clearing the first trench, rushed for the second. They went in three lines, and soon had seized both the fire and communication trenches. They lost a good number from machine gun and shrapnel fire as they advanced, but that seemed to make no difference to them.

It was a fine sight to see them pushing on so gallantly and so well on the whole. We gained two trenches, which we still hold. Holding on to the trenches was nearly as costly as taking them for the first twenty-four hours, for the Turks tried to drive our men out again with bombs. Out of 200 men, my regiment lost 110 in the twenty-four hours, but they were game and spirited throughout. The Turks must have suffered very heavily, for a lot of their dead were in and about their trenches—in one trench lying three deep.[39]

The Australian renewed assault further to the right was less successful. As soon as they rose from the trenches they were literately cut to pieces by machine gun and rifle fire. Two-thirds of the Australians became casualties in no more than a few minutes. As it drew dark, reinforcements in the shape of two Australian Light Horse regiments were sent forward to help the New Zealanders expand their gains. During 27 August the New Zealanders had managed to capture two lines of trenches that took them close to the summit; however they could not retake the D-C trench. This trench ran from the seaward side of the hill directly to the summit, and although in previous assaults troops had managed to get a footing in the trench, it was holding onto it that became the problem. It was now the turn of the light horsemen to try.

At 11.30 pm, 140 men from 9/LHR from South Australia, led by their newly appointed commanding officer, Lieutenant Colonel Carew Reynell,[40] charged towards the summit. They managed to gain a footing in the D-C Trench, and from there Reynell ordered another rush forward. Reynell was killed, whilst his men who still retained parts of this trench were very quickly overwhelmed by a subsequent Turkish counter attack. A second party of the regiment, led by Major Harry Parsons, managed to recapture the seaward end of D-C Trench, which had been originally held by 18/AIF on 22 August, and the Connaughts on 27 August. Even though they were driven back from most of their gains, Parsons held onto about seventy metres of this trench. It was now getting light, so after dawn on 28 August the Australians and New Zealanders set about consolidating their gains, deepening the trenches and building parapets for extra protection. This had to be done under a constant rain of Turkish bombs and deadly sniper fire.

Lieutenant Colonel Carew Reynell, commanding 10/LHR.

On 28 August, Godley informed the officers of 10/LHR that he wanted them to seize a trench on the summit of Hill 60, and added, 'I know you will get it. It's the holding that's the difficulty'. As well as the summit he also wanted them to take the remainder of the D-C Trench. The next assault, timed for 1.00 am on 29 August, would happen without artillery support, thus trying for the element of surprise. It was now the turn of the Western Australians, 10/LHR. We have seen how depleted some of the units were and the 10/LHR were no exception. Only three weeks earlier they had been mauled during the attack at The Nek, and what should have been a regiment of 600 could now only muster 180 men. To make matters worse, they had also lost their commanding officer and founder, Lieutenant Colonel Noel Brazier, who was wounded by shrapnel earlier that day when moving to the new bivouacs on Damakjelik Spur.

At 1.00 am, under a moonlit night, 10/LHR charged. Captain Phil Fry led the combined but weakened A and B Squadrons, whilst Captain Horace Robertson led C Squadron. The assault was made in silence as the men climbed out of the forward trench to charge to the next line. Fry's attack was successful; however Roberston's was less so, as a cheer was let out that forewarned the Turks. Later published in the Westralia Gift Book (1916), Second Lieutenant Hugo Throssell recalled the moment he charged:

There was a fusilade of rifles. We could only get out of the trench one at a time, but we scrambled up and ran for our lives across the sixty yards that separated us from the Turks' trench. It was a strange sensation to leave the high walls and the confinement of the trench for the open air. We had timed our charge to the minute and it was a wonderful thing to see the fellows running across that strip of ground with bombs bursting all around them. Halfway across I got my foot stuck in a bush and fell, and, struggling up, struck something else and rolled over and over and over. But I was not hit, and, running for all I was worth, hopped down straight into the Turks' trench. Our first line had got several of the Turks, but by the time we arrived all that were alive had fled.

An artist's impression of the ferocious bomb and bayonet mêlée at Hill 60.

Despite a few casualties crossing the open ground, both groups managed to enter the D-C Trench, where a bloody bayonet, bomb and rifle melée ensued. Lieutenant J. M. McDonald, 9/LHR, then began to fight his way from the seaward end of D-C Trench to meet up with 10/LHR; they eventually met and joined up the whole trench. 10/LHR began to sandbag the eastern side of D-C Trench where it intersected with the rings of Turkish trenches on the summit. With this trench now won, the light horsemen set about consolidating the position and to await the inevitable Turkish counter attack.

At this intersection Second Lieutenant Hugo Throssell watched into the moonlit night for Turks whilst his men filled sandbags. He did not have to wait long. Walking down the trench a large Turk approached the Australians' position and immediately Throssell shot him dead. He then engaged another four Turks, shooting them also. The Turks pulled back to the next traverse and began to throw bombs into the West Australians' position. This did not prevent the consolidation of the trench continuing, as bodies and sandbags were thrown up on top in an effort to deepen the trench. Throssell wrote:

We had fixed up our sandbags as well as we could, but a lot of the sandbags had no string to them and as we placed them in position half the sand would run out. Although we could not see the Turks,

162

One of Throssell's Light Horse troopers in the trenches at Hill 60. Note the gramophone player. (The War Illustrated, 1915)

we could see the tops of their bayonets, and we could see them striking matches to light their bombs. Soon the bombs began to fall in our trench, and we had to pick the bombs up quickly and hurl them back into the Turks' trench to explode there. Often there was not time for this and we just picked up the bombs and heaved them out of the trench. At times it was impossible to do even this and we had to lie down flat whilst the bomb exploded, and trust to luck.

Several of the light horsemen would be killed or wounded in this duel, but Throssell was one of the lucky ones; the fight continued, reminiscent of the Lone Pine struggle, with close quarter fighting by bomb, bayonet and rifle. Because of the sheer volume of bombs that were exchanged, estimates put it at 3000 to 4000 in this two-day period - the Turks renamed the hill Bomba Tepe, or Bomb Hill. One of Throssell's men, Corporal Sid Ferrier, reputedly caught up to 500 bombs and threw them back until one exploded in his hand before he could throw it back. Ferrier would have his arm amputated after the battle but died of tetanus ten days later.

It was fairly easy to send the bombs back so long as we kept the bottom of the trench clear. All the fellows had been instructed that if they were wounded and had to clear out they must drop their equipment, rifles, ammunitions, tucker, water bottles etc, and leave them for us to use. Our practice was to put these things on top of the parapet out of the way, but when three or four fellows got hit at once we could not do this and the floor of the trench became encumbered with stuff, amongst which the bombs fell. It was a bomb falling in this way that ... killed Captain Fry straight out.

In the advanced part of the trench there was only room for about seven bomb throwers, as it was only five metres long, little more than two metres deep and about the same wide. In this position many performed brave feats that night. These included Trooper Frank McMahon, a nineteen year old who had never thrown a bomb before. He learned quickly and worked all through the night until killed in the counter attack the following morning. Sid Ferrier, Tommy Renton and Henry McNee were also amongst Throssell's bomb throwers and fought on throughout that murderous night; Ferrier lost an arm, Renton a leg and McNee was badly wounded in the head and hand. Much of Throssell's work that night involved returning the Turkish bombs, although the Australians had their own bomb supply, the numbers were limited.

To prevent the Turks throwing our bombs back into our trench we timed them carefully. After lighting the fuse we counted slowly: 'One, two, three', then threw the bomb, and the Turks never had the time to handle it before it exploded. During the whole long night we never got one of our bombs back, whilst we threw theirs back by the score to explode in their own trenches ... Frequently we all took a spell for five or ten minutes, it almost seemed as though it were done by mutual arrangement between us and the

Turks. They would throw just the odd bomb or two and we would pitch them back again without bothering them with any of our own; then they would liven up again and we would be at it for all we were worth.

We were very cheerful all the time; lots of laughing and joking, and each of us had wonderful escapes. One bomb hit Ferrier on the elbow and failed to explode; a spent piece of bomb struck me on the knee and blackened it, but without drawing blood. Several times I was hit like that, one smack on the foot causing a lot of pain, but for some strange circumstance I escaped any serious injury.

Early on 29 August Hamilton reported: 'Knoll 60, now ours throughout, commands the Büyükanafarta valley with view and fire – a big tactical scoop'. As day dawned, this proved not to be the case. The Turks still held the summit, and any tactical advantage was minimal. Just before dawn, on the same day, the Turks counter attacked again. Recently

Second Lieutenant Hugo Throssell.
(The War Illustrated, 1915)

reinforced by *17 Regiment*, they charged out of the thick scrub, crying out 'Allah!, Allah!' from the north of D-C Trench towards the light horsemen. Few Australians remained in the trench unwounded, but they fought for their lives with grim determination. Corporal Henry McNee, 10/LHR, had his account of the attack published in the *Reveille* in August 1932:

The Turks made a very determined counter-attack from the right and right rear of our position. They came in waves, crying, "Allah, Allah!", and at one time we could see a German officer standing on the parapet of their trench urging the men on, but he was soon put out of action. They came right up to the muzzles of our rifles and were only kept out by rapid rifle fire and bomb-throwing. They managed to smash down our first barricade, but another one was built at the next traverse and a stand was made from there.

Throssell, now shot through the neck, described this attack as their worst trial:

WILLS'S CIGARETTES

We were hopelessly outnumbered. We could see the bayonets above the Turks' trenches just as thick as they could stick. Then they crawled out of their trenches and came straight at us. In the dim light we could see them against the sky line. I passed the word to our fellows, and when the first Turks got within ten yards we cheered and shouted, and, standing up in the trenches, started firing as fast as we could. There was no thought of cover. We just blazed away until the rifles grew red-hot and the chocks jammed and then we picked up the rifles that wounded or killed men had left. Twenty yards was about our longest range, and I have no idea how many rounds we fire: I think I must have fired a couple of hundred, and when we were wondering

An artist's impression of bomb catching at Hill 60.

how long we could stand against such numbers, the Turks turned and fled.

In a few minutes they came at us again, and the same thing was repeated. We had no machine guns and had to fire away with our rifles as quickly as we could. After the second repulse they changed their tactics and came at us from front, rear, and flank as well, getting behind us, between our trench and that occupied by the New Zealanders. Someone must have said something about retiring, though I did not hear it, and all around there were angry cries of 'Who said retire?' The hubbub was awful. Every man was determined to stick to the trench, and along with the firing they were yelling and shouting like demons. The noise must have deceived the Turks as to our numbers, for they were all round us within ten yards, and if they had come on we should have been overwhelmed. Just at the critical moment, as it was getting daylight, a machine gun came across from the New Zealand line, and was quickly placed in position. It settled the Turks' third and final charge, and the trench was ours.

166

This machine gun, manned by a mix crew of New Zealanders and men from 18/AIF, added its devastating stopping power in support of the light horsemen. As the sun rose the Turks melted back into the scrub. Throssell and McNee had miraculously survived, although both were wounded in several places. For this action Throssell was awarded the Victoria Cross and McNee and Renton the Distinguished Conduct Medal. Fry and McMahon were mentioned in despatches. Even though Hugo Throssell had singled out Ferrier as well for distinction, he was one of the Hill 60 heroes that missed

Hugo Throssell (right) standing outside Buckingham Palace on 4 December 1915, when he received the VC from King George V. (The War Illustrated, 1915)

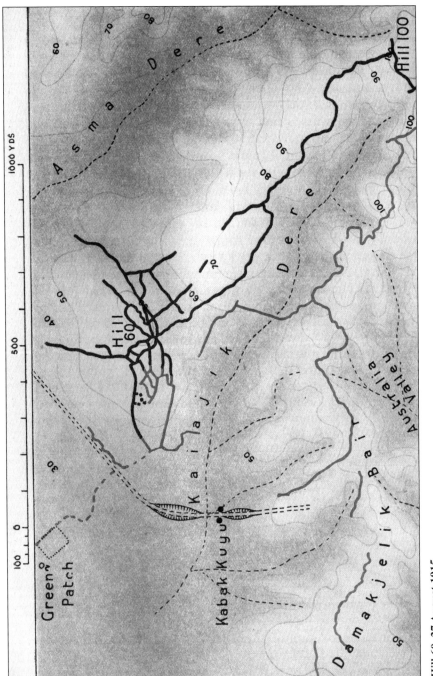

Hill 60, 27 August 1915.

out on any official recognition. Many more brave deeds have been lost to history and are today found but as names on graves and memorials.

This was the end of the August battle for Hill 60 and, despite the gallant efforts to capture the summit, the light horsemen were surprised to find that they were still short of the objective. The Turks would remain in control of the summit, thus preventing the Anzacs from overlooking their northern slopes of communication, whilst the Anzacs retained the southern slopes and, with the newly captured Turkish trenches, in a similar fashion denying the Turks a full view of the wells and lines of communication below. This would not be the end of the fighting. Hill 60 remained a hot bed of contention as each side raided, tunneled and bombed for each inch of advantage until the end of the campaign.

The invading army now resembled more the walking dead than the glorious troops that had left the shores of Britain, Australia and New Zealand months earlier. The writing was on the wall for the Gallipoli campaign. The August offensive gained some large expanses of territory but without the heights the gains gave minimal tactical advantage to the allies. Hamilton's force was dwindling by the day in fighting strength and physical ability, with little hope of further reinforcements, whilst the Turks continued to become stronger by the day. More and more Turkish troops were flowing into the area, whilst their ammunition and shell supply was also increasing. In September, when Bulgaria came into the war on the side of the Turks and Germans, this opened a railway link direct from Berlin to Constantinople, thus providing a land-based line of communication between the Central Powers. Hamilton's force was further weakened when he lost two divisions to the newly opened Salonika front that same month.

In October Hamilton was called back to London and replaced in the field by General Sir Charles Monro. A month later Kitchener visited Gallipoli and, along with Monro and Birdwood, decided that evacuation was the only option. A month later the troops left the Peninsula. Gallipoli was sold as a glorious defeat to Britain and her allies; a near run operation that almost succeeded. Studying the campaign today we now know that this was far from the truth; it was a disillusionment of a generation, a tragic blunder that turned this corner of a foreign field into England's graveyard. For the Turks it was a magnificent, but costly, victory that helped forge a nation after the war. Gallipoli means many things to many people and, because of this pull, will probably be studied for many more years to come.

Chapter Nine

The Battlefield Today
Advice to Travellers

Getting there: Turkey is very much on the tourist map and today Gallipoli and the nearby ancient city of Troy are firmly part of that industry. If you are not already in Turkey, most people would fly to the major international airports in Istanbul or Izmir, although a domestic airport in Çanakkale has recently opened. Because of the vastness of the Gallipoli battlefields, car hire is a must for the individual tourer, which can be arranged at the airports or locally in Çanakkale. If you have no vehicle, there are local tour companies in both Çanakkale and Eceabat that will take you to the battlefield, but for non-Anzac areas you may need to hire a taxi or bicycle. For the latest details see http://www.tourismturkey.org or, once in Çanakkale, visit the Tourism Information Office that is located near the jetty square, where you can get detailed information, maps and brochures of the area.

Equipment: When visiting the battlefields, preferably with at least one other person, always take a good supply of bottled water, a walking stick (also useful to fend off any shepherd's dogs), sun cream, wide-brimmed hat, long trousers for any bush walking, camera, binoculars, pen, notepad, penknife and a pair of sturdy boots with ankle support. If you are unfamiliar with the area and going off the beaten track, a map and compass is recommended. Put all this in a small rucksack with this book, and you should have a good recipe for an excellent tour. A mobile phone can also be useful in emergencies (with the number of hotel and, if applicable, the car-hire or tour company). It is also a good idea to tell someone else where you are planning to go for the day and what time you are planning to return. Most importantly, bring a camera with a good supply of film/digital storage and plenty of batteries. It is also worth noting that North Anzac, although a beautiful area to visit, is still very inhospitable and remote compared to the old Anzac area. It has a lack of toilets and refreshments for the modern visitor, indeed the lack of almost anything useful for sustenance and comfort, so travel prepared. Most hotels can provide packed lunches and the towns of course have shops, so stock up on food and drink before you depart for the day. If you are planning to visit a CWGC cemetery or memorial, please check the website for a plan/reference before arriving at Gallipoli, as there are no registers on the battlefield.

Accommodation: Most of the hotels in the area are not expensive and include breakfast and some an evening meal. To find a hotel of choice in the Eceabat and Çanakkale area it is best to search on the web or visit a local travel agent. Rooms are often basic, although many do have air conditioning and TV. There are also numerous camping sites in the area for those on a lower budget. Eceabat and Çanakkale have a good selection of restaurants and cafes and are all very reasonably priced. If you stay in Çanakkale you will need to take the ferry every morning to cross the Narrows. The crossing takes approximately thirty minutes, is quite frequent and is not only inexpensive but is also a picturesque way of starting and ending your day.

Warning: Be aware that the whole of the Gallipoli Peninsula is a national historical "Peace Park", dedicated to the memory of those who died on both sides. Please respect this. A lot of the area is still farmland and private property. When walking please be conscious of the crops and respect the privacy of the people who live here. If you do find a wartime relic, such as a shell, grenade or bullet, leave it alone. Photograph it by all means, but do not touch it as these things are often in a highly dangerous condition and can still cause death and injury. It is also strictly forbidden by the Turkish authorities to remove any artefact from the battlefield. Lastly, the area has many goatherds and small farm settlements that, of course, keep dogs. These can be quite ferocious if you happen to go too close, so keep at a distance, keep together and always carry a stick. There have also been sightings of wild boar in some of the more remote areas of the battlefield, and snakes are occasionally seen basking in the sun, both potential dangers if you get too close and disturb them.

Useful Addresses:

Çanakkale Tourist Information Office
Iskele Meydani, 67
Çanakkale
Tel: + 90 (286) 217 11 87

Commonwealth War Graves Commission (CWGC)
2 Marlow Road,
Maidenhead,
Berkshire, SL6 7DX
Tel: +44 (0) 1628 634 221   Website: www.cwgc.org

CWGC (Çanakkale Office)
Cimenlik Sohak,
Bagkur Ishani No.9,
Buro No.10
17100 Çanakkale.
Tel +90 (286) 217 10 10

The Gallipoli Association

An Association, established in 1969 and still going strong, whose objectives are to remember, honour and study the Gallipoli and Dardanelles campaign of 1914-1916. See website: www.gallipoli-association.org for details.

Most of these areas can be covered by car or similar vehicle in a day. You could equally do these tours on foot if you have more time, using your car as a base, but for this allow at least two days if you wish to attempt all the sites outlined below. Anzac is the most visited and accessible area of the Gallipoli battlefield and at the same time is also one of the most naturally beautiful. You will find that the Commonwealth War Graves Commission (CWGC) cemeteries in Gallipoli are different to those on the Western Front. The numbers of identified war burials are remarkably few. This is because of the years between the end of the campaign and the systematic recovery of the fallen after the war ended. Because of the nature of the ground, the identified burials have small, tilted, sandstone tablets for grave headstones. The Stone of Remembrance and white stone Cross of Sacrifice, a slightly different and more subdued style than those found in Europe, can also be found. They are also beautifully planted with small plants and shrubs that adorn the well-kept cemeteries, where mature trees grow majestically, providing valuable shade on a hot sunny day.

Anzac is within the Gallipoli (*Gelibolu*) Historical National Park, which also encompasses the battlefields of Suvla and Helles. On the northern outskirts of Eceabat (Maidos) is the National Park Main Information Centre, which was opened in 2005. This building has many modern facilities, including a library, cinema, conference centre, internet resources, souvenir shop, exhibitions and refreshments. From the main information centre it is approximately nine kilometres to Gaba Tepe (*Kabetape*).

On a clear day, looking out into the Aegean you can see the Turkish island of Gökçeada (Imbros), which was used as Sir Ian Hamilton's headquarters from June 1915. The island, then Greek, was captured from the Turks during the Balkan Wars of 1912-13. In February 1915 the Greek government offered Imbros to the British as a base for the invasion of Gallipoli. In 1923 the island was ceded to Turkey under the terms of the Treaty of Lausanne, which brought a final post-war settlement to the area. During the campaign, Imbros was a rest and recreation area for the troops on the Peninsula, where it housed a multitude of tented camps, casualty clearing stations, field bakeries, airfields and supply depots. Nestled behind this island to the northwest is the Greek island of Samothrace. It was on Samothrace that the statue of Nike, the Greek Goddess of Victory, was discovered and which today can be seen in the Louvre Museum in Paris.

Battlefield Navigation: To help with their location, cemetery, memorial and the main locations of interest are identified in the tour section using Google Map/GPS coordinates shown in Decimal Degrees.

Anzac Tours One, Two and Three.

Tour One:

Diversionary Assaults - Lone Pine to The Nek

If travelling by car, allow two hours for this tour; or five hours if walking. Walking is mainly on roads, so although relatively easy, beware of passing vehicles.

Begin this tour at the **Kabatepe Museum (1)** *(40.20722,26.28139)* and, following the signs to Anzac, take the immediate ridge road to the right. This road was built by the Turks soon after the evacuation and rises from the bottom of Legge Valley up onto Pine Ridge and then to 400 Plateau and the Second Ridge. Please note this road is one-way.

Continue on this road for about two kilometres, passing the Turkish soldier statue (*Mehmetcige Derin Saygi*) and the Turkish cemetery (*Karayörük Deresi*). As these sites do not relate directly to the August offensive, please refer to *Anzac: The Landing* for details. Continue until you reach the **Kanlisirt Turkish Monolith (2)** *(40.229128,26.291216)*, which stands on the Turkish slope of Lone Pine. The Lone Pine area became known to the Turks as *Kanlisirt* (Bloody Ridge) after the fighting in May 1915. The monolith inscription refers to the Turkish defence of Lone Pine during the August offensive. Continuing along the road, note the gully on the right-hand side that was called The Cup. On 6 August the Australians had fought their way to a position that overlooked The Cup, which they briefly held until being bombed back later in the battle. Continue on until you reach the **Lone Pine Memorial and Cemetery (3)**

Kanlisirt Turkish Memorial at Lone Pine (2013).

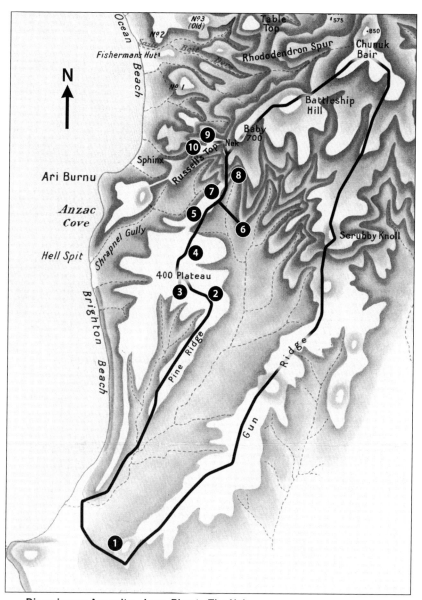

Diversionary Assaults – Lone Pine to The Nek

(40.23044,26.28715). Note the Ross Bastiaan Marker (No.5). Lone Pine is the southern spur or lobe of 400 Plateau that derived its name from the song *The Trail of the Lonesome Pine,* from a single pine tree that stood on this plateau during the early days of the campaign. This was a major tactical position as it overlooks Gaba Tepe to the south and the gullies leading up to it from the coast. Fortified by the Turks in May, it remained

Lone Pine CWGC Cemetery and Memorial. (2013)

in their hands until its recapture on 6 August, where the Australians won seven VCs for the action.

Lone Pine Cemetery, originally small and containing only forty six graves, was enlarged after the Armistice by relocating many of the scattered battlefield graves in the area and those removed from Brown's Dip North and Brown's Dip South Cemeteries that were originally located near the head of Victoria Gully. Today the cemetery contains 1167 graves, of which 651 are Australian, two New Zealand, fifteen sailors, soldiers or marines from the UK and 499 men who could not be identified. There are special memorial tablets in the cemetery that commemorate the names of 182 Australians and one from the UK who are believed to be buried in this cemetery.

Amongst the burials is **Private Victor Pinkstone** *(III.B.55)*, 3/AIF, who died in his brother's arms on 7 August at Lone Pine. Another burial is that of 2/AIF battalion commander, **Lieutenant Colonel R. Scobie** *(Sp.Mem.C.132)*, who was killed during a Turkish counter attack at Lone Pine on 6 August. There are many other 1 (Australian) Brigade burials here from that battle.

Within the grounds of the cemetery is the Lone Pine Memorial that commemorates 4,936 Australian and New Zealand[41] servicemen who died in the Anzac area and whose graves are either not known or who were buried at sea.

There are many names on the memorial that relate to the August Offensive, amongst whom is New Zealand born **Captain Alfred Shout VC MC** *(Panel 12)*, 1/AIF, who received a Military Cross for gallantry during the Anzac landings and in the fighting at Lone Pine was awarded the Victoria Cross. On 9 August, during the action, he was mortally wounded by a bomb that prematurely exploded in his hand. He died on a hospital ship and was buried at sea. Another of the Lone Pine VCs commemorated here is **Corporal Alex Burton**, 7/AIF *(Panel 28),* who was killed early on 9 August whilst defending a barricaded sap. Another Lone Pine casualty is **Lieutenant Hubert Meager** *(Panel 19),* 3/AIF, whose last words when mortally wounded were; 'Go on, boys; don't mind me'. **Lieutenant Colonel Alexander White**, 8/LHR *(Panel 5),* and many of his men from the disastrous charge at The Nek are named here, as are those from 10/LHR *(Panels 5-10),* which include the

Harper brothers, **Trooper Wilfred Harper** and **Trooper Gresley Harper**, the inspiration for the main characters in Peter Weir's film *Gallipoli*. Other Australian Light Horse casualties include those who fell on Dead Man's Ridge, such as **Major James Reid** and **Lieutenant Burdett Nettleton**, both on *Panel 1.* Nettleton's hip flask turned up in Turkey some years ago, which was probably souvenired from the body. New Zealander **Lieutenant Colonel Arthur Bauchop**, Otago Mounted Rifles, is also remembered here *(Panel 72).* He was mortally wounded during the bayonet charge on the hill that was named after him.

Much of the Gallipoli fighting became synonymous

Lieutenant Burdett Nettleton, 1/LHR, killed 7 August 1915.

The Lone Pine Memorial panel to the Australian 1/LHR.

Nettleton's flask, which was recovered from the body.

with the bomb (a grenade), and many on this memorial are casualties of the ferocious fighting at Hill 60. These include three men from the 10/LHR; **Captain Henry 'Phil' Fry**, **Corporal Sutton 'Sid' Ferrier** and **Trooper Francis 'Frank' McMahon** *(Panel 9)*. Fry, a popular officer, showed outstanding bravery; he was reported earlier in the attack to be running up and down the parapet, in full view of the Turks, encouraging his men. Eventually he jumped down, but was killed later by a bomb. Ferrier was fighting alongside Hugo Throssell VC when a bomb he attempted to catch and return exploded. His arm was later amputated and he died from tetanus aboard a hospital ship on 9 September. McMahon, a young but quick learner when it came to bomb throwing, was shot dead when he raised his head above the parapet and, falling back into the trench, was then blown to pieces by a bomb.

Leave Lone Pine. To the left of the road, near the area that was named the Pimple, you will find Australian trenches in various states of preservation, but worth the visit. Continue along the road for approximately 300 metres to **Johnston's Jolly Cemetery (4)** *(40.23269,26.28741)*. The cemetery is situated on Johnston's Jolly, the northern lobe of 400 Plateau, known to the Turks as *Kirmizi Sirt*. The Australians named it after Lieutenant Colonel George Napier Johnston, 2/Australian Artillery Brigade commander, who placed his field guns opposite this position in order to *jolly up the Turks*. The cemetery was

Australian trenches between Lone Pine and Johnston's Jolly. (2013)

Johnston's Jolly CWGC Cemetery with Lone Pine in the background. (2013)

made after the Armistice when graves were brought in from the battlefield. Today there are 181 burials, fourteen of which are unidentified. One grave from the 6 August Lone Pine attack is that of **Lieutenant Richard 'Dickie' Seldon** *(Sp.Mem.16)*, 4/AIF. He was hit in the face, losing an eye, during the initial charge, and then killed as he was working his way down a trench that led into Owen's Gully. By the side of the cemetery, close to Owen's Gully, is the preserved entrance to a war time tunnel. This whole area was honeycombed with tunnels; many probably still exist just a few feet down.

Continue along the road and after a few hundred metres you will come to **Courtney's and Steele's Post Cemetery (5)** *(40.23541,26.28899)*. Courtney's Post was named after Lieutenant Colonel Richard Courtney, commander of 14/AIF. Steel's Post (officially named Steele's) was named after Major Thomas Steel, 14/AIF. Both posts were steep niches, literally a slender foothold on to the ridge,

Courtney's and Steele's Post CWGC Cemetery. (2013)

which were defended throughout the campaign. The opposing front lines were separated by a No Man's Land the width of the road now running between them. It was near here that Lance Corporal Albert Jacka, 14/AIF, was awarded Australia's first Victoria Cross of the war for his heroism in repelling a Turkish bombing party on 19 May 1915 which had broken into Courtney's. The cemetery, built after 1919, contains 167 burials, seven are known graves but the others are all unknown. There are fifty four Special Memorials to men believed to be buried here. There are four burials of 6/AIF men who were killed during the attempt to capture German Officers' Trench on 6/7 August. Note the Ross Bastiaan Marker (No.6) by the entrance.

Leave the cemetery and continue along the road until you come to the sign for the grave of **Lieutenant Colonel Hüseyin Avni Bey** and the **Çataldere Cemetery and Memorial (6)** *(40.23293,26.29438),* on the right of the road. The grave is reachable on foot along a kilometre long track that descends into Mule Gully. Anvi Bey was the commander of *57 Regiment* until he was killed in August 1915. There is a plaque by the grave that commemorates soldiers from his regiment, many whom died during the August fighting at Lone Pine. A little further along the track is Çataldere Cemetery and Memorial. This newly constructed cemetery, near the site of the original, commemorates 2835 soldiers from various regiments including *27* and *57 Regiments* that defended this area. Return to the road.

Continue along the main road, stopping at **Quinn's Post Cemetery (7)** *(40.23815,26.29168).* Note also Ross Bastiaan Marker (No.7). This precariously positioned post was established here on 25 April, and in May became officially named Quinn's Post, after Major Hugh Quinn, 15/AIF, who was killed here on 29 May. The Turks later called this area

Quinn's Post CWGC Cemetery with the Turkish 57 Regiment Memorial in the background. (2013)

Bomba Sirt (Bomb Ridge) because of the concentration of bomb attacks that took place here. From the back of the cemetery there are fantastic views down to the sea along Monash and Shrapnel Valleys, the main supply routes to this part of the line. To the north-east is a gully that became known as The Bloody Angle, part of Dead Man's Ridge, where the Australian Light Horse attacked on 7 August from the direction of Pope's Hill, which is just to the left. Named earlier in the campaign after Lieutenant Colonel Harold Pope, 14/AIF's commander, this steep razor-backed hill runs in front of Russell's Top and The Nek.

Quinn's Post cemetery was made after the Armistice by concentrating 225 unidentified isolated graves and moving seventy three graves from Pope's Hill Cemetery (originally located at the foot of Pope's Hill). A further six graves were found later and also moved into this cemetery. 179 of the burials are identified. There are sixteen Australian Light Horse casualties from the attacks on Dead Man's Ridge and Turkish Quinn's on 7 August. These include **Major Tom Logan** and **Lieutenant Joe Burge**. There are also two brothers buried here, side by side, **Trooper Fred Sherwood** *(C.6)* and **Trooper Harold Sherwood** *(C.5)*.

Leave Quinn's, noting the grave to an unknown *57 Regiment* officer on the opposite side of the road, and continue up the road to the **Turkish 57 Regiment Memorial (8)** *(57 Alay Sehitligi ve Aniti) (40.24021,26. 29244)*. The memorial park, which was opened in 1993, is built on the area known as The Chessboard, named because of the concentration of criss-crossed trenches that were there. The area was held by the Australians on the first day but was relinquished when Baby 700 fell. The Light Horse attempted to capture the position during the morning of 7 August, but failed. The park comprises a symbolic 'martyrs' cemetery, with the names of the fallen chosen randomly and displayed as graves or memorial plaques. Note the bronze sculpture of Turkish veteran Hüseyin Kaçmaz with his grand-daughter. He was reputed to be the last surviving Turkish veteran of the campaign, dying in 1994 at the age of 110. On the opposite side of the road there is a Turkish Soldier statue, which is called *Askerine Saygi Aniti,* which translates as 'Respect to the Turkish soldier'. Behind the monument are the slopes of Baby 700 *(Kiliç Bayir),* where much of the devastating rifle and machine gun fire was directed towards the Australian Light Horse attacks. Baby 700 was captured by the Anzacs on 25 April 1915; after changing hands several times, it was finally lost under the weight of the Turkish counter attacks that day and never retaken. **NB**; There are toilet facilities and refreshments available here. Near 57 Regiment Memorial is a flight of steps that descends to **Kesik Dere Cemetery** *(40.23959,26.29291)*. Another newly constructed cemetery, built in 2006, it records the names of 1115 soldiers of *19th Turkish Division* who fell in the area. The original cemetery is on the opposite bank of the Kesik Dere.

Continue until the road forks at the head of Monash Valley; take the left hand turn, which is signposted *Mehmet Cavus Sehitligi,* Nek CWGC

Cemetery and Walker's Ridge Cemetery. This will take you onto Russell's Top, captured by the Anzacs on the first day of the landings. Park and visit **Sergeant Mehmet's Turkish Memorial** *(40.24267,26.29107)*. The Turkish memorial was erected soon after the evacuation and built over the Turkish trenches at The Nek, which the Australian Light Horse had attempted to capture on 7 August. **The Nek CWGC Cemetery (9)** *(40.24233,26.29035)* was built over No Man's Land. Note also the Ross Bastiaan Marker. Some of the Australian trenches still remain nearby, close to the cemetery wall. The Nek Cemetery was made after the Armistice and today contains 326 burials, 316 being unidentified. Of the identified burials, four are related to the Australian Light Horse attack of 7 August. Of the unidentified, without headstones, many would be Australian Light Horse.

Sergeant Mehmet's Turkish Memorial at The Nek. (2013)

Leave The Nek Cemetery and continue on foot along the track until you reach **Walker's Ridge CWGC Cemetery (10)** *(40.24163,26. 28842)*. As with the Nek cemetery, there are some spectacular views all along this ridge. To the north, below, and

Walker's Ridge CWGC Cemetery. (2013)

to your right, are the valleys and spurs leading back up to Hill 971 and Chunuk Bair. In the distance are the Suvla Plains, with Kireçtepe Ridge dominating the skyline. The curving sweep of Ocean Beach leads up to Nibrunesi Point, from where Suvla Bay opens into the Salt Lake, now permanently open to the sea. Walker's Ridge was the name given to the spur that stretches from the coast near Fisherman's Hut, running south-eastwards to the middle of Russell's Top, where you are now standing. It was named after Brigadier General Walker, who originally commanded the New Zealand Infantry Brigade. The cemetery was made during the campaign and originally consisted of two plots separated by eighteen metres of ground, through which a trench ran. The cemetery contains the known burials of forty

Trooper Harold Rush.

New Zealander soldiers, twelve Australian soldiers, one Royal Marine and twelve unidentified graves. In addition, eighteen soldiers from Australia and eight from New Zealand are commemorated by special tablets. Of the few August burials, one is **Trooper Harold Rush** *(II.C.4)*, 10/LHR, whose last words before charging at The Nek were, *'Goodbye Cobber, God Bless You'*. Also buried here is **Major Thomas Redford**

The grave of Trooper Harold Rush, 10/LHR, whose last words were 'Goodbye Cobber, God Bless You'.

183

(*II.C.9*), 8/LHR, who was killed at The Nek during the charge. During the night two troopers went out to recover his body, and he was laid to rest in this cemetery. An eyewitness of his death wrote: 'Our gallant major, whilst lying facing the enemy's trench (ten yards away) in front of his men, received a bullet through his brain as he raised his head slightly to observe. He died with a soft sigh and laid his head gently on his hands, as if tired. A braver and more honourable man never donned a uniform.'

Leave Walker's Ridge Cemetery and walk further down the track to the end of the ridge. Be extremely careful here! There are few safety fences and the drop is almost sheer down into the ravine below. There are some excellent views (for the non-faint hearted) of Mule Gully below, Ari Burnu and the Anzac landing and support areas.

Major Thomas Redford, 8/LHR, was killed 7 August 1915. His body was 'found lying facing the enemy's trench'.

Return to your vehicle and continue up the road, which will take you over the crests of Baby 700 and Battleship Hill. Continue on to Chunuk Bair (if you wish to stop here, see the latter Optional Tours for information relating to this area), or else follow the road along the Third Ridge, which gives a good perspective of the battlefield from the Turkish side, and return to the Kabatepe Museum.

End of tour.

Tour Two:

The Outpost Walks and Hill 60

If travelling by car allow two hours for this tour, or six hours if walking. Walking is relatively easy, and is a mix of roads and dirt tracks.

The tour begins at the **Anzac Commemoration area (11)** *(40.24079,26.28121)* on North Beach, the site of the Anzac Day Dawn Service. This walk is designed to take the traveller over some of the beach areas that served as headquarters, hospitals, casualty clearing station, store areas, the Big Sap and the sites of the jetties and piers that brought stores ashore and allowed wounded to be evacuated. The route follows in the footsteps of the path taken by the two major columns for the attack on Sari Bair.

   North Beach road was made during the campaign, involving night after night of work, performed by the 'resting' troops. In its own right this is a great feat of military engineering and amazing to think it was made in the dark in almost silence. With sniper, machine gun and shelling to respond to any movement during the daylight hours, the work in the dark was a little easier. Still, with the threat of attracting fire to any noise made, night in this area was owned by the scouts, of both sides, out on patrol. The dark and the fear of enemy fire took their toll on the men doing stressful work during the night, not made any easier by the physical strength needed to collect and position heavy stones to form the foundation of the road. The stones were set in with clay dug from the hillsides and mixed together with water poured over the surface to set the material. This was all performed in the dark, whilst harassed from

ANZAC Commemoration area by North Beach. (2013)

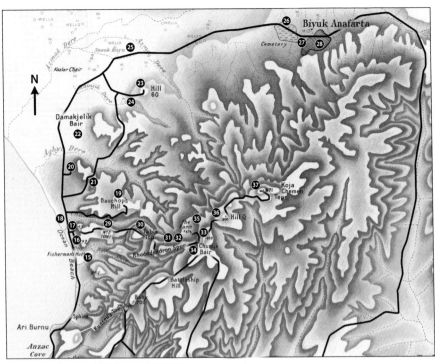

The Outpost Walks and Hill 60.

enemy fire and performed when the men's physical condition was already weakened by the heat of the day, the poor diet, lack of drinking water and poor sanitary conditions at that time, but the road consistently progressed north.

Walk along the beach road and after about 400 metres you will come to **Canterbury CWGC Cemetery (12)** *(40.24447,26.28292)*, sitting nestled in front of Walker's Ridge (*Serçetepe* – Sparrow Hill), one of the main communication paths to the front line. This small cemetery of twenty seven New Zealand graves was built after the war and named in honour of the Canterbury Mounted Rifles, who have sixteen identified burials here. Most of the burials are from May and June 1915 and reflect

Canterbury CWGC Cemetery with Walker's Ridge and the Sphinx behind. (2013)

casualties sustained whilst holding the outposts. One August burial is **Private Lawrence Stanley Trives** *(II.B.3)*, Auckland Regiment, who died of wounds on 12 August 1915. Trives was originally from Peckham in London. After the Turkish counter on 10 August, the New Zealanders were ordered back into the line on 12 August at The Apex and the Rhododendron Spur with orders to *entrench and hold on for ever*. It was here that Trives was mortally wounded.

On the beach directly opposite the cemetery are the skeletal remains of a boat, probably wrecked here later on in the campaign, and one of the few surviving craft that would have once littered the shoreline.

Return back to the road and walk on for a further 350 metres until you reach the **Commonwealth War Graves Commission Base (13)** (40.24712,26.28277), which contains a cottage and workshops. The CWGC workers that maintain the cemeteries in Gallipoli are based here. Within the grounds is a regulation grave tablet with the inscription *BILL – Australian Light Horse, 1914 to 1924, A waler and one of the best*. Bill was believed to be a war horse that served with the Light Horse in Palestine and went to Gallipoli with the Graves Registration Unit after the war. Much loved, he died on the Peninsula in 1924 and was given an honourable burial and grave marker. The grounds are not open to the public; however if there is a member of staff around, you should be able to seek permission to visit the grave.

No. 1 Outpost. (2013)

Behind the buildings is **No. 1 Outpost (14)**, which was sometimes known as Maori Post from it being garrisoned by the New Zealand Maori Contingent. In the area it is still possible to find faint remains of the Big Sap, which once ran past this outpost to connect those, further along the exposed shoreline. The beach road, although valuable, had its limitations; not only was it built during the night, but it could only be used during the night for the same reasons. To manoeuvre the troops safety and secretly from the old Anzac area to the outposts and deres where the assaulting columns would attack the Turks, it was necessary to expand the communication trench known as the Big Sap. This route had been evolved as the outposts were established; however, in many places the Turks from their positions higher up could enfilade within its channel. Thus not only did it need to be deepened but also widened to allow troops two abreast to march, for pack mules to pass and for riders to carry messages safely down on horseback. The soldiers feared the mule's steel-shod hoofs more than Turkish shell or bullet, and would exit the trench if a mule came the other way. Today there is little remaining evidence of this great trench.

Continue on and after a further 250 metres you will pass **Fisherman's Hut (15)** *(40.24941,26.28299)*, which sits at the foot of the Sazli Beit Dere. There is an old stone hut still on the hill, although not the original. As well as being linked to the original landings on 25 April, this site was also important for the breakout. Behind this small hill, to the north, is a larger knoll that was known as Maori Hill, named after the New Zealand Maori Contingent who played such an important part in breaking through the Outposts during the August Offensive. It was on this hill that it was reputed that the Maoris performed a pre-battle *haka*, the native warriors' war cry, before going into action. To its right is the Camel's Hump, a little higher and easily recognisable by its camel shaped form.

Leaving Fisherman's Hut, continue on for 400 metres, and on the right follow the track to **No. 2 Outpost CWGC Cemetery (16)** *(40.25218,26.28187)*. The cemetery is situated in front of No. 2 Outpost, which was known as Nelson Hill in the earlier days, named after the 10th (Nelson) Company of the Canterbury Regiment. Major General Godley moved the NZ&A Divisional Headquarters here during August, nestling it in a place called Otago Gully, by the steep banks of the Outpost. Shallow

Fisherman's Hut, with Sazli Beit Dere to the left. (2013)

New Zealand No. 2 Outpost CWGC Cemetery, showing No. 3 Outpost in the background. (2013)

remains of dugouts and the faint lines of the terraces are barely visible today. The Otago Mounted Rifles then took it over before it became Divisional Headquarters in August. The 16th Casualty Clearing Station and the New Zealand Dental Corps clinic were established near No. 2 Outpost, which also had a large well that supplied enough drinking water for 20,000 troops and 4000 mules a day. The valley to the south of the cemetery is Sazli Beit Dere.

By the end of the first week in April the New Zealanders had begun burying men killed in this area at No. 2 Outpost Cemetery. The cemetery contains graves from those early battles, as well as many from the August offensive. Of the 152 burials, sixty six are unidentified and special memorials commemorate forty eight casualties known or believed to be buried among them. The cemetery contains thirty one known burials from the August battles and are representative of the New Zealand brigades, Monash's 4 (Australian) Brigade and British troops, mainly from Baldwin's Brigade.

Captain Horatio Gordon Mann *(F.6)*, 6/Loyal North Lancs, was killed on 10 August in the same action as his brother, Second Lieutenant Horace Walpole Mann. Two other Mann brothers served at Gallipoli with the battalion, Roland and Neville. Neville was awarded an MC for Gallipoli, but was mortally wounded during an action in Mesopotamia.

Less than 100 metres away is **New Zealand No. 2 Outpost CWGC Cemetery (17)** *(40.25318,26.28060)*. There are 183 soldiers buried or commemorated in this cemetery, of which 150 are unidentified. Special Memorials commemorate thirty-one men who are known or believed to be buried among them. The Australian burials for August all belong to 13/AIF, a battalion in Monash's Brigade, who were killed or died of wounds between 6 and 10 August 1915.

Private Joseph Jones *(Sp.Mem.15)*, Otago Regiment, was a labourer in Dunedin, where he enlisted in October 1914. Jones was wounded by shrapnel in the mouth at Chailak Dere on 7 August. A tracheotomy was performed so that he could breathe, but he died shortly after.

Captain Charles Graeme Lutyens *(I.1)*, 6/East Lancs, was mortally wounded on 9 August 1915 and apologised to his commanding officer for having allowed himself to be wounded. He died at the dressing station later that day. From Hanscombe in Surrey, he had a brother who was killed at Ypres in 1918. Charles was a relative of Sir Edwin Lutyens, a leading twentieth century British architect who was responsible for many of the CWGC cemeteries and memorials, most notably that at Thiepval on the Somme.

Colonel Neville Manders *(Sp.Mem.20)*, Australian Army Medical Corps, was killed by a stray bullet whilst outside Godley's HQ on 9 August 1915. Manders, born and raised in England, entered the Army Medical Service as a surgeon in 1884. He served in the Suakin campaign of 1885 and with the Burmese expedition of 1887-89, during which he was severely wounded. He was appointed Deputy Director of Medical Services (DDMS) in Egypt in December 1914, a post he held until he was

Colonel Neville Manders, Australian Army Medical Corps, killed 9 August 1915.

attached to the New Zealand and Australian Division as Acting Director of Medical Services (ADMS). Manders was also an important entomologist, and a Fellow of both the Zoological and the Bombay Natural History Society. By the time of his death he had several species of butterflies named after him. Manders was at the ANZAC headquarters, along with Major General Godley, Major General Cox and the Assistant Adjutant-General, Lord Charles Cavendish-Bentinck, when he was struck by a bullet. Godley recalled in his autobiography, *Life of an Irish Soldier:*

Manders suddenly ceased talking, his head dropped on his shoulder and, remaining as he did in a sitting position, it was some moments before we realised that a spent bullet had noiselessly struck him on the temple and that he was dead.

On 9 August, the Hon. Aubrey Herbert, an Intelligence Officer and Interpreter to the ANZAC, wrote in his diary (published as *Mons, Anzac & Kut* in 1930), while at No. 3 Outpost:

Bullets came streaming down our valley, and we put up a small wall of sacks, 3 feet high, behind which we slept. I was sitting at breakfast this morning listening to Colonel Manders talking, when suddenly I saw Charlie B. put his hand to his own head and say: 'By G——, he's killed!' Manders fell back dead, with a bullet through his temple, he was a very good fellow … Came back for Manders' funeral. I was very fond of him. General Godley read a few sentences with the help of my electric torch, which failed. Four others were buried with him. Later I saw a great shell strike the grave. A cemetery, or rather lots, growing up round us. There are dead buried or half buried in every gully.

Manders had tried his best for the wounded and did not want a repeat of the complete breakdown of medical services that had happened during the April landings. Unfortunately, the process again broke down in August:

… Meanwhile, the condition of the wounded is indescribable. They lie in the sand in rows upon rows, their faces caked with sand and blood; one murmur for water; no shelter from the sun; many of them in saps, with men passing all the time scattering more dust on them. There is hardly any possibility of transporting them. The fire zones are desperate, and the saps are blocked with ammunition transport and mules, also whinnying for water, carrying food, etc. Some unwounded men almost mad from thirst, cursing. … We have a terrible view here: lines of wounded creeping up from the hospital to the cemetery like a tide, and the cemetery is going like a live thing to meet the wounded.

The Auckland History tells a similar story:

Close to the sea was one sap much travelled by all who passed No. 2 Outpost. This sap for nearly two hundred yards was crammed with badly-wounded men—all stretcher cases. For three nights they lay there without blankets; for three days they were scorched by the merciless sun. They had no food except scraps of hard biscuit, and no water save what was given them by passers-by. They were not even out of the fire zone, for many were hit a second time while they lay, waiting and waiting for the bearers who could not come. Some were killed, and to them death came as a merciful release. All wounded had to be evacuated by launch or lighter, and there had not been enough of these available. Remember, too, that it took four men three hours to carry from the slopes to the beach, and that stretcher-bearing is the hardest work, and taxes even the most powerful and courageous men to the uttermost. One trip was enough to tire anyone—the second brought a man to the limit of endurance, and after that the bearer staggered on, utterly spent physically and sustained only by that deeper spiritual side of human nature which gives victory over the flesh and its frailty. Remember, also, how many thousands of wounded men lay in the valleys and upon the mountain slopes. Was it any wonder that many a poor wretch died before succour reached him?

[Note: This is the starting point *(40.25302,26.28128)* for Tour Three: Walking the Rhododendron Spur]

Leave New Zealand No. 2 Outpost Cemetery and continue along the road for a further 150 metres. On the seaward side of the road is **Embarkation Pier CWGC Cemetery (18)** *(40.25477,26.28014)*, named after No. 3 Pier that was built here and from which the wounded were evacuated during the August offensive. The pier was short lived, due to the exposed position of the location and too shallow for most boats, and was abandoned only two days into the offensive. On the opposite side of the road, marked by a signpost, is the mouth of Chailak Dere and the road to Bauchop's Hill. This is also the approximate position where North Beach leads into Ocean Beach.

The headquarters of two divisions were located near here in August 1915, as well as a Casualty Clearing Station. Apart from five original burials, the cemetery is made up of graves brought in after the Armistice from the cemeteries known as Chailak Dere No.1 and 2, Mulberry Tree and Apex, and from isolated graves. There are now 944 Commonwealth servicemen buried or commemorated in the cemetery. Of these there are special memorials to 262 casualties known or believed to be buried among them but 662 of the burials are unidentified. One of those killed

Embarkation CWGC Cemetery.

nearby was **Lieutenant Commander Thomas Edward Greenshields**, Royal Navy. He had volunteered for shore duty on 7 August to command parties evacuating the wounded from Anzac; whilst superintending the work he was shot dead. He was buried at sea and so is commemorated on the Portsmouth Naval Memorial *(Panel 7)*.

The conditions at No. 3 Pier (Embarkation Pier) were far from ideal:

Chailak Dere. (2013)

Here must be traced the cause of this deplorable damming back of the stream of casualties, whereby the wounded were retained near the beach under conditions which entailed terrible suffering and loss of life within a few hundred yards of the roadstead, where the hospital ships lay undisturbed. As at the Landing, failure to carry the heights involved serious difficulty for the services responsible for supplies and for evacuation. Beyond the foot-hills, the open country and beach were by day continuously subjected to shell-fire and sniping, and in particular to a continuous rain of "overs".

No. 3 trestle pier was apparently intended only for evacuation of wounded, and it was at first so used, a Red Cross flag being flown. But early on the 7th it was used, under protest from the medical side, by beach parties under combatant officers for landing stores: thereafter the flag was, rightly enough, not respected by the enemy. Although at first, through his preoccupation, this fire was only intermittent, and was ignored by those conducting the evacuation, this advantage was offset by the fact that the pier was inaccessible to pinnaces and cutters, except at full tide, and that no lighters or barges were available.[42]

Amongst those buried here is **Private Donald Ferris** *(Sp. Mem.B.16)*, Maori Contingent. An accomplished machine gunner, he was killed alongside Private Colin Warden at The Apex on 8 August.

Trooper William Albert Baker *(I.A.12)*, 9/LHR, who was slightly wounded in support of the attack at The Nek, but killed later in November 1915, a casualty of a sniper. Baker, from Kangarilla, South Australia, was a station hand in civilian life, before enlisting in November 1914. Whilst on observation duty in the trenches on the Rhododendron Spur he was shot through the head. A recent heavy snowfall that covered the battlefield had the effect of pronouncing his head, silhouetted against the white background, a fatal mistake and a lesson others learned quickly. He was first buried in No. 2 Outpost, and then after the war his body was re-interred in this cemetery. His brother chose the words of the epitaph: *"Brother Bill A Sniping Fell, We Miss Him Still, We Ever Will."*

Reverend Andrew Gillison *(Sp.Mem.B.62)*, was the first AIF Chaplain to fall in the Great War, mortally wounded at Hill 60, dying some three hours later on 22 August. He was a Scotsman and a Presbyterian minister, who emigrated to Australia. Gillison was appointed as an army chaplain in 1906, and in October 1914 was appointed a captain and Presbyterian chaplain to 4 (Australian) Brigade. He was mortally wounded alongside Corporal Robert Pittendrigh, a Methodist minister from Lithgow, NSW. Pittendrigh died of his wounds on a hospital ship a week later and was buried at sea, and is commemorated on *Panel 36* of the Lone Pine Memorial. The Pittendrigh name is shared with two of his cousins who were also killed on Gallipoli: Edmund *(Panel 62)*, 18/AIF, who was killed at Hill 60 on 22 August, and Norman *(Panel 13)*, 1/AIF, who was killed on 6 August at Lone Pine. His brother Keith survived the war to return to Australia.

Another Hill 60 casualty is **Lieutenant Colonel Charles Ernest Thomas** *(I.A.17)*, New Zealand Medical Corps, who was commanding the Mounted Field Ambulance. He was killed on 28 August when leading stretcher bearers to the vicinity of Hill 60. He had entered a sap that led to the fire trenches when a shell burst over the party, wounding all four stretcher bearers whilst the concussion killed Thomas. Thomas was born in India, educated at Cheltenham College and became a surgeon in England. He emigrated to New Zealand in 1890, where he was a surgeon at Timaru Hospital. Serving in the Boer War, he returned to New Zealand and opened his own practice before joining the NZEF in August 1914.

Lieutenant Colonel Joseph Beeston, officer commanding 4th Field Ambulance, described the area:

We still had our swim off the beach from this position. It will be a wonderful place for tourists after the war is over. For Australians all along the flat land by the beach there are sufficient bullets to start a lead factory. Then searching among the gullies will give good results. We came across the Turkish Quartermaster's store, any quantity of coats and boots and bully beef. The latter was much more palatable than ours.[43]

Optional Walk - Bauchop's Hill

If travelling by car allow for a twenty minutes return journey along a rough track, or ninety minutes if walking.

Leaving Embarkation Cemetery, continue along the beach road for a further hundred metres. On the right, landward, side of the road, is a rough track that is drivable as well as walkable. This will take you initially into Chailak Dere before the road climbs up to the hill. After a distance of approximately 1500 metres the road will end on the top of **Bauchop's Hill (19)** *(40.25748,26.29133)*, about eighty metres high. There is a small white building nearby, upon which you get a panoramic view of the North Anzac battlefield. The hill is named after Lieutenant Colonel Arthur Bauchop, who commanded the Otago Mounted Rifles.

Bauchop, a veteran of the Boer War, was tasked with capturing the Turkish strongpoint on this foothill during the night of 6 August. As with No. 3 Outpost, seizing this hill was one of the few successes

---

of the offensive. Born and bred in New Zealand, he was a saw-miller before becoming a career soldier. He received gunshot wounds to the spine during the morning of 7 August and was evacuated to a hospital ship, HMHS *Delta*. He died three days later on 10 August and was buried at sea. He is commemorated on *Panel 72* of the Lone Pine Memorial.

From the top of Bauchop's Hill there are some great views of this 'mad country'. To the north is Aghyl Dere, and views into Australia Valley, the incorrect fork that Monash's Australians took when exiting Taylor's Gap, believing it to be Aghyl Dere. Aghyl Dere itself forks; the northern gully leading towards the objective of Hill 971; the southern is the route the Gurkhas followed on their route to Chamchak Punar and Hill Q. If you look to the east, at the Sari Bair ridge, all the landmarks are visible including; Chunuk Bair, with the two white memorials and with The Farm Cemetery nestled below. Moving left, along the ridgeline, is Hill Q and then the highest point, Hill 971, marked today by the forestry lookout tower. Below is the bare slope of the Abdul Rahman Spur. The narrow precipitous ridge line that leads in the direction of the Farm is Cheshire Ridge and the flat topped cliff in the foreground is Little Table Top. To the right of Cheshire Ridge is Rhododendron Spur, which leads up to Chunuk Bair from 'Big' Table Top.

Leave Bauchop's Hill and return down the same track back to Beach Road.

End of diversion.

Bauchop's Hill. (2013)

196

7th Field Ambulance CWGC Cemetery. (2013)

Continue on for a further 650 metres to **7th Field Ambulance CWGC Cemetery (20)** *(40.26156,26.28103)*. The cemetery is on low ground, called Walden Grove, under the shelter of the hill known as Walden's Point (sometimes spelt Waldron's Point), between Chailak Dere and Aghyl Dere. This area was secured during the night of 6 August. The area is believed to be named after **Private Colin Warden** (note the misspelling), who is commemorated on *Panel 11* on the Chunuk Bair Memorial. Warden was an accomplished scout, sniper and machine gunner who was killed at The Apex on 8 August whilst commanding a Maori Contingent machine gun. Captain Jessie Wallingford wrote: *had he lived, he was a marvel, and would have made an excellent brigade machine gun officer.*

The original cemetery was actually first created by the 4th Field Ambulance, but named after the 7th Australian Field Ambulance, which landed on Gallipoli in September 1915, but over 350 of the graves were brought in from earlier cemeteries after the Armistice. The majority of the burials are from 54th (East Anglian) Division and date from September onwards, and are not Australian as you might have expected. There are still numerous August casualties buried here, including burials of men of the New Zealand Mounted Rifles who cleared the Turkish outposts. The smaller burial grounds in the area were known as Bedford Ridge, West

Ham Gully, Waldren's Point, Essex, Aghyl Dere, Eastern Mounted Brigade, Suffolk, Hampshire Lane Nos. 1 and 2, Australia Valley, 116th Essex, 1/8th Hampshire, Norfolk, Junction and 1/4th Northants. There are now 640 Commonwealth servicemen from the campaign buried or commemorated in this cemetery. 276 of the burials are unidentified but special memorials commemorate 207 casualties known or believed to be buried among them. The graves represent three periods of the campaign; Sari Bair (7-10 August), Hill 60 (21-29 August) and those from September onwards.

Amongst those buried here are **Major Percy Overton** *(II.A.5)* and **Private Malcolm McInnes** *(II.A.4)*, Canterbury Mounted Rifles, NZEF. Overton and McInnes were scouts who had been actively reconnoitring the maze of valleys and scrub-covered spurs before the offensive, providing valuable intelligence of the country that led up to the heights of Chunuk Bair and Hill 971. Malcolm McInnes, who was from Canterbury, had a brother, Alex, who was killed at Gallipoli with the Canterbury Battalion in May 1915. During one of his reconnaissances behind Turkish lines, Overton took McInnes and a Corporal Young. They were out for two nights and a day and in his words: *we had a most exciting and interesting time dodging Turkish outposts.* It was from these trips that he was able to map this unknown country as well as to provide valuable information on the Turks' positions and movements. Percy Overton was from Christchurch, a sheep farmer before the war. He served in the Boer War as a trooper in the New Zealand Mounted Rifles, ending the war as a lieutenant in the NZ Contingent. On 4 August 1914, he was appointed a major in the Canterbury Mounted Rifles; he was killed in Aghyl Dere on 7 August 1915. He was originally buried in Warley Gap, but after the war his grave was moved here. He also had a brother in the war, Guy, who was mortally wounded at Walden's Knob with the Canterbury Mounted Rifles. Guy died of his wounds on a hospital ship on 10 August, and is commemorated on *Panel 71* on the Lone Pine Memorial.

Major Acton Adams, Canterbury Mounted Rifles, wrote about the two scouts:

For the general attack Major Overton was detached from the Canterbury Mounted Rifles and given the special mission of leading the Gurkha Brigade to their place of attack, they being ignorant of the country, whilst he, as you are aware, had been tireless in scouting, map-making, etc. To accompany him he chose Malcolm McInnes, one of my best scouts. We were all delighted, and were saying it would mean a D.S.O. for the major, as we all knew his absolute disregard of danger. The next scrap of news we heard was from an interpreter, who stated that the Turks were pressing hotly. Major Overton told him to look after a prisoner, and rushed back to see what he could do. Word of his fate came through, and here one feels that people at home have no conception of how little one knows beyond one's own regiment; everybody is working at top speed, and in a crisis such as this, there is no intercommunication. Still, on the word coming, I sent Sergeant Evans and Trooper Edwards to obtain all possible information and to mark the grave. Evans's report was that he crawled within a few yards and saw the grave, but it was right under Turkish fire; an officer was using his glasses and revolver, and begged to be allowed to purchase them, having none; that a sergeant of the Sikhs reported M. McInnes as having been wounded and taken away to hospital. The major's map case he brought back. Next morning I sent Evans back again for the revolver and glasses, which we judged would be precious relics to you and his sons. But before he returned, I was sent myself on to this ship, and can only hope that someone will be able to hold them for you. From a soldier's point of view, it is a lot to us that your husband was killed by no accident of chance shot but in a position that will always raise a thrill of pride whenever we of his regiment speak of our fearless major.[44]

There are two British battalion commanders buried here:

Lieutenant Colonel Sir William Lennox Napier (*Sp.Mem.A.105*), 4/SWB, was killed by a sniper on 13 August. Born in Canada, he succeeded his father to the baronetcy aged only 17. Educated at Uppingham and Cambridge, he was called to the Bar at the Inner Temple, becoming a solicitor in 1902. During this period he held a commission in the Royal Sussex Artillery, later transferring to 7/RWF, from which he retired in 1912 as lieutenant colonel. At the outbreak of war in 1914 he was gazetted into 4/SWB before proceeding to Gallipoli. Napier had three sons in the war, one was Lieutenant Sir Joseph William Lennox, 4th Bart., who served in the same battalion at Gallipoli and was twice wounded.

Lieutenant Colonel Arthur Richard Cole-Hamilton (*Sp.Mem.B.5*), he served in Egypt in 1882 with the Royal Scots and then saw out his military career in Ireland with the Royal Irish Rifles; when the Great War began he became the commanding officer of 6/East Lancs.

Close by to the south is Taylor's Hollow, a flat area used by the artillery as well as for bivouacs for troops. It was believed to be named after Lieutenant George Taylor, Canterbury Mounted Rifles, a school master before the war, who regularly scouted in this area. Between Walden's and Bauchop's Hill was a narrow path that became known at Taylor's Gap. Note the Taylor's Gap information panel by the road.

Optional Walk - Taylor's Gap

An hour's walk through fields and an overgrown track.

There has been a lot of emphasis placed on the use of the Taylor's Gap 'shortcut' as one of the contributing factors in the failure of Monash's Brigade to achieve its objective of Hill 971. However, even if Taylor's Gap had been by-passed, the outcome probably have been the same. The story was told that Major Percy Overton was using a local miller, of Greek origin, as a guide and when they were approaching Walden's Point, which according to the plan they should go around, the Greek suggested that a shortcut through Taylor's Gap would save them half an hour. Already conscious that the column was behind schedule, Overton eventually agreed that the 'shortcut' was the best option. This narrow pass would be fine for one man and his mule, but for a brigade it proved to be a disaster. Not only was it narrow and overgrown in many areas, but the Turks were in the hills and firing down onto the column. The pioneers had to be sent forward to cut a path through it and, even though the passage itself is less than 300 metres in length, it took over two hours for the head of the column to pass through it into Aghyl Dere.

Major Overton took the shortcut to save time and also to avoid the machine gun position that the Turks then had on Walden's Point. Unfortunately the delay caused by the overgrown, narrow goat track

Taylor's Gap information sign. (2013)

delayed the brigade reaching Aghyl Dere. When the brigade did emerge two hours later there was confusion in the dark and Overton lost his bearings and directed the Australians into the wrong valley.

From 7th Field Ambulance, walk across the fields in a southerly direction, keeping the beach road to the right. After about 200 metres there will be a large wide valley to the left. Follow this valley inland for a further 200 metres. You will then come to the opening of **Taylor's Gap (21)** (40.26042,26.28428) and a walking path which, depending on the scrub overgrowth, can be difficult to find. The gap itself only proceeds a further 250 metres until you exit into Aghyl Dere. This walk through Taylor's Gap and back will take approximately an hour and should never be attempted alone.

Walking Taylor's Gap today.

The track is hazardous and is still overgrown in places, and once through the other side the jumble of valleys ahead are confusing and so it is easy to get lost, as in 1915. This area is very remote and rarely visited by anyone, so do not expect rescue parties to be wandering by. However, it is worth the visit to understand the feat involved in squeezing Monash's and Indian brigades through it in single file, in the dark and under fire. Remember, the men were fully laden, sick and tired, and had not really encountered the Turks yet. There was no chance of them capturing Hill 971 before daylight, as their problems had only just begun.

As you stand at the exit of the gap, the valley that crosses in front of you is Aghyl Dere. The wide open valley, almost straight ahead (north east) and slightly to the left is Australia Valley, into which Monash's men marched.

It is possible to reach Hill 60 from this direction, along the bridle track that existed in 1915, but only attempt this if you have a guide or know the area well. Allow for a two hour return journey to Hill 60 and back.

Return the way you have come back to the road. From the road continue on a further 650 metres, where you will see the Turkish **Damakçilik Bayiri Memorial (22)** *(40.26758,26.27943)* to the right of the road. The memorial stands on the west section of the Damakçilik

Spur, which was lightly held by the Turks during the night of 6 August. The inscription says:

> Colonel Mustafa Kemal, commander of the Anafartalar Group, ordered the 7th Division to attack towards the Damakçilik Slope on 9 August 1915, thus preventing the ANZAC Brigade from linking up with the British IX Army Corps and eliminating the threat to Kocaçimentepe [Hill 971].

This position was defended by men from the Turkish *14 Regiment*, of which 150 were taken prisoner during the night of 6 August. Continue along the main road for 1.3 kilometres until you reach a crossroads. Turn right, signposted to Hill 60 CWGC Cemetery, and follow the dirt track for 650 metres to the cemetery and New Zealand Memorial.

Hill 60, named on period maps as Kaiajik Aghala, was known to the Turks as Bomba Tepe, or Bomb Hill, and this name speaks for itself. The hill was defended in August 1915 by elements of the Turkish *7th Division*.

Damakçilik Bair. (2013)

Hill 60 CWGC Cemetery (23) *(40.27271,26.29321)* was begun after the fighting and is situated amongst the old trenches that can still be found on the hill. It was enlarged after the war when the Graves Registration Units began the battlefield task of recovering the bodies from lone battlefield burials and from Norfolk Trench Cemetery. There are now 788

Bomba Tepe signs and information panel. (2013)

burials in this cemetery, 712 of them unidentified, leaving seventy six marked graves. Fourteen Australians have known graves here, with a further sixteen commemorated by Special Memorials. Twenty of the Australians either buried or commemorated here were serving with the 18/AIF or the 9/LHR, both units were heavily involved in the fighting in the area during August.

Amongst those buried in the cemetery are:

Lieutenant Colonel Carew Reynell *(Sp.Mem.4)*, the commanding officer of the Australian 9/Light Horse Regiment, who was killed on Hill 60 on 28 August. Reynell was the Regiment's second commanding officer, replacing Lieutenant Colonel Albert Miell, who had been killed on 7 August on Russell's Top whilst directing fire in support of The Nek attack. Lieutenant Colonel Carew Reynell was from South Australia, and educated in Adelaide. On leaving university, he joined his father in managing the family vineyard, but had also received a commission in the Australian Light Horse. The town of Reynella in South Australia is named after him.

Lieutenant Colonel Carew Reynell, commanding 9/LHR. Killed on 28 August 1915.

Killed alongside Reynell was **Captain Alfred John Jaffray** *(Sp.Mem.27)*, who had farmed in Wallacedale, Victoria. Before the war he had served for twelve years in the Light Horse.

In Darley's, *With The Ninth Light Horse In The Great War*, the author notes:

Hill 60 CWGC Cemetery and Memorial. (2013)

At a given signal the whole force rushed into the open to carry out their desperate venture, but were met by a terrible fire from machine gun, rifle and bomb. Cheering loudly, the gallant party rushed across the open and into the heart of the enemy, where hand-to-hand fighting was soon general. Our losses had, however, been extremely heavy, and the force was gradually driven back to its own lines, leaving the greater part of its number dead on the field. The following officers were amongst the slain: Lieutenant Colonel Carey Reynell, Captain Jaffray, and Captain Callery. This was a sad blow to the Regiment, especially the loss of their gallant Colonel, an officer and a gentleman of the best type, a splendid soldier and born leader… Desperate efforts were made to recover the bodies of our dead comrades, and during the night several were brought in, including those of Colonel Reynell and Captain Jaffray…We buried poor Reynell and Jaffray under the trees on the far side of our little gully, and had just concluded the service when the enemy, who had evidently seen us from their observation post on Hill 971, opened a very heavy shell fire on our position.

Within the circular cemetery is the **Hill 60 (New Zealand) Memorial**, one of four memorials on the Gallipoli Peninsula commemorating New Zealanders who have no known graves (the others are at Chunuk Bair, Lone Pine and Twelve Tree Copse Cemetery). The memorial records the names of 183 missing from the August fighting. As you will notice, they are predominantly from the New Zealand Mounted Rifles Brigade, and this place was chosen as so many were killed in this action. Of those who are commemorated, sixty five belonged to the Canterbury Mounted Rifles, forty eight to the Wellington, thirty one to the Otago, twenty seven to the Auckland, as well as nine to the Maori Contingent and two from the New Zealand Engineers. The general inscription on the memorial reads: *Here are recorded the names of officers and men of New Zealand who fell in the Actions of Hill 60, August, 1915, and in September, 1915, and whose graves are known only to God.* Amongst those commemorated on the memorial are:

Private Edward Brittan and **Lance Corporal Henry Brittan**, brothers, who served in the Canterbury Mounted Rifles who were both killed on 28 August. The Brittans lived in Christchurch and were to lose a third brother, Harold, who was killed on the Western Front in 1918. A fourth brother, Arthur, survived the war. Two Australian brothers, the Gillams, were also killed in the attack on Hill 60 and are commemorated on *Panel 10* of the Lone Pine Memorial. **Private Hubert Gillam**, known as Hughie, and his older brother, **Private Sydney Gillam**, known as Syd. Both served in the 10/LHR and died of wounds on 29 August. Syd made it to the Turkish trench in the initial charge, where he was mortally wounded by a bomb, which almost blew off one of his arms. Hughie was shot through the stomach and spine in the same charge. Both brothers were taken to the rear where they died within half an hour of each other. The Gillams had another brother who served in the war and survived. Four younger brothers went on to serve in World War II; they all survived.

Reverend Major William Grant, who served with the New Zealand Army Chaplains' Department, and was attached to the Wellington Mounted Rifles. Grant was shot and killed on 28 August whilst searching for wounded in the front line. Grant was born in Scotland in 1859 and emigrated to New Zealand in 1871 with his family. Commissioned in the Presbyterian ministry, he was appointed as Chaplain in the NZEF in August 1914. It would appear from eye witness accounts that Grant was keen to get back to the trenches in order to tend the wounded from the recent fighting. He teamed up with Chaplain Charles Dobson, who was attached to the Aucklanders, and together they went through the devastated trenches, tending and comforting the wounded and giving encouragement to those still fighting. As they worked their way along the trench they came to a barricade on the left flank and crossed this to see if any more wounded were lying the other side. Here they found two Connaught Rangers lying wounded, along with two wounded Turks; the wounds of both Christian and Mohammadan were tended alike. Walking on a little further, they rounded a traverse and came face to face with some Turkish soldiers. Alarmed by the sudden confrontation, the Turks raised their rifles and fired, not seeing the Red Cross armbands or

Chaplain William Grant, Wellington Mounted Rifles, killed on 28 August 1915 whilst tending to the wounded.

Grants original grave. (Alexander Turnbull Library, Wellington, New Zealand – ref: 22862232)

realising they were chaplains. Grant was hit, but the bullets had missed Dobson. The Turks then realized that they were non-combatants and waved Dobson away. Dobson returned with another chaplain, W.C. Blamires, attached to the Wellingtons, and a party of armed men to go back to find Grant, who was found dead. His body was carried back and buried by Blamires in a gully on the side of Hill 60 and a wooden cross was erected to mark his grave.

The actual summit of Hill 60 is behind the cemetery. Take the track that leads around the cemetery in a north easterly direction. From that track you will observe on the right hand side the re-entrant that descends back down into Kaiajik Dere. The British positions were on the cemetery side, the Turkish on the opposite bank, although some Australians, who managed to cross the Kaiajik, were able to establish a trench at the bottom of the bank. From the end of the cemetery you can see the summit as it rises slightly to the left of the track. There is evidence of mine craters in the wheat fields close by and also trenches within the scrub near the cemetery. It is worth continuing along the track for a few metres as there are some excellent views of the W Hills to the left (north) and the plain that leads off in the direction of Büyükanafarta and Abdul Rahman Spur to the east. The British never reached this point, but command of the surrounding area can be understood. Whoever held the summit could dominate the Azmak Dere plain, the communication route for the Turkish troops; whilst if the British had not captured what they did, they would have left the Turks in a dominating position to overlook their communication lines between Anzac and Suvla. The resulting positions that were established on Hill 60 at the end of August could be described as a mutual stand off.

In fact the battle for Hill 60 was as much for two wells as for capturing the summit. Both wells still exist today and can be found in their original positions. To locate **Kabak Kuyu (24)** *(40.27163,26.28980)*, retrace your steps along the track from the cemetery, in the direction of the main road, and after two hundred metres you will approach a cross-section of another track. This is the bridle track, sunken in places, that existed in 1915. Turn left in a southerly direction and walk for a further two hundred metres when you will reach a shallow stream bed, which the Turks used as a communication trench. At the junction of the stream and track you will find a well. The well, one of an original pair, itself is approximately three metres to the west of the track. Return to the cemetery.

Kabak Kuyu well, captured by 5/Connaught Rangers.

Leaving Hill 60, return to the main Anzac - Büyükanafarta road and continue by car along the road in an easterly direction, After approximately 250 metres, on the left hand side, is the well of **Susak Kuyu (25)** *(40.27808,26.28915)*, captured by the Gurkhas on 21 August. Much of this lowland area is rich, open ground, cultivated and with many irrigation ditches, hedges and an abundance of wells (the Turkish word *kuyu* means well). The wells in this area became tactically important for the British and the fighting was therefore intense. Continue along the road towards the village, approximately three kilometres distant.

Just before the village, on either side of the road, is the **Büyükanafarta Ottoman Cemetery (26)** *(40.28302,26.32342)*,

The grave of Lieutenant Colonel Halit Bey, commanding 20 Regiment. He died of wounds on 11 August 1915.

ANAFARTALAR MUHAREBESİNDE.
BOMBA TEPEDE ŞEHİT OLAN
7.Tüm.20.P.Al.K.Yb.
HALİT BEY RUHUNA FATİHA
II-AĞUSTOS-1915

containing many graves from the period. Two recently restored graves, which are sign posted, are those of two *7th Division* regimental commanders who were killed in the August battles: **Lieutenant Colonel (Yarbay) Halit Bey**, *20 Regiment*, who died of wounds received trying to push the British off of the Damakjelik Spur; and **Yarbay Ziya Bey**, *21 Regiment*, who had advanced alongside Halit Bey's regiment and was killed during the same attack on 9 August. Close by, nearer the cross roads, are two further graves of Hill 60 interest. They are **Lieutenant Hasan Tahsin**, *7th Division Artillery Regiment*, and the regimental mufti, who were both killed on 21 August. The mufti did similar work to the British chaplains, serving with the troops in the trenches, morally encouraged the soldiers in action, said prayers for the dying and wounded and whenever possible wrote home to the next of kin of the slain or wounded. Continue towards the village for a few metres until you reach **Büyükanafarta Turkish Cemetery and Memorial (27)** *(40.28229,26.32486)*, which was constructed in 2005 and lists the names of 749 Turkish soldiers commemorated in the cemetery, either buried here or in other smaller battlefield cemeteries nearby. The fallen were from the *3rd Division (31* and *32 Regiments)*, *7th Division (19, 20* and *21 Regiments)* and also units of *33, 45* and *17 Regiments* and the *Bursa Gendarmerie*.

Leave the cemetery and enter the village of **Büyükanafarta (28)** *(40.28180,26.33015)*. The village, evacuated of civilians and heavily shelled and bombed during the war, had to be rebuilt after the hostilities. Today it has a population of around 400 people, whose main living is from livestock and agriculture. There is a small café in the square where a good Turkish coffee or tea can be consumed. Public toilets are also nearby, the only toilets in the area, so take note! Whilst in the village it is recommended that you visit the small, but very good, Gallipoli Campaign Museum, situated between the café and cemetery. This museum contains many exhibits found locally on the Anzac and Suvla battlefield, making an interesting end to the tour.

Return to Anzac along the beach road or, alternatively, continue on the road out of the village, which will take you around the Sari Bair ridge, past the village of Kocadere, to the main Anzac-Eceabat road.

Büyükanafarta
Turkish Cemetery
and Memorial.
(2013)

209

Tour Three:

Walking the Rhododendron Spur

WARNING: This walk is not only spectacularly beautiful, but it is also in some of the most wild and remote parts of the battlefield, <u>so never try this alone.</u>

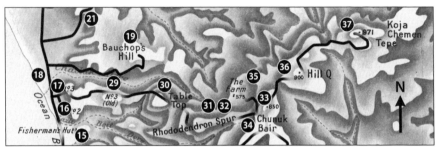

Rhododendron Spur – Walking the Heights.

Allow three hours if walking up hill, two if walking down. If you are not fit, do not attempt to walk it. The narrow, and in places overgrown, track is approximately five kilometres long over some rough ground which gets steeper as you near the end, when you are probably most tired.

• Wear sturdy walking boots, non-rip trousers, wide-brimmed hat and do not forget the sun block.
• Take plenty of water for the day.
• Keep to the itinerary. You will be able to see Chunuk Bair, your objective, throughout much of your walk, so stick to the track and do not be tempted to stray from the path.
• Inform someone who is not on this walk where you are going and roughly how long you will be. Mobile phones do not work in the gullies, but take one nevertheless and ensure it is fully charged with useful numbers pre-entered.
• Get someone to meet you at the end of the walk, with a vehicle, otherwise you will have to walk the same route again.

Anzac is a spectacular landscape and there is no better place to view it than from the spur that winds its way up from the Outposts on North Beach to Chunuk Bair and the heights of the Sari Bair ridge. The views are breathtaking and, mixed with the smell of wild thyme and the sound of the wind and wild birds, it is an experience to relish.

| Sazli Beit Dere | No.2 Outpost | Old No.3 Outpost | No.3 Outpost | Razorback Ridge | Chailak Dere |

The view from Table Top towards the outposts.

The walk is best tackled from the beach upwards, the route that the New Zealanders took, but it can just as easily be walked using Chunuk Bair as your starting point and down to the beach. Your choice should be based on fitness and, even though it is no less spectacular doing the walk in reverse, it is slightly easier going downhill, than up! Whichever way you chose to walk, ensure you take plenty of water. The vegetation can be quite thick in places and often is chest high or taller. The path is rough and has been reinforced in places with pine logs to form steps and, where hazardous, wooden railings. However, be careful, as much of the path is often in various states of decay.

This walk begins at **New Zealand No. 2 Outpost CWGC Cemetery (17)** *(40.25318,26.28060)*. At the bend in the track between the two cemeteries is a narrow and, in places, over grown, path *(40.25302,26.28128)* that

The path near Table Top looking down towards the Razorback Ridge. (2013)

211

Chailak Dere | Table Top | Chunuk Bair | Rhododendron Ridge | Battleship Hill | Sazli Beit Dere

Panoramic showing Chailak Dere to Ari Burnu. (2013)

takes you along the route the New Zealanders followed during the August assault on Sari Bair. This is one of the most rewarding walks on the Peninsula, going along Rhododendron Spur, given its name from the plant Arbutus, which is commonly found on the peninsula and which at the time was often mistaken for a rhododendron. It is also one of the most rewarding from a historical point of view, as you are following in the footsteps of the New Zealand assaulting columns.

Follow this trail, which takes you through the area known as Otago Gully, the site of the Godley's HQ, and then climb up on to No. 3 Outpost *(40.25360,26.28289)*, following the track onto No. 2 Outpost *(40.25255, 26.28375)*. The highest point of this ridge is the position known as Old No. 3 Post. This is the route that the Right Covering Force followed.

STAND 1: Old No. 3 Outpost (29) *(40.25350,26.28721)* was the site of a lightly entrenched Turkish outpost, captured by the Auckland Mounted Rifles during the night of 6 August. It was here that the Royal Navy assisted in its capture by its searchlight ruse. As it was then, today it serves as a good vantage point, from where you can clearly view the ground all around. To the immediate south is Sazli Beit Dere, where the Aucklanders assaulted the southern slopes of this hill, this route being chosen because of heavy Turkish wire on the western slopes whence you have just come. Look along the beach to Maori Hill and No. 1 Outpost and the CWGC buildings with the old Anzac area beyond. To the north is a wide mouthed valley known as Chailak Dere, with Bauchop's Hill (captured by the Canterburys and Otagos) on the other side.

Leave Old No. 3 Outpost and continue along the path until it descends and narrows onto a razorback ridge before it leads up on to Table Top, the sand faced cliff ahead.

STAND 2: Table Top (30) *(40.25324,26.29416)* was the next Turkish outpost to be captured, and again the searchlight ruse and bombardment was used. As the bombardment lifted, the Wellingtons, who had already climbed the cliff face, succeeded in storming the trenches on top. The unit also successfully captured Destroyer Hill, on the other side of Sazli Beit

Baby 700 | Destroyer Hill | The Nek | Sphinx | Plugges Plateau | No.1 Outpost | Ari Burnu

Dere. Continue along the path, taking care as the route narrows before the climb up onto Table Top itself. From this position are some notable views of the wild country to the north, all of which was undefended and unfortified at the time of the attack. To the left is Bauchop's Hill, marked by a small white building. This hill was also an objective of the Right Covering Force and was captured by the Otago and Canterburys. They had followed the beach further north and attacked Bauchop's by way of Chailak Dere. Although the hill was not as steep as Table Top, it was the stoutness of Turkish defence that had delayed its capture until 1.00 am. In this assault Lieutenant Colonel Arthur Bauchop was mortally wounded during the final bayonet charge to clear the position. With the Turkish outposts now captured, the path for the Right Assaulting Column was now open.

Orientation: From Bauchop's Hill the ridge leads up onto Little Table Top, a smaller version of the hill upon which you are now standing, which then leads up onto Cheshire Ridge, which narrowly connects to the Farm, marked by The Farm CWGC cemetery. The valley in between Cheshire and Rhododendron is still Chailak Dere. The valley on the other side of Cheshire Ridge is Aghyl Dere, which separates the ridge from Damakjelik Spur. On the other side of this is the valley of Kaiajik Dere, which prematurely ends before another valley, named Asma Dere, runs in front of the Abdul Rahman Spur, the path up to Kocaçimentepe (Hill 971), marked by the national parks fire lookout station today.

Continue along the path. In this area the main elements of the Right Assaulting Column climbed up from Chailak Dere in readiness for making their way along Rhododendron Spur and the assault on Chunuk Bair. This is the path we are following. Lots of criticism was made of this column for its inactivity, which was only missing one battalion and was only 1500 metres short of the unoccupied summit of Chunuk Bair. It was light by the time the column eventually moved forward, advancing to a small rocky knoll that became known as The Apex. Continue along the path; as you walk you will notice that it becomes much steeper and note the trenches within the scrubland on both sides of the path. You will soon come to a dirt road. To the left it will take you in the direction of The Farm CWGC Cemetery. Turn right and after ten metres you will see a wide fire track that will take you up towards Chunuk Bair. Take this path and walk

Bauchop's Hill   Damakjelik Spur   Agyhl Dere

Panoramic showing Bauchop's Hill to Chunuk Bair. (2013)

a further 450 metres until you reach a knoll on the path; this is The Apex which stands at 220 metres. If you have not already noticed how steep the walk has been so far, it now gets steeper, and you can understand the difficulties the troops faced fighting their way up hill. These same troops were heavily laden in battle order, weakened by dysentery and months of monotonous food, and had only one canteen of water.

STAND 3: The Apex (31) *(40.251250,26.303580)* was where Colonel Kannengiesser first spotted the New Zealander column advancing, and ordered the few Turks on Chunuk Bair to open fire. This helped stall the assault and any likelihood of capturing Chunuk Bair on 7 August. As you can see, it is tantalising close to the summit; and all that was separating the column from it was a Turkish platoon. Standing here you may feel isolated, as was the feeling of the New Zealanders, who had seen no sign of the other columns, namely the Indian Brigade and the Australian Brigade. Apart from sporadic fire coming from the Turkish platoon, all around was quiet. With no support and the British IX Corps at Suvla, off in the distance, it was probably as quiet at this stage in the fighting as it is today.

Continue along the track. Between The Apex and The Pinnacle are the remains of tunnels, their entrances exposed during recent erosion of the ground. DO NOT enter these, as they could collapse at any time. There are two galleries, at different levels, that remain, and which run in the same direction as the track. These are New Zealand tunnels from later in the campaign and connect what were the front line trenches overlooking Chailak Dere to the rear of The Apex. The whole of the Anzac area is honeycombed with tunnels, which were used for fighting, communication and shelter. Continue on to The Pinnacle which stands at 226 metres. Note that all the ground was open scrubland in 1915 and there were no trees.

Little Table Top · Chailak Dere · Abdul Rahman Spur · Cheshire Ridge · Hill 971 · Hill Q · The Farm · Chunuk Bair

STAND 4: The Pinnacle (32) *(40.251379,26.304542).* If you can imagine this track without the trees you will get an understanding of how open and exposed this position was in 1915. It was across this ground that the Aucklanders were cut down as they tried to cross this narrow saddle in broad daylight later on 7 August. The steep amphitheatre hollow below Chunuk Bair was the only shelter the New Zealanders had and an area where the battalions that were being pushed into the line took shelter. It was up these slopes where Corporal Cyril Bassett, NZ Divisional Signal Company, laid and continuously repaired the telephone wires to Chunuk Bair, which earned him his Victoria Cross. All of this ground was lost during the Turkish counter attack on 10 August.

Continue up the track (fire break), passing the sign to The Farm CWGC Cemetery (see the optional tour), until you reach the top of Chunuk Bair. This is the second highest hill of the Sari Bair range. The Turks know Chunuk Bair as Conkbayiri. Once you have reached the top you can reward yourself with a sit down in the shade, and even indulge in a cold drink and/or an ice cream from a local tradesman. The views back down over the countryside are spectacular.

Looking from The Pinnacle towards Chunuk Bair. (2013)

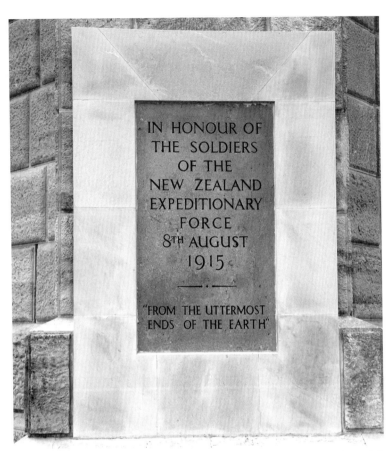

'From The Uttermost Ends of the Earth' plaque on the New Zealand Memorial.

On the northern knoll of Chunuk Bair (272 metres) you will find the **Chunuk Bair New Zealand Memorial (33)** *(40.25230,26.30825)* with the inscription: *IN HONOUR OF THE SOLDIERS OF THE NEW ZEALAND EXPEDITIONARY FORCE 8TH AUGUST 1915 "FROM THE UTTERMOST ENDS OF THE EARTH"*. Rising some 20.5 metres high, this stone monument, built in 1925, is the site of the official New Zealand Anzac Day ceremony each 25 April. It should be noted that the New Zealanders never reached this position, as Malone's northern flank was at the edge of this hill about sixty metres further south, closer to the fire track. Men from 7/Gloucesters briefly occupied this summit but, under fire from Hill Q and Hill 971, were compelled to withdraw. Malone's main position was where the five Turkish monoliths are positioned on the southern knoll of Chunuk Bair, called Hill 261.

Close by is the **Atatürk Memorial,** which shows Kemal with his whip clearly seen behind his back. It was with this whip that he signalled the counter attack on 10 August. Thousands of Turkish soldiers were now

216

assembled in the dark below Conkbayiri. It was 4.30 am, 10 August 1915. Kemal wrote: *The blanket of night had lifted. Now was the hour for the attack ... I ran forward at once ... 'Soldiers! There is no doubt we shall defeat the enemy opposing us. But don't you hurry, let me get in front first. When you see me wave my whip all of you rush forward together' ... Then I went to a point forward of the assault line, and, raising my whip, gave the signal for the assault.* The memorial also has a reference to Mustafa Kemal being hit on the right hand side of his chest by shrapnel and saved from being mortally wounded by his pocket watch. The shattered watch he gave to General Liman von Sanders, commander of the Turkish *Fifth Army*, as a souvenir; he, in turn, gave him his gold watch. It was probably not at this actual location that he was wounded in the charge, which would almost certainly have been some metres further south, on the eastern slopes and nearer the British positions. Close to the Atatürk Memorial is a memorial to a company commander, **First Lieutenant Nazif Çakmak**, Turkish *64 Regiment*, who was killed on 8 August on Chunuk Bair. Nazif Çakmak was the younger brother of Fevzi Çakmak, who became a field marshal after the war.

Memorial to Lieutenant Nazif Çakmak, 64 Regiment, killed on 8 August.

To the south east is the **New Zealand Chunuk Bair Memorial to the Missing and Cemetery** *(40.25197,26.3085)* which bears 856 New Zealand names of those missing who were killed in the Sari Bair operation. The inscription reads: *IN MEMORY OF THESE OFFICERS, NON-COMMISSIONED OFFICERS AND MEN OF THE NEW ZEALAND EXPEDITIONARY FORCE WHO LOST THEIR LIVES IN THE HEROIC ASSAULT ON THE HEIGHTS OF SARI BAIR, 6TH-10TH AUGUST, 1915, IN THE CAPTURE OF CHUNUK BAIR, AND IN SUBSEQUENT BATTLES AND OPERATIONS FROM AUGUST TO DECEMBER, 1915, AND WHO ARE NOT DEFINITELY RECORDED AS BURIED IN THIS OR ADJOINING CEMETERIES.*

Names on the memorial include:

Lieutenant Colonel William George Malone *(Panel 17)*, Commanding Officer, Wellington Regiment, who was killed by a shell on 8 August whilst defending Chunuk Bair. Only seventy of his men, out of 760, survived to walk away from that hill. Of those left behind, twenty one became prisoners. Malone was born in London in 1859, emigrating to New Zealand in 1880. In his pre-war life he had several careers, from serving

The Atatürk Memorial, New Zealand Memorial and Chunuk Bair Cemetery. (2013)

in the Armed Constabulary, working as a farmer, a clerk, a treasurer and a solicitor, ending his law career as a barrister and head of a law firm. In 1900 he was appointed captain in the Wellington (Taranaki) Rifle Volunteers, and in 1910 was their commanding officer. In August 1914 he was appointed a lieutenant colonel in the NZEF. He had four sons in the army, two of whom were wounded with the Wellington Mounted Rifles at Gallipoli, and a daughter who served as a nurse in France. **Major James Elmslie** *(Panel 4)*, Wellington Mounted Rifles, is also named on this memorial, His body was brought down from Chunuk Bair and buried in Old No. 3 Outpost, but after the war his grave could not be located.

Private John Dunn *(Panel 20)*, a machine gunner in the Wellington Regiment, was killed on 8 August on Chunuk Bair. Less than a month before the attack he was sentenced to death for sleeping whilst on duty at Quinn's Post. The sentence was confirmed but later remitted by General Sir Ian Hamilton, as Dunn had not been relieved from sentry duty at the correct time. Dunn was from Wellington and in civilian life was a journalist. Through his time at Gallipoli he was regularly writing to the *Wairarapa Daily Times* with stories of the New Zealand troops at the front.

There are several brothers on the Chunuk Bair Memorial, which include the **Mellor brothers** *(Panels 18 and 22)*, Clement and Arthur, both of the Wellington Regiment, who were killed on 8 August. Also in the same battalion were the **Stokes brothers** *(Panel 23)*, Sydney and James. All four of them were posted as missing after the fighting on Chunuk Bair, later confirmed as killed. There were also the **Corlett**

218

brothers *(Panels 22 and 24)*, Alfred and Frank, who were also killed on 8 August. In the local New Zealand paper, *Hawera & Normanby Star*, a letter appeared in April 1916, titled 'Hero Brothers – Officer's Kindly Letter'. This is just one example of many letters officers would have written to the next of kin. This one, addressed to the Corletts' father, is from Captain Frank Hartnell:

> *I take the liberty to write you a few lines. I write believing you to be the father or brother of the late Private F. Corlett, 10/307 and Private A. H. Corlett, 11/407, and because I was the officer in charge of the platoon to which the two brothers belonged while we were on the Peninsula. I was not privileged to know these two men in private life. I only knew them as the magnificent soldiers that they were, and very proud of them I was, always ready and willing, never complaining, I looked upon them as model soldiers. A few days before their death I required six men to perform a job that was particularly dangerous and I called for volunteers. There was no hesitation, no consultation between the two. The elder brother steps forward and quietly says: 'My brother and I will make two, sir." On the evening of the 7th I lost the sergeant and corporal of their section, and I had no hesitation whatever in placing Frank in command of this section, little thinking that before another sun was to set the whole of the ten men he was to, and did, lead so well, would be either killed or wounded. It was just before noon on the 8th, the Wellington Regiment were holding at this time with desperate courage Chunuk Bair—that these two splendid fellows met a gallant death. They were fighting side by side. One went down, hard hit; the other bends over him to see if anything can be done, hut hardly had he done so when he fell lifeless across his brother. The battle raged round them, but to them it had no terrors. They had fought their last fight, and had fought it well.*

Also killed side by side during the early hours of 9 August were the **Statham brothers** *(Panel 14)* from the Otago Regiment, Frank and Clive. The Otagos were in support of the Wellingtons on Chunuk Bair; tragically they were killed by friendly fire. Clive was a corporal and a sheep farmer, whilst his brother, Frank, a major and company commander in the battalion, was a mining engineer in civilian life. The following letter, by Lieutenant L.G. Wilson, 10th (North Otago) Company, to Major Statham's father was published in *The Auckland Weekly News* on 4 November 1915:

Major Frank Statham, Otago Regiment, killed on 9 August alongside his brother.

The battalion was almost decimated, and the only information we could get was one man's statement that he had seen the Major wounded and in an unconscious state early in the afternoon. After that he had not seen him. Now, however, three men who were wounded state that the major and Clive were standing together and were killed by the explosion of one shell, which landed very close to them. Beyond that I regret that I have been unable to gain any more details. It has been a terrible business and a loss that will never be fully realised. The major, as an officer among officers, was placed on the highest pedestal of respect and admiration, by the men was loved, and was a born leader. In every operation in which our battalion was engaged it was the Major and his Company who led the offensive.

Another eye witness reported similar circumstances of Statham's death and which Charles Bean included in his *The Story of Anzac*:

About 5 am, while the Turkish attack upon them was still at its height, three high-explosive howitzer shells, coming from the right rear, burst among them, one exploding in the front trench on the left, wrecking the trench, and killing the gallant Major Statham together with his brother beside him, as well as Sergeant-Major Porteous and six or seven men. The shells almost certainly came from one of the howitzer batteries inside the old Anzac lines.

The **Chunuk Bair CWGC Cemetery** was made after the Armistice and contains 632 British and Commonwealth burials of soldiers killed during the same operations. Only ten are identified. Of these, one is **Havildar**

View of the Dardanelles Narrows from Chunuk Bair CWGC Cemetery.

Punahang Limbu, 10/Gurkhas *(Grave 7)*, who was killed on 10 August. Many Gurkhas were in fact Buddhist, even though their religion was listed as Hindu. At Gallipoli it was not always possible to respect the rites of the dead and cremate the dead, as was customary for the Gurkhas, as this buried soldier shows.

Grave of Havildar (Sergeant) Punahang Limbu, 10/Gurkha Rifles, killed on 10 August 1915.

Sergeant David Lascelles *(Grave 1)*, Wellington Regiment, was killed on 8 August. One of Malone's men, he had already been wounded in May 1915 when shot in the arm, before returning to the front. He was from Napier in New Zealand and in civilian life was an accountant. Close by is buried **Private Richard Tonkin** *(Grave 12)*, Otago Regiment, who was killed on 7 August at The Apex. Born in Cornwall, his family emigrated to Australia in 1902 before moving to Auckland. Dick was a member of the Auckland Motor Cyclists' Club before the war and was employed by the New Zealand Railways. There is also a grave of a British soldier, **Private Edwin Marsden** *(Grave 10)*, 6/Loyal North Lancs, who was from Chorley in England. He was reported killed on 10 August during the Turkish counter attack, and is one of the few identified bodies recovered and buried here after the Armistice.

On the southern knoll of Chunuk Bair, **Hill 261 (34)** *(40.25084,26. 30744)*, are five large monolith panels that tell the Turkish side of the battles from the landings in April 1915 to the last major action on 10 August. The five monoliths, built in the 1980s, represent the fingers of an upturned hand praying to God. The position is important for two reasons. Firstly it was here, on 25 April, that Mustafa Kemal stopped the Turkish soldiers from retreating, ordered them to fix bayonets and counter attack. It was also this exact position, on 8 August, that was captured by Malone's men. So it was here where Mustafa Kemal stemmed the Turkish retreat during the April landings, but also it was from here where Kemal pushed the British from the top during the August offensive.

Re-created trenches close to the area Malone defended. (2013)

221

About 250 metres further on, just off the left-hand side of the Third Ridge road, was the site of the *8th Division* 'River-bed' Headquarters, which is signposted *8 Tümen Karagahi Su Yataği*. Mustafa Kemal stayed here during a restless night on 9/10 August, just prior to the famous Turkish counter attack that finally sealed the fate of those holding Chunuk Bair.

There are two optional walks in this area, The Farm and both Hill Q and Hill 971.

Optional Walk – The Farm

An hour walk along a very steep path.

The Farm CWGC Cemetery (35) *(40.25418,26.30500)* is located off of the path down from Chunuk Bair. To visit the Farm you can either extend the Rhododendron Spur walk and visit it from the CWGC track that follows the contours of the ridge from The Apex. Along this contour, below the Farm plateau, a mix of British units (Gurkhas, Warwicks, Maoris, Royal Irish Rifles and Hants), held the line just prior to the counter attack on 10 August. When Bean returned to the battlefield in 1919, he found many bones of British soldiers. He wrote 'we came across the remains of men, thick; all below the seaward edge of the shelf. The slope for a hundred yards down was simply covered with them. The bodies of Tommies were thick, their helmets everywhere.' Alternatively, from Chunuk Bair, by following the fire track down about ninety metres, there is a sign that points down the steep path (435 metres) to the Farm. The Farm is a very moving and evocative place to walk to; although once open, it is now covered

The steep track that leads down to The Farm. (2013)

---

thickly with trees. It was from the slopes above that the Turkish troops swarmed down on 10 August, twenty-two lines thick, and when they reached the Farm desperate hand-to-hand fighting ensued. There were few survivors on either side when the fighting stopped, which is why no clear accounts of the fighting here exists. Brigadier General Baldwin and his brigade major were killed in the struggle as 29 Brigade HQ was overrun. These were mainly Kitchener's men, who fought to the last. The Turks had also suffered heavily, and were caught in the open by Wallingford's machine guns, as well as the guns of the fleet and the supporting field artillery batteries.

In 1915 the Farm was a simple stone hut, known to the Turks as Aghyl, or sheepfold. The area was passed by the troops who held Chunuk Bair, but later on 8 August it was occupied by 10/Gurkhas, part of the 9/Warwicks and the Maoris. The 6/East Lancs, 10/Hampshires, 6/Royal Irish Rifles and 6/Leinsters reached it the following day. The cemetery was made after the Armistice and contains 652 Commonwealth burials or commemorated in this cemetery. Most of these would be from Brigadier General Baldwin's brigade. There are special memorials that commemorate seven soldiers who are believed to be buried here; four are from 9/Worcesters, one from the 10/Hampshires, one from the 8/Welsh and one New Zealander, who was killed at The Apex. All the remainder are unidentified.

On 10 August the 9/Worcesters were in a position about 400 metres north east of the cemetery, just below the crest of Hill Q, and were virtually annihilated by the Turkish counter attack. The regimental history records that:

The Farm CWGC Cemetery – Their Name Liveth For Evermore.

At dawn on 10th August, the enemy on the crest line above the position of the 9th Worcesters opened fire and commenced a bombing attack. Great bombs were rolled down to burst in our lines. Then the enemy came over the crest of the ridge in wave after wave of densely packed troops. Firing as rapidly as possible, the 9th Worcesters held their ground, meeting and repulsing the enemy's rushes. For some three hours a desperate struggle raged. By 7 am Colonel Nunn had been killed. Captain Rolph, mortally wounded, fired his revolver up the slopes as he lay dying. At last, when nearly all the officers and most of the men were down, the remnant of the 39th Brigade fell back to the more sheltered position in the dead ground at the head of the ravine.

Lieutenant Colonel Mervyn Nunn *(Sp.Mem.7)*, commanding officer of 9/Worcesters, was killed on 10 August during the Turkish counter attack, and rests today in this cemetery, one of the few marked graves. Born in 1864 and educated at Harrow, he began his military career in 1886, seeing service in the Nile Expedition of 1897 and during the Boer War in 1902. Having retired from the army in 1906, he rejoined the regiment at the outbreak of war. His epitaph reads: "*I have fought a good fight*". Bean wrote of his visit here in 1919:

Lieutenant Colonel Mervyn Nunn, 9/Worcesters, killed on 10 August 1915.

We could see the bones of men on two hills ahead of us, somewhat as in the above sketch, and (so we) cut across the valley intervening. We found on both the further heights (they were steep, lofty spurs, leading to the crest of the range just north of Chunuk Bair) the remains of the Worcestershire Regiment and a few South Lancashires. Those at the very top seemed to have been attacking a Turkish trench or redoubt on the hilltop. None had gone quite to the top, but we found them very near to it, and some of those on top had bombs, old jam tin bombs, lying near them. Hughes came across what seemed to be a colonel's [probably Nunn's] coat; and the buttons showed that he belonged to the Worcestershire Regiment ... I have nowhere, except at The Nek, seen the dead lying so thick as on these slopes and those of The Farm. We searched for signs of the general [Baldwin] but could not find any.[45]

Major Ernest Boyd-Moss DSO *(Sp.Mem.2)* was in the 4/Worcesters, but attached to the 9/Worcesters for the attack. Born in Charlwood in Surrey and resident in Worthing, Sussex, Boyd-Moss had a brother who was a brigadier general in France. He was educated at Tonbridge School in Kent and later gazetted in the Worcestershire Regiment in 1900. He served in Sierre Leone (1898-99) and during the Boer War from 1900 to 1902, when he was awarded the Distinguished Service Order. He landed with 4/Worcesters at W Beach on 25 April 1915, and was later attached to the 9th Battalion in 13 July 1915. Mentioned in Despatches for Gallipoli, he was killed in action during the Turkish counter attack on 10 August. Buried close by is **Second Lieutenant Leonard Hiscock** *(Sp. Mem. 5)*, 9/Worcesters, who was killed alongside Boyd-Moss.

A letter from an unnamed Worcestershire private gave an account of this action:

We had been fighting almost continually since the night of August 5th. This (August 10th) made our 5th day of it, when the Turks brought up their reinforcements (about 50,000) to try and gain back the hills which our troops had so gallantly occupied at great cost. In those five days our company was the first line on the crest of Hill 971. When the alarm was given there was only Maj. Moss and Lieut. Hiscock, the only two officers left with our company. They dashed off, calling to us men to follow them with fixed bayonets. It was fine the way they led us, but the numbers told. I don't think there were many 9th Worcesters left when I was wounded myself. A bomb thrown by the enemy killed both officers and many men.[46]

The graves of Major E. W. Boyd Moss and Major C. W Crofton, 9/Worcesters, killed during the 10 August Turkish counter attack.

The following report appeared in the *Berrows Journal* of 31 October 1915. It related to Major Boyd-Moss' servant, **Private Joseph Rowberry**, 9/Worcesters:

Mr. W. J. Rowberry, Oak Villa, Worcester Road, Malvern Link, who had had no news of his son, Joseph Rowberry 9th Battalion Worcestershire Regiment, for about three months, has now learnt the worst news, conveyed in a letter by Sgt. Hopkins to his mother, Mrs Hopkins of Brook Street, Worcester. Sgt. Hopkins says "I am more than sorry to say that I can tell you about poor Joe Rowberry. He was killed in "the hill" fight where I lost all my pals the 10th August. He died fighting beside his officer, Major [Boyd-] Moss, to whom he was servant. The Major was killed by a bomb and poor Joe, a second after, was shot through the heart. I saw him drop but could not get near him on account of the dead and wounded. It was hell. Tell his friends he was very brave, but careless. I am sure he killed the bomber who killed his officer as he was the only one left near the spot after the bomb had fallen.

Major Charles Crofton, also of 9/Worcesters, is known to be buried here. Private Rowberry is commemorated on the Helles Memorial to the Missing *(Panel 103-113)*, but it is quite possible that his body was one of those unidentified and buried here.
End of diversion.

Optional Walk - Hill Q and Hill 971

An hour walk along the Sari Bair Ridge road.

It is possible to walk further along the Sari Bair ridge from the road that runs by the New Zealand Chunuk Bair Memorial, to both Hill Q (Besim Tepe) and Hill 971 (Kocaçimentepe). Leaving the New Zealand Memorial, follow the road on foot for about 250 metres (at the time of writing this road was closed to vehicles). Along the narrow saddle that connects Chunuk Bair and Hill Q is where Major Cecil Allanson's 6/Gurkhas reached the top, and in this area Gurkha bodies were found and cremated after the war. Remains of trenches, possibly some are those dug by Allanson, can be found down the seaward slopes. From the southern side of the saddle you can see the narrows in the distance, a prize so close, but in fact so far away. Carry on along the road; the high ground to the left of the road is **Hill Q (36)** *(40.25584,26.31139)*, the crest being another 250 metres from the

Sari Bair Ridge looking from Hill 971 across to Hill Q, Chunuk Bair and Su Yatagha. (2013)

saddle. Hill Q has two summits, north and south, and today trenches are still very much evident around the twin hills, although all of these were dug after the August offensive. Rejoin the road and continue for a further kilometre, which will take you onto **Hill 971 (37)** *(40.25937,26.31903)*, which stands at 305 metres. A viewing platform is located next to the national parks' fire watch station, and offers some spectacular views of the north Anzac and Suvla sectors. There is also a Ross Bastiaan Marker (No.10) located here. An objective of the offensive, Hill 971 was never captured or even threatened; down in the 'mad country' below are the twisted valleys, the scenes of some of the most bitter and confused fighting on the Peninsula.

End of diversion.

The view of the Abdul Rahman Spur from Hill 971. A Ross Bastiaan Marker is in the foreground. This would have been Monash's path to the top, but he got no further than the foothills in the middle distance. (2013)

Order of Battle – August 1915

Australian & New Zealand Army Corps
G.O.C. Lieutenant General Sir W. R. Birdwood, KCSI
General Staff: Brigadier General A. Skeen
1st Australian Division
Major General H. B. Walker, DSO
1 Brigade (New South Wales): Brigadier General N.M. Smyth
1/AIF, 2/AIF, 3/AIF,4/AIF
2 Brigade (Victoria): Brigadier General J.K. Forsyth
5/AIF, 6/AIF, 7/AIF, 8/AIF
3 Brigade: Brigadier General E.G. Sinclair-MacLagan
9/AIF (Queensland)
10/AIF (South Australia)
11/AIF (Western Australia)
12/AIF (South & Western Australia and Tasmania)

I (NSW) Field Artillery Brigade
II (Victoria) Field Artillery Brigade
III Field Artillery Brigade
1st, 2nd & 3rd Field Companies, Australian Engineers
4/LHR (Victoria)

New Zealand & Australian Division
GOC: Major General Sir A. J. Godley, KCMG
New Zealand Brigade: Brigadier General F. C. Johnston
Auckland Battalion
Canterbury Battalion
Otago Battalion
Wellington Battalion
4 Brigade: Brigadier General J. Monash
13/AIF (NSW)
14/AIF (Victoria)
15/AIF (Queensland & Tasmania)
16/AIF (S. & W. Australia)
New Zealand Mounted Rifles Brigade: Brigadier General A. H.
    Russell
Auckland Mounted Rifles
Canterbury Mounted Rifles
Wellington Mounted Rifles

1 Australian Light Horse Brigade: Lieutenant Colonel H. G. Chauvel
1/LHR (NSW)
2/LHR (Queensland)
3/LHR (S. Australia & Tasmania)

Maori Contingent

I New Zealand Field Artillery Brigade
II New Zealand Field Artillery Brigade
1st & 2nd Field Companies, New Zealand Engineers
NZ Field Troop, Engineers
Otago Mounted Rifles

2nd Australian Division
GOC: Major General J. G. Legge
5 Brigade (NSW): Brigadier General W. Holmes
17/AIF, 18/AIF, 19/AIF, 20/AIF
(Note: 6 and 7 Brigades were in Egypt in August 1915 and not involved.)

CORPS TROOPS
2 Australian Light Horse Brigade: Lieutenant Colonel G. de L. Ryrie
5/LHR (Queensland)
6/LHR (NSW)
7/LHR (NSW)
3 Australian Light Horse Brigade: Lieutenant Colonel F. G. Hughes
8/LHR (Victoria)
9/LHR (Victoria & S. Australia)
10/LHR (Western Australia)
7 Indian Mountain Artillery Brigade

Attached to New Zealand & Australian Division
29 (Indian) Brigade: Major General H. V. Cox
14/Sikhs
5/Gurkha Rifles
6/Gurkha Rifles
10/Gurkha Rifles

13th (Western) Division
GOC: Major General F. C. Shaw
38 Brigade: Brigadier General A. H. Baldwin
6/King's Own Royal Lancs

6/East Lancs
6/South Lancs
6/Loyal North Lancs

39 Brigade: Brigadier General J. de S. Cayley
9/Warwicks
7/Gloucesters
9/Worcesters
7/North Staffords

40 Brigade: Brigadier General J. H. du B. Travers
4/South Wales Borderers
8/Royal Welsh Fusiliers
8/Cheshires
5/Wiltshires

8/Welsh (Pioneers)
72 Field Company RE

Attached 13th Division

29 Brigade: Brigadier General R. J. Cooper
10/Hampshires
6/Royal Irish Fusiliers
5/Connaught Rangers
6/Leinsters

OTTOMAN *FIFTH ARMY*
General Otto Liman von Sanders

Order of Battle, Chunuk Bair, 6-10 August 1915

NORTHERN GROUP
GOC: General Esat Pasha
Chief of Staff: Lieutenant Colonel Fahrettin

5th Division
GOC: Lieutenant Colonel Hasan Basri
Chief of Staff: Major Mehmet Arif
13 Regiment: Lieutenant Colonel Ali Reza
14 Regiment: Lieutenant Colonel Ali Rifat *(died 10/8/15)*, then Major
    Ismail Hakki
15 Regiment: Major Ibrahim Şükrü *(kia 7/8/15),* then Major Veysel
    Özgür

16th Division
GOC: Colonel Rüştü
Chief of Staff: Captain Mehmet Nazim
47 Regiment: Major Tevfik *(kia 7/8/15)*
48 Regiment: Major Hüseyin Ilhami
77 Regiment: Lieutenant Colonel Saip
125 Regiment: Lieutenant Colonel Abdürrezzak

19th Division
GOC: Colonel Mustafa Kemal *(until 7/8/15)*, then Lieutenant Colonel Mehmet Şefik
Chief of Staff: Major Izzettin
18 Regiment: Major Mustafa *(kia)*
27 Regiment: Lieutenant Colonel Mehmet Şefik *(until 7/8/15)*, then Major Halis
57 Regiment: Major Avni
72 Regiment: Major Mehmet Münir

ANAFARTA GROUP
GOC: Colonel Mustafa Kemal *(from 7/8/15)*
Chief of Staff: Major Izzettin *(from 7/8/15)*

4th Division
GOC: Lieutenant Colonel Cemil
Chief of Staff: Major Alaaddin
10 Regiment: Lieutenant Colonel Kemalettin
11 Regiment: Major Mehmet Emin
Artillery Group: Major Ahmet Azmi

8th Division
GOC: Colonel Ali Reza
Chief of Staff: Major Ali Galip
12 Regiment: Major Bayatli Arif
23 Regiment: Lieutenant Colonel Recai
24 Regiment: Major Nuri
28 Regiment: Major Hunker
41 Regiment: Lieutenant Colonel Fuat
33 Regiment: Lieutenant Colonel Sabri
8 Artillery Regiment: Major Saffet

9th Division
GOC: Col Hans Kannengiesser *(wia 7/8/15)*, then Lieutenant Colonel Pötrih

Chief of Staff: Major Hulusi
25 Regiment: Lieutenant Colonel Kisiklili Nail
26 Regiment: Lieutenant Colonel Hafiz Kadri
64 Regiment: Lieutenant Colonel Servet
2 Artillery Regiment: Lt-Col Izzet

7th Division
GOC: Colonel Halil
Chief of Staff: Captain Şemsettin
19 Regiment: Lieutenant Colonel Irfan
20 Regiment: Major Halit
21 Regiment: Lieutenant Colonel Yusuf Ziya

Order of Battle, Second Anafarta (*Hill 60*), 21 August 1915

ANAFARTA GROUP
GOC: Colonel Mustafa Kemal
Chief of Staff: Major Izzettin

4th Division
GOC: Lieutenant Colonel Cemil
Chief of Staff: Major Alaaddin
11 Regiment: Major Memmet Emin
14 Regiment: Major Reşit
1/32 Regiment: Major Kazim
1/33 Regiment: Major Hulusi

7th Division
GOC: Colonel Halil
Chief of Staff: Captain Şemsettin
20 Regiment: Lieutenant Colonel Ali
21 Regiment: Major Ahmet Zeki
33 Regiment: Lieutenant Colonel Sabri

8th Division
GOC: Colonel Ali Reza
Chief of Staff: Major Ali Galip
23 Regiment: Major Ahmet Fuat
24 Regiment: Major Nuri
28 Regiment: Major Hunker
41 Regiment: Lieutenant Colonel Fuat
3/70 Regiment: Major Reşat

Bibliography and Recommended Further Reading

Bean, C.E.W., *The Story of Anzac,* (Sydney, AWM, 1924).

Bean, C.E.W., *Gallipoli Mission,* (Sydney, AWM, 1948).

Byrne, A., *The History of the Otago Regiment, NZEF, 1914-1919,* (Wilkie & Company, 1921).

Byrne, J. R., New Zealand Artillery in the Great War, (Auckland: Whitcombe and Tombs Ltd, 1922).

Burton, O., *The Auckland Regiment*, (Auckland: Whitcombe and Tombs Ltd, 1922).

Butler, A., *Official History of the Australian Army Medical Services,* (AWM: 1938).

Browning N., & Gill, I., *Gallipoli to Tripoli:History of the 10th Light Horse Regiment* (Hesperian, 2011).

Cameron, D.W., *Sorry, Lads, But The Order Is To Go,* (Sydney: UNSW, 2009).

Campbell, D., *Forward The Rifles, The War Diary of an Irish Soldier*, (Dublin: The History Press, 2009)

Carbery, A., The New Zealand Medical Service, (Auckland: Whitcombe and Tombs Ltd, 1924).

Chambers, S.J., *Anzac: The Landing,* (Barnsley: Pen & Sword, 2008).

Chambers, S.J., *Suvla: August Offensive,* (Barnsley: Pen & Sword, 2011).

Chataway, T., *History of the 15th Battalion 1914-1918,* (Brisbane 1948).

Cooper, B., *The Tenth (Irish) Division at Gallipoli*, (London: Herbert Jenkins Ltd, 1918).

Cowan, J., *The Maoris in the Great War*, (Auckland: 1926).

Cunningham, T. H., *The Wellington Regiment*, (Wellington: Ferguson & Osborn, Ltd, 1928).

Erickson, E.J., *Gallipoli: The Ottoman Campaign*, (Barnsley: Pen & Sword, 2010).

Ferguson, D., *The History of the Canterbury Regiment,* (Auckland: Whitcombe & Tombs Ltd, 1921).

Gőncű, G., Aldoğan, S., *Gallipoli Battlefield Guide,* (Istanbul: MB Books, 2008).

Hamilton, Sir. I., *Gallipoli Diary,* (London: Edward Arnold, 1920).

Hamilton, Sir. I., *Ian Hamilton's Final Despatches*, (London: George Newnes, 1916).

Hamilton, John, *Goodbye Cobber, God Bless You*, (Australia: Pan Macmillan, 2005).

Hamilton, John, *The Price of Valour*, (Australia: Pan Macmillan, 2012).

Hart, P, *Gallipoli*, (London: Profile Books, 2011).

James, R., Rhodes, *Gallipoli*, (London: Pan Books Ltd, 1984).

Kingsford, C. L., *The Story Of The Royal Warwickshire Regiment*, (London: Country Life, 1921).

Mackenzie, Compton, *Gallipoli Memories*, (London: Cassell and Company Ltd, 1929).

Nichol, C., *History of the Auckland Mounted Rifles Regiment*, (Auckland: Wilson & Horton 1921).

Oglander, Aspinall-, *Military Operations Gallipoli*, (London: Heinemann , 1929-32).

Olden, A., *Westralian Cavalry in the War*, (Melbourne: McCubbin, 1921).

Oral, H, *Gallipoli 1915 – Through Turkish Eyes*, (Istanbul, Türkiye Iş Bankasi, 2007).

Powles, C., *The History of the Canterbury Mounted Rifles*, (Auckland: Whitcombe & Tombs, 1928).

Pugsley, C., *Gallipoli: The New Zealand Story*, (New Zealand: Reed 1998).

Snelling, S., *VCs of the First World War – Gallipoli*, (Stroud: Sutton Publishing, 1995).

Çelik, K., *A Turkish View of the August Offensive*, (Onsekiz Mart Uni, Cannakale, 2000).

Travers, T., *Gallipoli 1915*, (Stroud: Tempus, 2001).

Walker, R., *To What End Did They Die: Officers Died at Gallipoli*, (Worcester, 1985).

Waite, Maj, *The New Zealanders at Gallipoli*, (Auckland: Whitcombe and Tombs Ltd, 1921).

Wanliss, N., *The History of the Fourteenth Battalion AIF*, (Melbourne: 1929).

Wilkie, A., *History of the Wellington Mounted Rifles*, (Auckland: Whitcombe & Tombs Ltd, 1921).

Notes

1 Atatürk, *Memories of the Anafartaler Battle*, p.28.

2 Published in, *The North Western Advocate and the Emu Bay Times*, 22 January 1916.

3 Published in, *The Western Mail*, 7 July 1932.

4 Published in *The Sydney Morning Herald*, 5 October 1915.

5 Published in, *The Sydney Morning Herald*, Friday 8 October 1915.

6 Published in *The Sydney Morning Herald*, Wednesday, 29 September 1915.

7 Published in, *The Queenslander*, 4 December 1915.

8 H. Oral, *Gallipoli Through Turkish Eyes*, pp.244-245.

9 C. Bean, quoting Zeki Bey in *Gallipoli Mission*, (AWM, 1948), p.185.

10 Published in, *The Examiner*, Monday, 11 October 1915.

11 P. Goldenstedt, *Attack and Defence*: 3rd at Lone Pine (*Reveille*, 1/8/1932), pp.26-27.

12 The manuscript history of the 20/AIF, pp.24-25. White's burial place was lost after the evacuation, so his name is commemorated on the Lone Pine Memorial.

13 Şefik Aker, *Çanakkale-Ariburnu Savaşlari ve 27. Alay*, (Askert Mecmua, 1935).

14 Haluk Oral, *Gallipoli 1915: Through Turkish Eyes*, (Türkiye Iş Bankasi Kültür Yayinlari, 2007)

15 Letter from P.Gooch, *Rockhampton Daily Record,* 29 September 1915.

16 J. Cowan, *The Maoris in the Great War: a History of the New Zealand Native Contingent and Pioneer Battalion,* (Auckland: Maori Regimental Committee, 1926), p.39.

17 C.T. Atkinson, *The History of the South Wales Borderers 1914-1918*, London, The Medici Society Ltd, 1931, p.156.

18 O.E. Burton*, The Auckland Regiment.*

19 Aspinall-Oglander, Official History p.190.

20 T. A. White, *The Fighting Thirteenth: The History of the Thirteenth Battalion, A.I.F.* (Tyrrells Ltd., Sydney 1924), p.46.

21 T. A. White, *The Fighting Thirteenth: The History of the Thirteenth Battalion, A.I.F.* (Tyrrells Ltd., Sydney 1924), p.48.

22 H. Kannengiesser, *The Campaign in Gallipoli*, (Hutchinson & Co. Ltd., 1928)

23 F. Shaw, IWM DOCS, F. Shaw, diary, entry 8/8/1915.

24 J. Cowan, *The Maoris in the Great War*, p.46.

25 C. Pugsley, *Gallipoli: The New Zealand Story*, Auckland, 1984, p.314.

26 W. Cunningham, *The Wellington Regiment, NZEF, 1914-1919*, pp.74-75.

27 T. A. White, *The Fighting Thirteenth: The History of the Thirteenth Battalion, AIF,* Tyrrells Ltd., Sydney 1924, p.49.

28 W. Meldrum, *Evening Post*, Volume XC, Issue 117, 13 November 1915, p.13.

29 Lieutenant J. Le Marchand, 56 Punjabi Rifles, attached 6/Gurkhas, is commemorated on the Helles Memorial, Panel 263. His body was recovered by Captain Phipson during the night and buried close to where he fell.

30 Subadar Major Gambirsing Pun was later seriously wounded in the head during the attack on Hill 60. As a result of this wound, three and a half years later he became paralysed and had to leave the army.

31 The damaged watch was given to Liman von Sanders after the battle as a souvenir, and Sanders gave Mustafa Kemal his family crested watch in return.

32 Jessie Wallingford was a champion shooter, winning numerous medals before the war. He had won bronze in pistol shooting, and also competed in the rifle event during the 1908 Olympics. He won the Military Cross for his actions as brigade machine-gun and sharpshooting officer during the landings of 25/26 April 1915. Wallingford is credited with over 700 kills, and that was only the figure reported in late June 1915. Exaggerated or not, he was deadly with the rifle.

33 Private William Cowley's body was never identified and he is today commemorated on the Basra Memorial. The author cannot explain why his name is not on the Helles Memorial to the missing, so believes this to be a CWGC clerical mistake.

34 B. Cooper, *The Tenth (Irish) Division in Gallipoli*, (London: Herbert Jenkins Ltd, 1918).

35 N.Wanliss, *The History of the Fourteenth Battalion, AIF,* pp.69-71.

36 H. Jourdain, *Ranging Memories*, (Oxford: University Press, 1934).

37 G. Garland, Letter published in *The Mercury*, February 1916.

38 J. McIlwain, personal diary (IWM Catalogue Number: 5537 96/29/1).

39 W. Meldrum, letter published in *Evening Post, Volume XC, Issue 117*, 13 November 1915.

40 Lieutenant Colonel Albert Miell, the former CO, had been killed on 7 August when he made the mistake of lifting his head above the parapet to witness the attack at The Nek. 9/LHR were not directly used in The Nek attack and were thus relatively unscathed at this time.

41 The NZEF names are those who died prior to August 1915. For the Chunuk Bair offensive and subsequent fighting in the area the names are commemorated on the Chunuk Bair Memorial. There are further New Zealand memorials at Hill 60 (North Anzac) and Twelve Tree Copse (Helles).

42 Butler, Australian Medical History, pp.306-307.

43 J. Beeston, *Five Months At Anzac*, p.23.

44 Published in the *Otago Daily Times*, on 6 November 1915.

45 C. Bean*, Gallipoli Mission*, (AWM, 1948), pp. 233-234.

46 *Tonbridge School and the Great War of 1914 to 1919*, p.40.

Index